morbo

Phil Ball began life in Vancouver, was brought up in Cleethorpes and ended up in the Basque Country, after spells in Peru and Oman. He has written for *When Saturday Comes* since 1987 and lives with his partner and two children in San Sebastián. He is the author of *White Storm: 100 Years of Real Madrid*.

morbo

The Story of Spanish Football

Phil Ball

First published in 2001 by WSC Books Ltd
This edition published in 2003 by WSC Books Ltd
Reprinted 2006
17a Perseverance Works, 38 Kingsland Road, London E2 8DD
www.wsc.co.uk
info@wsc.co.uk

ISBN 0 9540134 6 8

Cover design by Doug Cheeseman
Printed by Biddles Ltd, King's Lynn, Norfolk

To the three Ds
David, Doris and Diana

acknowledgments
I would like to thank the following for their help.
David Lindsay, Juanjo Moran, Juan Bautista Mojarro García,
Toni Strubell, Duncan Shaw, Simon Inglis, Maite Ibañez,
Joaquin Bueno, John Mills, Angus MacDonald and everyone at
When Saturday Comes: Mike Ticher, Andy Lyons, Doug Cheeseman,
Richard Guy and Shane Simpson

cover photo
Real Madrid's Luis Figo finally manages to take a corner in a hostile
Camp Nou, Barcelona, November 2002. *Firma Rafa Casal*

back cover
Athletic Bilbao's 'Pichichi' and his future wife, Avelina Rodríguez
Miguel, painted by Emilio Arteta. *Maite Ibañez*
(with thanks to the Museo Centenario de Athletic)

Marca signals the return of Javier Clemente to Seville for his first game
in charge of Real Sociedad, October 1999. *Marca*

contents

spain

REGION

● Towns & cities of significant football interest

○ Capital

La Coruña
Santiago
Vigo
GALICIA

Gijón
Oviedo
ASTURIAS

Santander
CANTABRIA

Bilbao
San Sebastián
Irún
BASQUE
COUNTRY
Vitoria
NAVARRE
Pamplona
Logroño
LA RIOJA

FRANCE

CASTILLA–LEON
Burgos
Valladolid
Salamanca

Zaragoza
ARAGON
Lérida
CATALONIA
Barcelona
Tarragona

MADRID
Madrid
Toledo

CASTILLA–LA MANCHA
Albacete

Castellón
VALENCIA
Valencia

MALLORCA
Palma

EXTREMEDURA
Mérida
Badajoz

Elche
Murcia
MURCIA
Alicante

PORTUGAL

Huelva
Seville
ANDALUCIA

Málaga
Cádiz

100miles

0   100km

CANARY ISLANDS

Santa Cruz
TENERIFE

Las Palmas
GRAN CANARIA

50miles

0   50km

N

Note on Spanish, Catalan and Basque usage

Certain words appear in different guises in this book for distinct reasons. The Barcelona-based club Espanyol have officially spelt their name in Catalan since 1994, using the 'y' instead of the previous Castilian 'ñ', as in Español. The spelling appears in the latter form when the text refers to the club's pre-1994 story, for reasons of historical coherence.

The spelling of Barcelona's former president Josep Sunyol is in Catalan, in spite of family objections (see page 101). The same club's founder, the Swiss Hans Kamper, changed his name to the Catalan Joan Gamper – a change that is respected in the temporal progress of the chapter on Barcelona. In other cases, Catalan is used wherever it is appropriate.

The spelling of the city Seville and of the football club of the same name is differentiated in order to distinguish between the two. The English spelling Seville is employed for the city, and the Spanish spelling Sevilla refers to the club.

Basque place names have not generally been used, for the simple reason of familiarity. San Sebastián is known as Donostia in Basque, Vitoria as Gasteiz and so on, but it would have been unnecessarily unwieldy to have included all this information in the flow of the text. The Spanish versions are merely employed as terms of general convenience and not as political statements.

introduction

When I was a kid, I saw an item on the news one tea-time about the running of the bulls in the *fiestas* of Pamplona. I was at that age when you didn't really listen to the news, but just looked up at the screen from time to time as you ate your scrambled eggs. I never questioned what I saw on that night long ago, but the madness of the scene etched itself into my memory in that twisted, dreamy sort of way it does in childhood, and I spent the subsequent years convinced that the Spanish ran through the streets of their country on a daily basis, pursued by fearsome bulls.

So convinced was I that the natives spent their days peering gingerly from left to right as they stepped from their doorsteps that I could not bring myself to ask several schoolfriends, whose parents had actually taken them on holiday to this curious country, how they had coped with that particular inconvenience. I preferred not to know. The idea was enough, and, as with the death of Santa Claus, the truth would have proved simply too mundane. I never dreamed that one day I might come to live in and write about this same country and that my own children would be born there – half an hour's drive from Pamplona. And the madness I thought I saw all those years ago is certainly here, albeit in a different guise.

This book is about Spanish football, but it is not football which defines the peculiar character of the country. Within the European frame, Spain's has always been one of the most difficult cultures to paint. It has always been a state of mind, not just for the British but for the rest of Europe as well, despite the shift in perception that has taken place over the past decade as to the desirability of maintaining all those corny cultural stereotypes we grew up on.

Most people probably know now that Spain is really a loose federation of fiercely autonomous regions, and that in only one of them do people actually waft fans and dance *sevillanas* with any sort of regularity. But deepest Spain is still a strange beast, way beyond the one that is now packaged for the British middle-classes. As VS Pritchett wrote back in the Fifties, Spain breaks with 'Europe' – whatever that is – when you pull up at its frontier:

> England is packed with little houses; France lies clearly like green linoleum, a place of thriving little fields; but, cross the dark blot of the Pyrenees and Spain is reddish brown, yellow and black, like some dusty bull restive in the rock and the sand.

Plenty of writers have made similar observations about Spain, that it is somehow out on a limb, isolated, literally 'down there'. When you live there for any length of time you begin to feel that the rest of the world is beginning to melt away. The newspapers have their international sections, but they read like a reluctant afterthought. In any case, Spain has almost the lowest percentage of newspaper sales per head of population in Europe. People lead their own lives here, and the rest of the world can get on with whatever it's getting on with.

In some ways, it's a much odder place in reality than it seemed to me back then as a kid. Many Spaniards are still formal and conservative in both dress and manner, but at the same time wildly anti-authoritarian, giving the poor police and referees a hard time of it. The nouveaux middle-classes flock to their gyms to work out, then relax afterwards in the bar in their tracksuits surrounded by plumes of cigarette smoke. Men, women, children and grannies all swear like proverbial troopers, invoking their muse to soil every garment of Catholic sensibility imaginable, only to dress up like Lord and Lady Muck on Sunday morning and stride head-high to church as if the Lord had never heard them. Guilt is a grey area, and is consequently a no-go zone for the Spanish. Pity the poor outsider who dares to throw into a conversation a mere suggestion of doubt. He or she will more than likely be howled down. To the average Spaniard, publicly at least, there is black and white, and anything in between is the stuff of the limp-wristed and the feathery.

Enter football and the biggest paradox of them all. The Spanish insist on outward shows of confidence, but their fatal weakness is their inferiority complex. Quite why they have one is unclear, but it may have had something to do with the Armada. Cervantes, their greatest writer, wrote a long and funny book suggesting that it was a result of their reluctance to see things straight, to see them as they really are, while 300 years later

Picasso was saying very much the same thing. This fatal chasm in the Spanish psyche, between how things really are and how the average person would like them to be, seems to have been the cause of the country's particular national dysfunction.

Football offered a chance to bury the past. Back in the early 1870s, in the parched Cerro Colorado of the Rio Tinto region in Andalucía, the Spanish labourers who had begun to work the English-owned copper mines north of Huelva were already beating their employers at 'football'. Here was something that could throw off the debilitating disease of inferiority – a game with a simple objective and a quick-fix aesthetic that 80 years later would convince a dictator that it might bring his struggling country back into the international fold after too many years in the wilderness. And, of course, Real Madrid, during one of the toughest periods of economic hardship in Spain this century, did indeed manage to change the image of the country with their wonderful displays. The period of their European triumphs is looked back upon as if it were a Golden Age – a lie, of course, but one that has persisted because it relieved the country of its feeling of underachievement and international isolation.

Spanish football is in a sense so wonderful that the country needs little else these days to sustain it. The great artists and poets may have gone, but football is here. The game unites an otherwise divided country in a collective frenzy of talk, talk and more talk. You can start up a dialogue about football with a perfect stranger in any bar, in the sure knowledge that he will respond. Or indeed she, for here women are less marginalised by the game, despite the fact that *machismo* is a Spanish word. Everyone knows the issues, and everyone has an opinion. There is a daily football tabloid, *Marca*, whose own particular tittle tattle is so astonishingly tedious in its detail that it numbs the mind, but it nevertheless sells more copies than any other newspaper in Spain. In it you really can read, without irony, what the Real Madrid players had for breakfast.

But it would have been both futile and dishonest to have written this book as if football in Spain were merely a sporting phenomenon. Any contemplation of the history of the sport leads you inevitably to the confluence of the two turbulent rivers where football and politics meet. And although several Spanish writers will try to suggest that the waters only met after Franco had appeared on the scene, it seems to me that they did so right from the off, from the moment Madrid and Barcelona discovered the game. The book is about them, and others, of course. It does not pretend to be a complete record, but an investigation of some of the more interesting cultural and political aspects of the game here, as far as I understand them.

In Europe in general, and Britain in particular, many of Spain's other teams are now much better known than was previously the case. The Champions League final between Real Madrid and Valencia in 2000 and the exploits of several other previously disregarded clubs have all contributed to an improved knowledge of the Spanish scene. Valencia may have been reasonably well known in British circles, if only thanks to Graham Rix's penalty miss against them in the 1980 Cup-Winners Cup final, but teams from the wilds of Galicia, like Celta de Vigo and Deportivo de La Coruña, were hardly household names.

Celta's sudden swashbuckling appearance in the 1998-99 UEFA Cup, in which they knocked out Aston Villa and Liverpool in some style, and Deportivo's excellent 1999-2000 campaign which ended with the league title, have all contributed. Real Mallorca forced their way into the European reckoning in the summer of 1999 when they narrowly lost to Lazio at Villa Park, in the last of the Cup-Winners Cup finals. Even more astonishing was the brief rise of Alavés, whose extraordinary progress in the 2001 UEFA Cup culminated in a still more extraordinary final against Liverpool.

Thanks also to Sky and Eurosport, people now seem to know that Espanyol are the other team in Barcelona, and that Rayo Vallecano are also from Madrid. Moreover, the existence of books such as the European football *Rough Guide*, with its emphasis on both the historical and cultural aspects of the region's major clubs, would seem to point to a new, more inquisitive audience.

While Italy was the first focus of recent British interest in other European leagues, thanks to the 1990 World Cup, groundbreaking coverage by Channel 4 and the prominence of the great Milan side, Spain has proved an unexpectedly successful challenger since the late Nineties, not least through its ability to lure the best players in the world from Serie A and elsewhere. This has been most evident in the series of high-profile transfers since Florentino Pérez took over the reins at Real Madrid. The signings of Luis Figo, Zinedine Zidane and Ronaldo over the first three years of Pérez's mandate raised the European profile of Real Madrid to great heights, but the capture of David Beckham – whose official presentation in Madrid was witnessed by a television audience of two billion – took interest in Britain to unprecedented levels.

Such manic collecting of art treasures might seem to run counter to the other most significant trend in the Spanish league – its ability to throw up numerous contenders for the big prizes rather than locking out the medium-sized clubs as the Premiership has done. But since the Beckham signing was widely perceived (and indeed promoted) as a shameless marketing operation, it was not seen at the time as a major threat to the sense of on-field democracy that had broken out in previous years.

Deportivo's league title in 2000 and their enduring credibility as challengers were emblematic of a general levelling-up of the competition, in what used to be considered a two-club race. Barcelona and Real Madrid still rule the roost when it comes to television coverage and general media chit-chat, but there has been, if you will excuse the phrase, a definite shifting of the goalposts. Rich presidents have been popping up like mushrooms, probably mirroring the wider distribution of wealth in Spain since a more buoyant economy left the Franco years far behind. More teams than ever can now compete with the financial packages that only the big two could previously offer and as a result your average fan will now hesitate before automatically backing Real Madrid and Barcelona to win on *la quiniela*, Spain's version of the pools.

While Spanish football has never been solely about those two giants, the new map of the game provides scope for even more interactions between the big two and the regions than before. The game here mirrors and represents its regional cultures, much more so than any other country in Europe. One could go further and say that football has become inseparable from the expression of regional culture in Spain – that it has become one and the same thing. Each town, each region, feels its special identity so keenly that it is hardly surprising that football prospered as a willing catalyst to this phenomenon. It continues to prosper on the back of this regionalism. In this book, I use the word 'Spanish' and 'Spain' as terms of convenience, but it must be borne in mind that there are many of the country's citizens who would object to being described as such.

In the end, Franco's 40-year exercise in centralism was so intransigent that it succeeded in creating regional nationalist movements in all sorts of previously docile places like Murcia and Extremadura. Things fell apart, and the centre could not hold – not that anyone ever really expected it to. Regions remembered who had fought for whom, and they have still not forgotten. Football clubs grew up out of the divided earth and have not forgotten either.

Finally, before this little journey begins, I would like to quote my mother, whose daily incredulity at football's popularity was summed up in the immortal phrase: 'I cannot see why anyone should get so excited about 22 silly men kicking a piece of leather about.' The essential absurdity of football – that it has become so important – is nine-tenths of the poetry. If you can see that, then I would hazard a guess that you'll enjoy this book.

Phil Ball
San Sebastián, October 2003

1. *morbo*

Morbo is the word, as they say in Spain. Trouble is, it's one of those awkward ones that defies easy translation. No matter how you try, you can't quite nail the word down. It entails a lot of slippery little notions that just won't rub shoulders with a convenient English synonym. Don't bother with a dictionary, for it will only confuse you further, the word having other meanings that are not applicable to football. Most treat it as a noun and translate it as something like 'disease', which is hardly appropriate to this context. Nevertheless, since no history of Spanish football can pretend to be complete without it, the word has to be confronted. At the very least, it may be worth mentioning at this stage that it crops up regularly in the phrase *mucho morbo*, and there is indeed a whole lot of *morbo* going on.

Take Real Madrid and Barcelona for starters – the easiest introduction to the idea, and to Spanish football in general. There is so much *morbo* festering between these two sides that they would have to employ a very powerful priest to exorcise the phenomenon, always presuming that they wanted to. It's not merely that they hate each other with an intensity that can truly shock the outsider, but that each encounter between them always has a new ingredient. This is the essence of *morbo*. It feeds off itself and keeps growing until it becomes a self-regulating and self-perpetuating organism, like some sinister creature from a science fiction fantasy. The creature could carry on quite happily with no new ingredients, because by definition, once the *morbo* is up and running it can never die.

Spain is something of an unforgiving country – one which, as the writer Jan Morris once put it, dedicates itself to the art of the self-inflicted wound and which is 'committed to acts of cruelty against its own kind' rather too often. While there are people still around who fought and suffered in the Civil War and whole swathes of the populace who lived under Franco and either hated or loved every minute of it, you

17

have a recipe for a very spicy soup indeed. The cat and dog synergy that has always existed between Barcelona and Madrid, even before the Catalans began to get assertive, is the basis of the *morbo*, but the Spanish are most adept at stoking and fanning the flames.

The football tabloid *Marca* is the unrivalled expert in the art of creating the new season's spice between these two great clubs. Based in Madrid, although it originated in the Basque Country just after the Civil War, it makes no secret of its allegiance to its local heroes, nor of its antipathy towards the Catalans in general and FC Barcelona in particular. In July 2000, Luis Figo became the world's most expensive player on being transferred from Barcelona to Real Madrid, the paper went into a veritable frenzy. The transfer was perceived by the Barcelona faithful as an affront to their image and their soul.

There were few precedents. Only Michael Laudrup and Bernd Schuster in recent years had dared to make the move and while Laudrup, like Figo, was popular with the supporters, he had fallen out publicly with Johan Cruyff, then Barcelona's manager. Schuster's move in 1988 was greeted with derision in the Catalan capital, but few were sorry to see him go. Figo, by contrast, had the Barça faithful in his pocket, was at the height of his fame and form and appeared to be another convert to the Catalan cause.

When he returned to the Camp Nou on October 22, 2000, three months after his transfer, the reception he received was positively thermonuclear. *Marca*, proud of its reputation as a troublemaker, published a simple picture of Figo's ear under the headline **Figo: Te van a calentar la oreja** (Figo, they're going to make your ears burn). And they did. Figo, famed for his consistency, was unable to function. Every time he ventured near a corner flag he was met with a barrage of abuse, angry gestures and various objects – including three mobile phones, several half-bricks, a bicycle chain and a shower of coins, all meticulously noted in the referee's report.

In the run-up to the match, several thousand supporters had dedicated themselves to creating enormous copies of the 5,000 peseta note with Figo's face superimposed and the line *Figo, pesetero* (Figo, money-grabber) emblazoned above. In many ways the transfer generated at least as much heat as the Di Stéfano affair in 1953 (outlined in chapter five). Both were classic cases of *morbo*.

Two years later, in November 2002, the famous '*Derbi de la Vergüenza*' (Derby of Shame) demonstrated that issue was still very much alive. For no obvious reason, Figo's presence in the Camp Nou that season seemed to be resented more than ever by the Barça fans, and the game was held up for ten minutes while he attempted to take a corner. Among the objects hurled in his direction this time were the head of a suckling pig and a full bottle of whisky. Roberto Carlos led the Madrid players off in protest as Figo's repeated attempts to approach the corner flag were repulsed, but the worst part of the episode came after the match, when Joan Gaspart, Barcelona's troubled president, declared that Figo had been instructed to take the corners in order to 'provoke' the home supporters. His comments caused a furore the like of which had not been seen since Johan Cruyff told the European press in 1973 that he had chosen Barcelona over Madrid because he could not possibly play for a team 'associated with Franco'. After the smoke drifted away, Barça had their ground closed for two games and life went on, but better examples of *morbo* are few and far between.

Back in 1997 Luis Enrique, one of the most consistent and affable Spanish players of the Nineties, moved from Madrid to Barcelona. *Marca* – just in case the player's appearance was not going to be greeted with sufficient abuse – decided to remind the Spanish public the day before the two clubs met that he was a 'traitor'. 'And we all know what happens to them,' they added helpfully. Unlike Figo, Luis Enrique scored in the game, and has subsequently continued to add value to his own particular *morbo* quotient by such acts as kissing the Catalan shield on his shirt whenever he scores against his former club (he is not a Catalan – no matter) or telling the press how happy he is to live in such a vibrant and open city such as Barcelona – the implication, of course, being that Madrid is exactly the opposite.

Booed and vilified ever since by the Bernabéu crowd, the player exacted his revenge in February 2002, a month before the official celebrations of Real Madrid's centenary were scheduled to begin. All former players had been invited to the opening bash, but Luis Enrique (according to *Marca*) was the only one who failed to RSVP. He nonchalantly told the press that he had better things to do with his time. This calculated and wounding snub turned Luis Enrique overnight into the most hated man in Madrid. No suckling pigs flew his way on his subsequent visit to the capital (in which he had the further effrontery to score) but his every touch was accompanied by the predictable chorus of *Hijo de puta* (son of a whore), a phrase that John Aldridge claimed was the only Spanish he needed to learn during his spell with Real Sociedad, so well did it serve him on the field of play.

The Dane Michael Laudrup moved the other way in 1994 and ended Barcelona's so-called 'Dream Team' sequence of four consecutive titles by linking up instinctively with the Chilean forward Ivan Zamorano and helping to return the title to the Bernabéu in his first season there. A more decent and modest chap than Laudrup it would be hard to find, but his reception at the Camp Nou that season was so astonishingly hostile that the player, like Figo six years later, simply could not function during the game. Perhaps he thought that his previous role as architect of the Dream Team's aesthetic would count as a mitigating circumstance in the troublesome context of a move to Real Madrid. Yet the mere sight of him in a white shirt that night guaranteed the country a substantial dose of its beloved *morbo*.

Before the game, in the bars around the country, men, women and children would have been turning to each other and saying *'bueno – mucho morbo esta noche en el Camp Nou'* (hmm... lots of *morbo* in the Camp Nou tonight) over their drinks. Poor Laudrup seemed to lose his appetite for the Spanish game the following season. Tiring of the circus, he moved back to Denmark to play out his career and to pursue his interest in wine, far from the taunts and accusations his upbringing had not taught him to confront.

Morbo can thrive just as well away from the field of play. In the early 1980s, Barcelona's new marketing team decided to impress their employers with a new money-making initiative. The Catalans are obsessive ideas people, and have a reputation in the country as being the 'Jews of Spain' because of their financial adeptness and all-round hard-working ethos. The idea was that the members of the club, who already numbered some 90,000 at that time, could further cement their relationship with their beloved club by purchasing a small brick with their own name and membership number on it, subsequently to be inserted into the back wall of the new stand that was being constructed at the time.

The idea went down well, and for a smallish fee thousands of supporters came forward to become physically as one (in name) with their club. Of course, what the club had failed to see was that the system was open to abuse. It has still not been established which member was responsible for the heinous deed, but a wealthy Real Madrid supporter discreetly joined Barcelona with the intention of buying himself a brick on which he subsequently had carved the name Santiago Bernabéu – ex-president of Real Madrid, friend to Franco and the godfather of

Barcelona's rival club during the Fifties and Sixties. It was he who gave his name to their present-day stadium, smack in the centre of downtown Madrid.

That the brick was actually inserted somewhere with Bernabéu's name on it is possibly apocryphal, but the Madrid press had a field day with the story, mercilessly poking fun at the Catalans. It may be difficult for outsiders to understand, but to desecrate the cultural temple of Catalanism in this way is akin to urinating in the font of your opponent's church. The Spanish are not too renowned for being able to laugh at themselves, but it is difficult to believe that, say, Rangers or Celtic followers would be tolerant of a similar trick. When Paul Gascoigne pretended to play the flute to celebrate a goal against Celtic it was widely reported in Spain and well understood as a classic act of *morbo*. Indeed, Celtic v Rangers is a fine example of the concept, should it need any further illustration. All cultures must logically possess their version of the phenomenon, but in Spain it has always been the driving force behind the public's relationship with the game.

In 1902, FC Barcelona were three years old and Madrid FC, as they were then called, a year younger. Alfonso XIII, already a patron of the fledgling game, was to be crowned that year, and a certain Carlos Prados, the new president of the Madrid club, hit on the idea of organising a football tournament to coincide with the various festivities surrounding the coronation in the capital. Five teams turned up: Vizcaya (the name of the north-western region of the Basque country), Barcelona, Madrid, New Football de Madrid and the other team from Barcelona, the provocatively named Español – the club did not change its name to the Catalan spelling (Espanyol) until the mid-1990s.

The tournament was to feature the first recorded game between Barcelona and Madrid, the Catalans drawing first blood with a 3-1 win. Vizcaya eventually beat Barcelona 2-1 in the final, but more of the Basques later. There is no explicit *morbo* present in the press cuttings of the time, although the tournament aroused plenty of interest. By all accounts the old Hippodrome in the centre of the capital was packed to the rafters, even though the public were asked to fork out between ten and 25 centavos to get into the final.

The interesting detail for *morbo* watchers is that the organisers, most likely miffed at the fact that the final had been disputed by Catalans and Basques, decided to cobble together a quick *concurso de consolación* as they put it (third place play-off, in modern parlance) the same afternoon, won by Madrid of course. The newspapers used the word *trofeo* to define what Madrid picked up that afternoon, although it must have been something hastily brought along from somebody's personal silver collection, because Vizcaya had already been given the official trophy – a cup which was to become the King's Cup the following year and which would thereafter be presented to the winning teams of the national competition by royal hands.

Madrid's reputation as poor losers seems to have been born immediately, in the improvised spirit of the country's first attempt to put on a national football tournament. Indeed, it took the two teams three years to get around to playing each other again, this time in Barcelona. The Catalans won again, 5-2. According to one account, in the rather posh restaurant Francia, where the hosts entertained their beloved guests after the game:

> ...certain rather unfortunate and unhappy references were made by the visitors from Madrid as to the alleged unsporting nature of the encounter, the partial nature of the referee's decisions and the indelicate phrases used by certain sections of the spectating public, thus bringing into some disrepute the nature of this sporting event.

So began a century of mutual antipathy. Indeed, it might not be going too far to say that the strife and struggles between the two clubs from 1905 onwards accurately mirror the main contests of 20th century Spanish history. The two cities have always been moving in different directions, partly through bloody mindedness, partly through political allegiance, but mainly through clear cultural differences. A supporter of Real Madrid seems a very distinct creature from a supporter of Barcelona, a fact that cannot be attributed wholly to the fact that they probably talk about football in a different language.

Madrid is a bourgeois, grand, rather suffocating sort of city on first acquaintance. From its airport lounge you stare out over barren, brown rocks and brooding little hills, baking in the sunlight. The surrounding countryside is bleak and bare, watching you without interest as you drive into Madrid – suggestive of some harshness in the citizens who shelter under its awnings and scurry about beneath its dark, rather imposing buildings. To an outsider it does not seem a welcoming city at first, although on further acquaintance nothing could be further from the truth. Madrid is now as much a melting-pot as any European capital of similar size, and the inhabitants have well earned their nicknamed *Los Gatos* (the cats) – which some say derives from their tendency to come out at night for a good time. Yet the capital's attractions are the sort that need time to announce themselves.

Madrid was built on and sustained by the notion of centralisation – in the 20th century exemplified by Franco's obsessive opposition to regional nationalism which he regarded as one of the principal reasons for the turmoil of Spain's ill-fated Second Republic. Madrid is in the geographical centre of the country, put there by Felipe II in the mid-16th century. Good symbolism, poor urban planning. Madrid has no harbour, it is not at the meeting place of two rivers, it boils in summer and it freezes in winter. It does, however, sit on an escarpment that commands good views over the surrounding plain, just in case the Moors should ever have decided to get their revenge and organise their own *reconquista*.

The first time I saw any Real Madrid fans was at a game in San Sebastián between Real Sociedad and Madrid in 1994. The infamous *Ultras Sur* had stayed at home, just as many citizens from Madrid will still avoid the Basque Country when travelling up to France, as if fearing a reprise of the ambush of Charlemagne's troops at Roncesvalles – such is the fearsome reputation of the Basques. There were just two of them, early thirtyish, sitting in the expensive seats, both wearing dark business suits and expressions of polite but distinct *hauteur*.

Their hair was slicked back and they wore their Armani smoothness on their sleeves, ruffled only when Real Sociedad equalised in the second minute of injury time, a goal which unleashed all the fury of Basque *morbo* down upon their unfortunate heads. Their reaction to the abuse around them was to sit it out, staring forward with scared rabbit expressions into the distance, as if nothing had happened. I was impressed by their stoical dignity in the face of such verbal assault, but curious as to why they had risked their necks up in the wilds of the north. Whatever, the image of them has remained – smooth, hard-looking, self-important, from a city that despite its modern changes, still feels rather too acutely its sense of being literally at the centre of things.

It is part and parcel of the Madrid-Barcelona *morbo* that the latter seems to inhabit a different planet. While Madrid has the Prado, the seat of government and the royal family, according to John Hooper's *The New Spaniards* almost all the radical ideas that have shaped Spain's modern history – republicanism, federalism, anarchism, syndicalism and communism – have found their way into Spain by way of Catalonia.

Fashions, whether in clothing, philosophy or art, have tended to take root in Barcelona's more welcoming soil years before they gained acceptance in Madrid. The whole city seems to be up to something and it seems to like itself, not in a narcissistic way but rather in a confident, breezy manner that conveys a sense of ease with itself. It is not everyone's cup of tea, of course, and later in the book Catalan nationalism in the guise of FC Barcelona will come under more critical scrutiny, but for the purposes of explaining the background to some of football's biggest helpings of *morbo*, the contrast is illuminating.

Barcelona fans labour under the touchingly innocent belief that everyone else in the world, apart from Real Madrid and Espanyol fans, is happy to accept that their club is the biggest on earth and quite simply the bees' knees of the whole footballing cosmos. When you first step into the Camp Nou, the pretension begins to look a little more justified, for it is indeed an astonishing sight. The whole place seems so taken up with its own socio-cultural significance that you can only marvel at the immense conviction of it all, a conviction that can at least suck you in for the 90 minutes that you have forced yourself to sit among its pervading triumphalism. No wonder the *madrileños* hate it all so much.

The Bernabéu is a colder place, as beautiful as the Camp Nou but more brooding somehow, more edgy. Its rounded, concrete solidity is suggestive of a sort of parochial arrogance, as if the rest of the world ceases to exist once you are inside its walls. You have been invited in to witness its past and present glories, but no one is too concerned about where you have come from and what you might have to offer: 'Look on my works ye mighty and despair!'

Barça fans, by contrast, will ask you where you are from, what you think of their team, what you think of the city, who you support, and so on. Apart from their ludicrous *Boixos Nois* thugs, when their travelling supporters visit other Spanish cities there is rarely trouble. They have four *morboso* encounters a season, two each with Madrid and Espanyol, and apart from a smidgeon of nastiness between themselves and Atlético Madrid, they cannot believe that there is any more of the stuff to be found in the rest of the country.

Of course, lest it need repeating, the history of Spain in this century has served to drive the two cities apart. Franco banned the Catalan language and all public use of it, even encouraging people through public notices in telephone booths that they should communicate, when the pips stopped pipping, in Castilian, or 'the Christian language' as his administration called it. As with the Basques, this legislation was deeply unpopular, of course, but thanks to the efficiency of Franco's police state, the policy worked, on the surface at least.

Spain's neutrality in the Second World War meant that football could carry on, subject of course to a certain degree of political manipulation and tampering. By and large, in the early years of Franco's reign, people who were opposed to him decided that discretion was the better part of valour and kept a low profile, if they had not already fled into exile. Games between Barcelona and Real Madrid continued, albeit on a slightly more anodyne basis. Nevertheless, our old friend *morbo* was never very far away.

By 1943, the Copa del Rey, the King's Cup, had been renamed the Generalísimo's Cup, in Franco's honour. The previous season Barcelona had had the temerity to win it, though they had struggled in the league – a failure attributed by those brave enough to speak out to a widespread bias in the refereeing. Or, more likely, to a feeling among referees that they knew which side their bread was buttered on. It may well have been true that certain officials had been receiving specific instructions (and payment) to act against the Catalan club, but Franco was probably cleverer than that. To take away all the *morbo* of the encounters between the clubs at one fell swoop would hardly have served his purposes.

By allowing Barcelona the occasional triumph, if that is indeed what he did, he ensured the pre-eminence of Real Madrid, and the symbolic light that it shone on his regime, appeared in a more authentic, more dangerously convincing way. Nevertheless, for the conspiracy theorists, the semi-finals of the cup in 1943 make very juicy reading indeed. The two games ensured that every subsequent encounter between the two sides would be forever burnt by the flames of *morbo*.

The first game, at Barcelona's old stadium Les Corts, ended in a 3-0 win for the Catalans. The victory was a somewhat pyrrhic one, however, since José Escolá, Barça's star of the early Forties, was stretchered off in the first half with José María Querejeta's stud marks in his stomach. The fact that certain sections of the crowd began to berate Madrid's players and the leniency of the referee was a red rag to the bull of the Madrid-based press, which toed Franco's line whenever necessary. The newspaper *Ya* (Now) reported that there had been lots of ungentlemanly whistling and booing – 'unpatriotic' the journalist should have written – and that this had been symptomatic of a 'clear intention to attack the representatives of Spain'. Say no more.

In the return match in Chamartín, Madrid's former ground, Barcelona were defeated 11-1, something of a blot on their statistical history when the trivia merchants trot out, year after year, the facts and figures surrounding the two teams' encounters. The fact that the Catalans had a player sent off before half-time hardly seems a sufficient explanation for the rout. Perhaps it had more to do with the fact that the director of state security went into their dressing-room before the game and allegedly told the team that some of them were only playing because of the regime's generosity in permitting them to remain in the country.

On way or another, it would seem Real Madrid were destined to overturn the three-goal disadvantage from the first leg. Franco's biographer, Paul Preston, points out that the dictator was fond of doing *la quiniela*. Perhaps someone should begin a research project into the possibility that Spain's bookies were being tipped off as to the kind of odds they could have offered on a game where paid-up thugs of the state wandered into dressing-rooms and made it clear to those assembled that they should sacrifice the match for the good of their benevolent regime.

There is much more to *morbo* than Barcelona and Real Madrid, of course. Nor is it only a function of rivalry between Spain's regions, occurring as it does with equal virulence between clubs from the same city. Liverpool and Everton fans may have some problems with each other, but if you look at a comparable Spanish example, such as Sevilla and Betis, the gap in *morbo* terms is of Grand Canyon proportions. Most commentators agree that the astonishing enmity that exists between Seville's two clubs can be attributed chiefly to reasons of social class. Betis have always represented the poorer, more working-class side of the city, and Sevilla the more prosperous, bourgeois side. The twain, it is said, only ever meet at bullfights – but even there it has been noted by the better-heeled spectators, tut-tut, that only a Betis fan would be naff enough to turn up to the *corrida* in a replica shirt.

The teeth-baring between the two sides is curious, for while it may be true that the working and the middle classes do not, as a rule, cavort together in harmony, the gap between the two in Spain is not such an abyss as it is in England. Perhaps Spain requires something like football to allow class consciousness to manifest itself. There are echoes of it in the awkward coexistence between Barcelona and Espanyol, Oviedo and Sporting Gijón and between Real Madrid and Atlético, although in Madrid the true working-class side is the more obscure outfit, Rayo Vallecano. But nowhere is it as fierce and as long-standing as in Seville.

When the Betis manager Francisco Antúnez made the forbidden journey from employment with Betis to employment with Sevilla in the late 1940s, Radio Moscow declared:

> Sevilla, the capitalist team of the city, have trampled upon
> their noble proletarian neighbours Betis, abusing the
> power handed to them by the fascist Francoist regime.

As with Madrid and Barcelona, the *morbo* has been steadily building since the early part of the century until it has reached quite epic proportions. During the last month of the 1998-99 season, with Sevilla pushing hard to reach the Second Division play-offs, the Betis president Manuel Ruíz de Lopera, a self-made man and a hard-line Sevilla hater, was accused of paying Albacete players in order to motivate them to get a result at Sevilla – which they did, a 1-1 draw. The result threatened Sevilla's chances of making the play-offs (although they were eventually promoted) and was the cause of much public vitriol between the two clubs, culminating in a written death threat to Lopera from an anonymous Sevilla supporter.

Lopera, of course, denied all charges and veritably frothed with righteous indignation, but could not resist adding that he didn't see what the problem would have been even if he had actually offered the incentives to Sevilla's opponents. 'I reserve the right to do what I like,' he announced to the press, a statement that rather sums up the current moral state of the game in Spain. If Lopera's middle-man really had offered Albacete money to get a result – and there were those in the squad who told the press that someone did – the mind boggles at the motivation for that grubby little incident. It could hardly have been in the financial interests of Betis, then in the First Division, to deny themselves the spectacle and pay-day of a couple of *morbo*-charged derbies per season. Yet such was their dislike of their neighbours that they were prepared, allegedly, to pay another club to beat them.

No Betis fans could be found who thought there was any problem with the practice, as if after decades of being in Sevilla's shade they simply preferred to retain the status quo and remain a division higher. Betis are now as rich as, if not richer than Sevilla, to which their £22 million purchase of the over-hyped Brazilian Denílson in 1998 was meant to be public testimony. Lopera, a somewhat unbalanced man despite the chips on both shoulders, was declaring to the other side of the city that he was a man of wealth and circumstance, while the Sevilla fans were merely laughing up their expensive sleeves at such *nouveau* behaviour.

However, at the end of the 1999-2000 season no one was laughing, as both sides were relegated. History repeated itself with lamentable consistency when Sevilla, already relegated, took on Oviedo at home and were 3-0 down by half-time. Oviedo were involved, coincidentally enough, in the struggle to avoid the third relegation place with Betis. Sevilla even took off their best player, the Norwegian goalkeeper Frode Olsen, at half-time, because he had clearly misunderstood instructions and was manfully keeping the score down. Sevilla made a token comeback in the second half and the game ended 3-2, but the result as good as relegated Betis. The circumstances provoked some hot air in the press and a threat from the Spanish federation to investigate, but they never did.

Two seasons later, both clubs were back in the top flight, where matches between the two were routinely labelled high risk by the police. In October 2002 at Sevilla's Sánchez Pizjuán stadium, a security guard was set upon before the derby when he tried to stop five youths from stealing one of the practice balls being used by Antonio Prats, the Betis goalkeeper. The guard's beating was so severe that he was hospitalised.

While class is notionally the key in Seville, a more common arena where *morbo* takes hold is Spain's particular sense of place. The vast majority of Spaniards define themselves by where they come from, their *pueblo* as they will call it, whether it is a village or a sprawling conurbation. Indeed, footballers and managers are constantly referred to as *él de Badajoz* (the one from Badajoz), *él de Ordizia*, or wherever they happen to hail from. For the Spanish, provenance is all. It is as if they are not totally satisfied in their judgement of someone unless they know, as the ultimate proof of their hunches, the town (and by extension the region) where they were born and bred.

Although Spain has seen a few large waves of internal economic migration – notably from the poor south to the industrial cities of the Basque country and Catalonia – the idea of moving *pueblo* in order to gain promotion at work or simply to experience something new is anathema to most Spaniards. It is significant that Spanish footballers have by and large proved to be poor or reluctant travellers. The Spanish league was quick to cotton on to the advantages of employing foreign players, but there was never much movement out of the country, the success of Luis Suárez in Italy in the Sixties being something of an exception.

Parochialism, or *pueblorinismo*, is something the Spanish wear unashamedly on their sleeves. Even now, post-Bosman, the Premiership has not exactly attracted a glut of Spanish players. In an interview with Chelsea's Albert Ferrer in 1998, the newspaper *El País* reported that the ex-Barcelona full-back was very happy in London and that he and his family were of the touching view that London was a very interesting city, with 'lots of things to do'. The interview gave the impression that Ferrer and the readers of the paper were actually learning something new in this observation. Perhaps Barcelona really is the centre of the universe, but at least one of its former inhabitants now knows that other cities can be of interest too.

Ivan Campo, who arrived at Bolton during the 2002-03 season, only found himself there because no one else in Spain would have him after his unhappy spell at Real Madrid resulted in a nervous breakdown. In Spain's football magazine *Don Balón*, Campo noted with approval not only the friendliness of the Lancashire town, but also that 'no one cares where I'm from. It's great.'

Morbo exploits this parochialism, gathers it up and flings it back into the circus of Spanish football. The country's most popular football programme, *El día después* (The Day After), is hosted on Monday nights by Michael Robinson, once of Brighton and, among others, Osasuna. Robinson has made a remarkably good living in Spain by devising a programme which is less about football and more about the variety of cultures, rituals and small-town stories that proliferate in Spain, all revolving in some way around football. The fact that this pot pourri of local colour is presented by a foreigner makes it somehow more attractive, as if it is gratifying to be commented on by a famous and, it has to be said, extremely funny outsider.

Robinson hit on the formula of highlighting what the folks do on a match day, before and after the game, and ensuring that it was placed firmly inside a local cultural framework. You can hear Franco turn in his grave as Spain is shown up as a bewildering collection of local *fiestas*, regional languages, obscure rituals and obsessive rootsiness, all expressed ultimately in undying love for the local football team. English football coverage pales in comparison, despite its recent growth in more unconventional and off-beat types of presentation, probably because England cannot call upon such obsessive regionalism.

Nowhere is more obsessive or more particular than the Basque Country. The pugnacious, chain-smoking little Basque, Javier Clemente, sacked from his post as national team manager in early 1999 after a humiliating defeat in Cyprus, was forever at war with the media because of his tendency to include substantial numbers of his 'fellow countrymen' (his phrase) in the national squad. The fact that his sister was married to one of ETA's most wanted men was hardly a point in his favour either, so far as the solidly Madrid-based *Marca* was concerned.

29

His spats with the paper were legendary, and his love of fuelling the *morbo* all too apparent.

When asked by the paper why he had continued to use the ageing goalkeeper Andoni Zubizarreta at the 1998 World Cup instead of Real Madrid's Santi Cañizares, Clemente explained calmly that it was like inviting people around to your house for dinner. 'You don't ask people round who you feel uncomfortable with. It's as simple as that. Zubi's my friend. End of story.' The words were to haunt him after his friend and fellow Basque failed to get his creaky knees down to a tame shot in Spain's opening 3-2 defeat against Nigeria.

The Madrid press had always wanted Clemente's blood, having never forgiven him for breaking up the *quinta del Buitre* (Butragueño's gang) shortly after taking the job in 1992. Clemente's contribution to the latter part of the century's *morbo* cannot be overestimated and he was to distinguish himself in this particular field, a year after he was pushed from the national job. Taking on the manager's post at Real Betis for the 1998-99 season, his dour approach made him few friends in Seville, where supporters demanded, and usually got, attacking spectacle.

The cautious welcome the club gave him that September was reciprocated by Clemente's subsequent and obvious discomfort, so far from his native Bilbao. As the team stuttered to yet another 0-0 draw, he was spat on by a home fan as he walked down the tunnel, an incident which he described to the press after the game as 'the kind of thing that is normal down here. I'm sorry to say it, but I come from another country.' The insult to Andalucía, a region all too accustomed to receiving snide remarks from anywhere north of Seville, was all the worse in that it came from a northerner who made no secret of his Basque nationalist sympathies and who had just converted their previously exciting side into a team of negative dullards. **Another country!** screamed the local press, swallowing the bait and turning the pages purple with rage. The president of the club, a diehard local himself, now had the perfect excuse to send Clemente back up to the dole queue in Bilbao.

Morbo watchers could hardly wait for Clemente to return with his new team, whoever they were going to be. The gods of football usually manage to deliver the goods, and the first club to take him on the following season was Real Sociedad. His managerial debut, needless to say, turned out to be against Betis, in their Benito Villamarín Stadium. The night before the game I asked a barman in Seville if he thought the spitting incident had been a bit over the top. 'No,' he said. 'And when he comes out of the tunnel tomorrow, I'll be the first to spit on him again.'

He presumably went home happy with the 1-0 scoreline in favour of the home team, but there were no reports of any sputum flying through the air, just plenty of insults.

The *morbo* between the Basques and the 'centre' is by no means simply a modern phenomenon. As far back as 1920, when a Spanish national team first travelled abroad, to the Antwerp Olympics, the press complained about the fact that of the 21 players who travelled (third class, by train) to the tournament, 14 were Basque, four were from Barcelona and the remaining three were Galician. Though separatism up in the wilds of Galicia has never really been a serious issue, and Franco himself was born there, the region does have its own language, and its people describe themselves as Galicians first and Spaniards second. What worried the Madrid press, even back then, was that there was not a single player from the heartlands to represent the country in its first official trip beyond its own borders.

The presence of the 14 Basques was a fairly accurate reflection of the region's overwhelming influence on the early years of Spanish football. There are tales told, similar to those of the north-east of England, in which scouts in the region are forever hollering down holes in the ground, out of which would pop monstrous defenders, solid goalkeepers and prodigious goal-scorers. In fact the Spanish talk of the *cantera* (quarry) from which good young 'uns emerge, hewn from the rock of their particular regions. The Basques have always had more cause to celebrate the philosophy of the *cantera* than most, due to their insistence, from the early years of the century, on using only local players in their teams. This policy is still carried on by Athletic Bilbao, courting controversy in certain circles because their approach has always been coloured by suggestions of Basque racial purity and xenophobia – predictably and strenuously denied by those who support the practice.

The Basque Country was a booming place in the first half of the century due to its central role in Spain's long delayed industrial revolution. Bilbao, with its iron, steel, shipbuilding and chemical industries, was one of Spain's first modern urban disasters, but the region was seen as a land of opportunity for many Spaniards trapped in even grimmer rural poverty. The subsequent migrations north contributed to a burgeoning population and helped make the region renowned for producing tough little tykes from the quarries by the thousand. As proof of this, Athletic Bilbao were not the only Basque team represented at the 1920 Olympics. Real Unión, from the eastern border town of Irún, Arenas de Getxo, a prosperous suburb of Bilbao, and Real Sociedad of

San Sebastián, a city in the Gipuzcoa region to the east that the Spanish royal family had made fashionable by choosing it as their annual summer resort, all contributed players to the cause.

Arenas and Irún had won the King's Cup in the two seasons leading up to the Olympics, but the absence of any players from Real Madrid was still a trifle odd, given that the team from the capital were hardly an insignificant force in the game. They had, after all, managed to win five King's Cups between 1903 and 1920. It seems that the circumstances surrounding the selection of the squad for Belgium were themselves subject to Spain's peculiar socio-cultural games, the haphazard rules of which would come to guarantee another 80 years of related *morbo*.

The polemics surrounding the Olympics were a fairly mild precursor of what was to come, but in the classic style of *morbo*'s juiciest moments, the issue could not be separated from the personalities involved, in this case the Catalan, Paco Bru. As with Clemente, and Johan Cruyff before him, the more difficult or outlandish the human element, the richer the controversy. Paco Bru was certainly one of the first 'characters' in the Spanish game. Born in 1885, he played for Barcelona during the first decade of the century and went on to represent Español, before hanging up his boots in 1917. On retiring, he decided to become a referee. Before his first game in charge he is alleged to have walked into the dressing-room and pulled a Colt pistol from his haversack. Saying nothing, he threw the gun on to a table in the middle of the room and began to put on his refereeing gear. Once he was changed, he picked up the gun and stuffed it down his shorts, explaining to a player who had the temerity to ask him why, that he had merely wished to 'guarantee a quiet match, given that it is my first in charge'.

Once the Spanish Football Federation had decided to send a representative team to the Olympics – the country's football still being officially amateur – three selectors were chosen to pick the squad. Sensibly, they were chosen from the three regions that were producing the most footballers, José Berraondo from the north, Julián Ruete from the 'centre' (Madrid) and Bru from Catalonia. Then, in an act which beautifully illustrates Spain's unique habit of forming committees only to bypass them completely, the federation sent along a rag-bag selection of *probables* and *posibles* to the first training session in Vigo. None of the selectors had been consulted as to which players were to attend this initial session, but it hardly mattered, since neither Berraondo nor Ruete turned up, both citing 'family problems'. Bru, finding himself alone in Vigo with some 30 players he was to describe as 'totally crap', noticed that no Basques had been sent by the federation. Sensing a conspiracy between Julián Ruete and the administrators, he abandoned the sessions and insisted the federation agree to his recommendations.

Bru got his way and Spain came home with the silver medal, though more by dint of a series of bizarre circumstances than by their talent. In terms of *morbo*, the problem was that the coach and the emerging star, the goalkeeper Ricardo Zamora, were Catalans, and the majority of the players Basque. During the tournament, the federation, sensing that Spain might go all the way, sent a *madrileño* to act as 'delegate' to Bru, even though Bru had no idea who he was. Bru was no fool, and suspecting that the ad hoc post was merely an attempt to make the party more 'Spanish', ignored his new helper and just got on with the job, only to find that on returning triumphantly to Spain, the National Assembly had decided to award only the two absentee selectors, Ruete and Berraondo, Gold Medals of the State. Bru got nothing, until the Catalan press kicked up such a stink that there was nothing for it but to give him his just reward.

Since 1920 the Basque Country has always shown itself capable of making a generous contribution to *morbo* and you don't need a doctorate in political history to understand why. Franco suppressed the Basque language just as fervently as Catalan and, despite much bluster in the annals of Catalan *resistencia* history, it was the Basques who really did him harm. ETA's violence was a lurking threat from the Sixties onwards, which occasionally came spectacularly into the open. Two years before Franco's own death, the Basque separatists killed Admiral Carrero Blanco, eliminating the man who had been most likely to carry on the old dictator's legacy and striking a death blow to the image of invulnerability the regime had enjoyed for so long.

There was so much dynamite packed into the bomb that blew up his car in a Madrid side-street in December 1973 that the vehicle actually took off and landed on the roof of one of the overlooking buildings, an event still celebrated in Basque nationalist circles by a song which begins 'He flew, he flew...'. It was sung regularly when Real Madrid visited either Real Sociedad or Athletic Bilbao during the late Seventies, the period now officially termed the *transición* – meaning the transition to democracy and the election of Felipe González's Socialist party. Most young Basques of that generation still know the song, and the tune is so pretty that some fathers may still sing their children to sleep to it – especially on the night before a game against the old enemy.

The Basques are certainly a race apart. They talk of the Spanish – and anyone else – as *erdaldunak* (those who speak a different tongue) and still refer to families of Spanish migrant workers, whether second or third generation, as 'immigrants'. The Basque Country has a different feel to it, and not only because of the extraordinarily complex language which, unlike Catalan, has nothing whatsoever in common with Spanish. In fact it has nothing whatsoever in common with any language on earth today, a mystery that still represents the linguist's Holy Grail. I don't know if the Basques have their own word for *morbo*, but the concept is certainly alive and well up there in the misty mountains.

As with the Catalans, the only legal manifestation of Basque identity during the Franco years was through football. Nevertheless, the Basques waited for a year after the Generalísimo's death until they decided to 'come out' in an explicit gesture, although had the fixture list permitted they might have done it sooner. In December 1976 the captains of Real Sociedad and Athletic Bilbao walked on to the pitch at the Atocha stadium in San Sebastián carrying the Basque flag, the *Ikurriña*, which they placed ceremonially on the centre-circle before one of ETA's anthems, *Eusko Gudariak* (Basque Soldiers), was played over the tannoy – a politically seminal act which all Basques remember.

The two captains, Ignacio Kortabarría and José Angel Iribar, both became involved in Basque nationalist politics at a local level on retiring, and the connection between football and politics has always been well to the fore in the region – José Antonio Aguirre, a Bilbao player from the Twenties, was president of the Basque government during the pre-Civil War republic. The flag-carrying act must have struck a rich seam of *morbo*, especially as the game was on national television. Indeed, it is said that it was seen by one Lieutenant-Colonel Tejero and some of his army cronies in a cafe in Madrid, leading to the first mumbles among those gathered that 'something had to be done'.

It doesn't say very much for their speed of planning that it took Tejero almost six years to actually do anything about this awful plague of democratic expression, but when he did he certainly did it in some style, striding into parliament in Madrid and firing a gun into the rafters shouting 'Get down you bastards!'. Which of course they did. Fortunately, no one took him too seriously, and he ended up behind bars. Neither did anyone bother to ask him what his precise motives were, but he might well have replied: 'To stop any more of that nationalist flag-waving at football matches.'

It must have been tough on him and his mates, watching four months later on the prison telly as Real Sociedad went on to win their first

Spanish league title, pipping Real Madrid at the post with the last kick of the match up in Gijón. It is difficult to convey what it must have meant to the supporters of the San Sebastián club to win the league so soon after the tribulations of the Franco years, but the fact is that the city has lived off the event ever since, despite winning the title again the following year, 1982. There is a black and white photograph which adorns at least half the bars in San Sebastián's cobbled old quarter, in which Jesús Zamora, Real Sociedad's legendary mustachioed midfielder, is pulling back his right foot, eye fixed on the ball, about to pound home the goal that secured his team that coveted first title.

The year before they had lost it at the last gasp to their enemy from the capital by losing unexpectedly in Seville, having gone the whole season undefeated. The *morbo* surrounding the game in Gijón stems partly from that loss, partly from the whole swath of years in which they'd had their noses rubbed into the dirt in both sporting and political terms. Barcelona had always had their powerful team to dilute the effect the Franco years had on the general community spirit, but in the Basque country this was not the case. Athletic Bilbao, always the biggest Basque side until the 1980s, won four of the first eight championships between 1928 and the outbreak of the Civil War in 1936. That they won only two more in the next 40 years seems significant, to say the least.

Although there is now little love lost between the two principal Basque sides, Bilbao also rejoiced in their rivals' league title back in 1981. Zamora's goal came 12 seconds before the end of the game against Sporting Gijón, 150 miles to the west of San Sebastián, on a rainy afternoon in the grim Asturias mining town. The picture shows a mass of umbrellas among the wall of supporters behind Zamora, opened up against the torrential rain on the steep side of El Molinón, Sporting's ground. Real Madrid were winning their game, as expected, and Sociedad needed a point. Zamora himself recounts that, with Sporting winning 2-1, he was overcome by a sudden wave of depression:

> I looked around. It was bucketing down. I was freezing.
> The supporters had come a long way and I thought – we
> can't blow it again. I saw one of our defenders hoof it up
> one last time, but I felt too tired to chase it. Bixio [Gorriz]
> was up with the attack and he just swiped at it. The miskick
> came straight to me and I didn't even think. I just clouted
> it. It went in…

The emotions released by that goal were greater than all the negative energy that the Luftwaffe exploded on Guernica 40 years earlier under the satisfied smile of Franco. Every picture of the goal on the walls of the bars says the same: 'Are you watching Madrid?'

These days, the Basque country can no longer be portrayed as a united front of nationalists, all desperate to rid themselves of the central hegemony of Madrid's government. There are serious divisions, for example, between those who accept ETA's violence and those who reject it, between ethnic Basques and more recent arrivals and between Basque speakers and non-Basque speakers. Nor are the region's football teams on such friendly terms that they are immune to *morbo*. Real Sociedad in particular have long resented the fact that Athletic Bilbao consider themselves the top side in the region and the main flagship in the fleet of nationalist Basque sentiment. Athletic's connection with the Partido Nacionalista Vasca, the conservative nationalist party formed around the same time as the club, lends credence to Bilbao's claims, as do their trophy-laden history and their policy of sticking to the *cantera*. All good *morbo* fodder, even if, as will be seen in a later chapter, the claims often fall short of the reality.

Such complications are not always apparent from the outside. The BBC fell into the trap of simplifying the issues when attempting to film Ian Gibson's series *Fire in the Blood*, a documentary illustration of the Irish author's book on Spain, in 1992. Gibson, resident in Madrid for many years, seemed to have been seduced by the assumption that any Madrid-Basque *morbo* would have to be sought out in Bilbao, despite the fact that a majority of Athletic's supporters cannot even speak Basque.

Moreover, the film chose to focus on a game in San Mamés, Bilbao's stadium, between Athletic and Atlético Madrid, a curiously inaccurate choice to say the least. Atlético have certainly had some brushes with fascism in their past, and their infamous former president Jesús Gil y Gil is not exactly a liberal. However, the fact remains that the club was founded by students from Bilbao at the turn of the century and was actually a subsidiary of the original Basque club for the first few years of its life, sporting the same red and white stripes, as they still do today.

There is actually more rivalry and *morbo* between Atlético and Real Madrid than there is between these two clubs, and yet Gibson was determined to create some where it hardly existed. 'Why do you hate this team so much?' he asked a group of young supporters on the film, to which they predictably replied: 'Because they're Spanish aren't they? And we're Basque.' As if this wasn't enough, the next question was: 'And what would you do if you saw a Spanish flag in the stadium?' to which the gleefully predictable response was: 'We'd burn it!'

A focus on the dislike between Bilbao and Real Sociedad would have illustrated a much more interesting phenomenon, a sort of fratricidal *morbo* that lends the lie to the easy assumption that all one-fingered salutes are necessarily done in a southerly direction. The smash-and-grab transfer in 1996 of the young Joseba Etxeberría from Real Sociedad to Athletic caused a vast amount of bad feeling in the region and led to the clubs formally breaking off all official relations for almost two years.

Etxeberría, subsequently one of the brightest and most talented players in the Spanish squad, was clearly a star from the moment in 1995 when, as a 17-year-old, he scored twice on his debut for Real Sociedad in Gijón. That summer, his father, catching the whiff of pesetas in the air, became his son's agent and Bilbao moved in with the equivalent of £3 million – a record for a teenager in Spanish football and a transfer that broke the gentleman's agreement between the two clubs that there should be no poaching of each other's junior players.

The next season, with Etxeberría the new thing in Spanish football, he curiously failed to take to the field in San Sebastián, his club citing a mysterious back injury. It seemed that the *morboso* build-up to the game had got to the poor young chap. Among other welcoming delights, the Real Sociedad supporters had been busy all week designing gigantic peseta notes, which, as with Figo, accused Etxeberría of being a *pesetero*. The transfer guaranteed a healthy dose of extra *morbo* for many derbies to come. In January 2001, Etxeberría scored twice in San Sebastián to secure Bilbao's first victory there in 13 years, earning him a permanent chorus of *hijo de puta* and a hail of bottles, which cost Real Sociedad a 100,000 peseta fine.

Enough of the untranslatable substance for the time being. If these examples have provided some initial insights into the special nature of Spanish football, then it has served its purpose as a framework for the following chapters. Nevertheless, it will never be far away from whichever topic is under scrutiny, for as much as the Spanish federation would like to consider themselves in control of the game's destiny, it is clearly *morbo* that is its true governing body.

2. brave and bold

Huelva, birthplace of Spanish football

In a sleepy Andalusian town called Gaucín, 30 kilometres to the south-west of Ronda, you will find an old *fonda* (inn) down a small cobbled street off the main road. Even though most tourist guides suggest it would be worth your while to take a look, you get the impression there is some element of Hobson's choice in the recommendation, since Gaucín is not exactly bursting with things to do and places to see.

Its church is mundane, its bars small and scruffy and its shops practically non-existent. Wealthy expatriates hide away in the surrounding hills – Cecil Parkinson, Michael Douglas, to name but two you always wanted to meet – while the British chattering classes found out long ago that *Homes and Gardens* could be read in peace in the bougainvillea silence of their *fincas*, far from those frightful *Mirror* readers down on the sweaty coast.

The inn's door is covered by a swath of purplish brothel beads which tinkle as you draw them back and push open the small door to the dark interior. The inn was used by the officers of a series of British garrisons stationed between Huelva and Málaga, left behind to help protect the area after the Carlist War of the 1870s. The food is still good, and although the place could use a spruce-up, it remains unclear as to whether the owners have left it deliberately in its present state of decay for reasons of authenticity, orders from the town council or simply because of a lack of funds.

Looking around at the yellowing walls and the cold black and white tiles it is difficult to take yourself back 125 years and feel how comfortable and welcoming the place must have seemed after a march that might have begun some 85 miles to the west. But the cool, dark dining-room must have been a blessed relief during the summer months, when the area is as hot and unforgiving as anywhere in southern Europe. Several large visitors' books are now the main attraction of the place once you've finished your dessert. They are the originals, dating from the 1850s to the present day although, unless you ask, it is assumed that you want to see the oldest ones.

The elderly owners nod politely at your request to see the books, since they know that you have read about them in your tourist guide, and that the food has not been mentioned as the highlight. The two books they place on the dining table for your inspection are huge, with thick brown covers and surprisingly white pages, yellowing only in the corners. Most of the entries are written carefully in fountain pen, with that lovely joined-up handwriting that reminds you of childhood birthday cards from grandparents long since departed. All the scribes are officers, and most of them make similar, inoffensive observations such as: 'Good to be back again, after such a tiring few days. Food and company as good as always, and a most welcome shade!' Or: 'Left Cadiz yesterday morning and arrived here after a long march. We leave tomorrow at dawn, but meanwhile thank our hosts again for such friendly fare.' Then, however, a certain Captain WF Adams remarks that he and his men 'marched out from Huelva on Wednesday. Played foot-ball with some railmen at about an hour out. The only diversion we truly had.'

The entry is dated September 1874 and must refer to locals who were laying the railway line between the port of Huelva and the Rio Tinto copper mines, 40 miles to the north. The area lies some 80 miles south-west of Gaucín, and the line, built between 1873 and 1875, must have been built by locals only, since there is no reference in the historical documents to any foreign involvement, apart from financial.

Further north, in the godforsaken lands of the Cerro Colorado, English engineers, surveyors and workers were busy putting together an infrastructure that would help to satisfy the demand for copper occasioned by the second phase of the British industrial revolution, a demand that led Spain, hard-up and exhausted after the second Carlist War, to put up one of its prize assets for sale and to let it go cheaply to the first and most insistent bidder, who just happened to hail from London.

Captain Adams and his small bunch of men must have stumbled that day upon a group of local workers who would have been among the first to have actually played the game of 'foot-ball' in Spain. The date certainly puts them officially ahead of any ball-kicking activities that were taking place on the banks of the river Nervión, 800 miles to the north in Bilbao, as much as the Basques may wish to dispute it. Eleven years after the formation of the Football Association, Adams still uses the quaint 'foot-ball' compound, painting the game with an air of the innocence it must still have had, even in its country of origin.

The locals would have learned the game from the British workers who had already begun to make their way north in those early days of the mines, but who would have spent time in the port of Huelva before travelling up by horse-drawn carriage to the copper reserves. It would have been nice to have known the result, for, however good Adams and his men were, the heat of September in Huelva would certainly have favoured the local workers. Little did they know that 105 years later the town that would grow around and over their improvised pitch would resound to the delirious celebrations of an unlikely promotion to a Spanish First Division whose existence would bear testament to a socio-cultural phenomenon that in their wildest flights of fancy they could not have imagined.

Modern-day Huelva (pronounced 'Wellva') is not the kind of place you would choose for your honeymoon. It is tucked away in the south-west of the country as if it neither welcomes nor expects visitors. The countryside around is harsh and arid, waving you along to the damper delights of the Portuguese coast to the west. The industrial estates on the outskirts of the city seem a long way removed from the fabled romance of Andalucía – flamenco, Lorca, bullfights and dark-haired beauties behind wafting fans. As you drive around the back of the city on the ring-road, the buildings stop suddenly on the raggedy fields that straggle out towards the flat horizon, punctuated only by the occasional factory chimney. The flats on the outer edge of the city look neglected and crumbly, with washing hanging sadly from every window. If Huelva was once prosperous on the back of mining, time seems to have readjusted its accounts.

I had flown the length of Spain, from north-east to south-west, for the dubious privilege of seeing Recreativo de Huelva play Villareal, to take some time out in the original cradle of Spanish football. The guide books are dismissive, if they even mention the place at all. The *Rough Guide* calls it 'the least interesting city in Andalucía' and suggests you move on as quickly as possible – unless you've come to watch a game of football, of course.

The game against Villareal, from near Castellón, north of Valencia, is in the Segunda A, equivalent to the English First Division. Villareal had spent the previous season in the top flight, but I have not come because they are an 'attraction', rather because it is the only weekend I can squeeze in when Recreativo have a home game. I tell the taxi-driver why I have come to his city, in that chatty way the Spanish will accept as an alternative opener to the weather. He is nearing retirement, and looks a little bit like Steptoe.

'That's wonderful,' he enthuses through broken teeth. 'Everyone has forgotten about us down here, and it's not fair because we started it all.' I reassure him that I know this and that I have come to put the record straight. 'Years before any of them,' he continues, and takes me down a wide thoroughfare which I take to be the main street in the centre of the city, although the whole place is alarmingly quiet for Spain.

It's midday and sunny, the perfect combination for bar-life on the late autumn streets, but the weekend fiestas have seriously curtailed what little atmosphere the city might have to offer, the folks having gone away. When the driver points out the Casa Colón (Columbus House) in a way that suggests we have arrived at the city's only building of any interest, I ask to be dropped off. As I pay he tells me that the English built it in the 1870s, with the first profits from the copper mines, and that the gardens to the side of the building were the original site of the pitch where Huelva's first football team played.

Pointing further down the deserted road he tells me I will find the old Velódromo, Huelva's first stadium, and the *barrio de los ingleses* (the English quarter) which was built to house the mining company's directors, engineers and doctors. They were more or less permanently on-site but their professional status meant they could enjoy the luxury of the rail trip back to Huelva every night on one of the trains that carried the precious loads of copper to be shipped out to England. According to a journalist I was to meet later at the match, many of the houses there are still occupied by folks with curious names such as Pedro Smith and Alvarez Mackay, the great-great-grandchildren of the pioneers who chose to stay.

The taxi-driver's desire to tell me all this reminds me of one of the websites I had checked out before flying down, run by a certain Mauricio. He introduces the page by telling the reader that '*Soy Mauricio – del Recre, decano del fútbol español*' (I'm Mauricio, a fan of Recreativo, grand old man of Spanish football). The word *decano* will crop up time and again during my brief stay in Huelva, and it seems to be used in order to emphasise the point that Huelva were the first, just in case anyone had forgotten – a sort of clarion call to respect your elders, to remember your roots. The fact that Recreativo have done nothing significant since their official foundation in 1889 seems to further underline the importance of this, especially to the diehards who are left to carry on the cause.

After checking in to my hotel, conveniently situated about 100 yards from the *barrio inglés* and right next to the old Velódromo site (now a tennis court) I wander down into what I assume is 'town', past the Casa Colón and down the sun-shadow streets of late October to find somewhere for lunch. The Villareal players are staying in my hotel, and they have reserved the whole dining-room for themselves, forcing me to find sustenance elsewhere.

I take a photo of the Colón, an attractive orange-red building, decorated with some neo-colonial flourishes and now converted into a *casa de cultura*, a sort of low-profile arts centre you can find in any reasonably sized Spanish town. It was here, on the cold night of December 23, 1889, that the Huelva Recreation Club was founded. The meeting had been organised a month earlier on the initiative of the Anglo-German William Sundheim, one of the key figures in the purchase of the Rio Tinto mines, and the man who originally managed to convince the director of the Bank of London, one James Mathesson, that the English should put their money into the venture.

Sundheim is quoted by the club's historians as being the 'father of the club' mostly because of the time he spent in and around Huelva between 1870 and the turn of the century. He was certainly at the forefront of both the sporting and industrial web that began to spin itself into life during the latter part of the 19th century in Huelva, although his reasons for helping to found the club seem to have been very much part of the upper-middle class expatriate British tradition, something misinterpreted by the Huelvan historians as an altruistic gesture towards the 'land that he had come to love', as Placido Llorden puts it in his book on the club. The idea is an attractive one, but a reading of the minutes of that meeting back in December 1889 rather suggests that the founding of the club was merely another way in which the substantial expatriate community could make itself feel at home.

As with Bilbao and Barcelona ten years later, and, more controversially, Tarragona three years earlier, the club seems to have been founded with more general sporting principles in mind. Athletic Bilbao were formed by young students who hung out in a fashionable city gym, Barcelona were formed by a Swiss expatriate who certainly wanted to play football but who wasn't that fussy to begin with. According to most accounts he just wanted some healthy exercise and a bit of sweaty bonhomie. Club Gimnástico Tarragona, due south of Barcelona, were formed in 1886, and there are those (particularly from Tarragona) who claim that they are the *decano* and not Huelva. The problem with their claim is that they didn't get round to kicking a ball until 1914, whereas

Huelva Recreation Club certainly did – three months later in Seville, in the first officially reported match on Spanish soil.

Nevertheless, the elected secretary, one EW Palin, records seven separate motions in the minutes of the meeting, all passed unanimously by the largely British gathering and none of which mentions foot-ball. Tennis gets some attention, since the grounds to the side of the Colón already had three courts, and athletics figures high on the agenda too, with a 'meet' planned for February 1890.

The week after the meeting, just before New Year, some ground was cleared to the side of the courts – the pavement from where you can now stand and gawp over the fence at the attractively landscaped gardens (there is still a tennis court) – and a game was played between the elected members of the club and the crew of a ship that was docked in port. The only Spanish player was one of the *vocales* (committee members), a certain José Muñoz. The club won 3-1, a surprising result, given that the crew should all have been strapping lads bursting for a game after several days at sea, and the club members' average age must have been pushing the mid-thirties, at a conservative guess.

The fact that football seems to have been of secondary importance should not come as any surprise. The game, such as it was back then, could hardly have generated the sort of jolly-hockey-sticks networking so crucial to the health of expatriate life because it still lacked any defined ritual or cultural focus, whereas tennis and athletics offered a clearer framework of social possibilities for all the family, including cucumber sandwiches and lashings of ginger pop. This emphasis on the mainte-nance and development of a decent social life – given the lack of natural attractions in a place like Huelva – can be clearly seen in the text of the very first item on the night's agenda, which proposes that at the beginning of January 'a Grand Ball be held at the Casa Colón'.

Indeed, the whole meeting seems to have been organised a month previously on the condition that it included a 'sumptuous supper' which continued into 'the early hours'. So much for the founding of a football club. At least the participants had the foresight to put it all down on paper, elect a committee and file it away for posterity. That the locals should in time come to misinterpret the whole thing as having been done for the love of Huelva shows how strongly they have maintained their affection for England and the people who brought work and football to their region.

When it comes to confirming the date of the founding of the club and the date when football first came to Spanish shores, the jury is still locked in session. It becomes a question of whether you interpret a founding date as a matter of fact or as a matter of faith. In Bilbao they insist that their club was founded in 1898, but there are no surviving documents to support this claim. There was certainly a meeting that year, but the retention of the date for the archives looks suspiciously like an attempt to pip Barcelona by a year – a club definitely formed in 1899.

Such statistical one-upmanship is important in Spain, as it makes a deep and significant contribution to the concept of *pueblo*. Like a person's accent in England, in Spain people are identified by their provenance, by their *tierra*, whether they like it or not. The difference between 1898 and 1899 can change and colour many things, in all sorts of ways. The *Historia del Fútbol Español* (1994) even claims that Huelva were founded in 1880, though it fails to make clear on what basis. Sure, some games were going on between the English workers of the Rio Tinto mines and the Scottish workers at the Tharsis mines to the west, probably even before 1880, but this hardly constitutes a reason for bringing Huelva's founding date back a whole nine years. Locals must have been playing in these games, but that date marks the spirit of the enterprise, not the rubber-stamp.

About a hundred yards down from the Casa Colón, I find a small plaza lined on all four sides by book stalls. It is a *feria de libros*, a sort of Sunday-market second-hand book sale subsidised by the local town council. This one is completely empty of people. I wander across to a stall and ask the man behind the pile of books if he has anything on Recreativo de Huelva. He shakes his head and mumbles something to the effect that the man on the stall opposite with the glasses might have something. I thank him and walk across the empty square. The man with the glasses looks like he's about to pack up for lunch so I pop the question straight away. Without replying, he reaches down to a small pile of books and pulls out a copy of *Real Club Recreativo Huelva: Historia de un ascenso* (Story of a promotion) by Plácido Llorden, written in 1979, the year after Recreativo's famous promotion season. The author should of course have called the book *Historia de un ascenso y descenso*, since they went straight down again, but he obviously decided to dwell on the happier aspects of the story.

I ask him how much and he shrugs. 'What do you want it for?' he asks me, clearly surprised that anyone should want to buy it, and a foreigner to boot. 'Ah, but this is gold-dust,' I reply. 'I'm writing a book on Spanish football and I want to mention Huelva in it.' At this, he brightens considerably. 'You can have it for 400 pesetas (£1.70) then. I haven't sold one of these for years. There are only four left, and I've got them all,' he explains. 'I knew the publisher and he gave me a pile of them just before he died – of cancer,' he adds, as if I should be made aware of this. He beckons to his wife. 'This man is English and he's writing a history of Recreativo,' he tells her, already changing the details. 'Ooh, send us a copy when you've finished,' she implores, and she wafts her business card into my hand. 'It'll be in English,' I tell her, but she replies: 'Then all the better. We like our stall to be international.' They seem genuinely happy at the fact that their home-town club is to be back in the news, shaking my hand effusively as I leave.

In the first chapter of the book, the author wrote that Recreativo's second ground, the Estadio Colombino, was inaugurated in the 1956-57 season, when the old Velódromo was bulldozed to make way for a new sports complex. When I get there later in the afternoon, the white autumnal sun over to the west is almost touching the roof of the stand, casting dark shadows over the pitch. I squint into the sun and try to make out the players down below, warming up on the patchy grass. An obese young chap sits at an old wooden table a few steps up from me selling Coca-Cola, and since there is no one else around this part of the terracing, I ask him who the star of the team is. He wheezes on his cigarette. 'Stars? You must be joking. We haven't got any of those. Stars are in the sky, mate. They don't come down to Recre.' 'Not doing so well this year?' I continue. They actually lie 18th of 22 in Segunda A, only two points clear of the relegation places. 'That's right,' he nods, his face lost in a billow of smoke. 'They're crap. Always have been, always will be.'

As it turned out, his pessimism was misplaced, though it was easy to share it at the time. Three years later Recreativo would be back in the First Division in a spanking new stadium, although they were to display admirable consistency by returning to the Second straight away. But at least they made a better fight of it, and even reached the King's Cup final (losing 3-0 to Mallorca) for the first time in their long history. Back then, on that sunlit day, none of these things seemed remotely possible.

As if to show me that he wishes to take matters no further, the man begins to pack up his stock into a wooden crate, turning his back on me. I walk down to the high perimeter fence and gesture an official towards me. The press secretary has given me a pass, on the solid grounds that I have come to write his club back into the archives, and this time in English. 'Go and find Cotán Pinto,' he told me, 'he'll tell you all you need to know.' Cotán Pinto, according to the press secretary, is a legendary journalist who has been reporting on Recre since the dawn of time, and who will be more than happy to help in my research.

The official nods and unbolts the gate, gesturing me over to the West Stand. As I walk around the perimeter track, the soothing murmur of the gathering crowd is suddenly pierced asunder by the raucous screech of a woman howling out a traditional Sevillana, blasted out of a large metal speaker sitting on the edge of the running track. The volume is brain-shattering. At the very least, the noise begins to bring some life to the place.

I stop behind the goal and take a snap of Gica Craioveanu, the Romanian international who used to buy his bread from the same bakery as me when he played for Real Sociedad. Just before the 1998 World Cup I had asked him if he could wangle me some tickets for the England v Romania match. He laughed and told me he'd wait and see how many he was allocated, but I never saw him in the shop again. The next season he was transferred to Villareal after a bust-up with Real Sociedad's then manager, Bernd Krauss. In the hotel I had bumped into him in the bar having a coffee, just before leaving for the game. Jokingly I had reminded him of the tickets, at which point he recognised me and said: 'You – San Sebastián!' Now he notices me behind the net and does a mock little curtsey.

I walk around to the West Stand, still darkened by the shade. The central parts of the old wooden structure have been tainted by the standard bucket seats, but the open terracing to the north and south is a real throwback to pre-Hillsborough days. The central stand is filling up and I begin to feel conspicuous, dwarfed by the height of the structure and unprotected by the glare which had led me to believe there were fewer in the ground than there really were.

I ask an official to let me through the high gate that gives on to the central walkway of the stand, high up to where I can see the journalists gathered. There's a nice pre-match murmur and a smell of cigar smoke in the air as I walk up between the seats. The ground reminds me suddenly of my boyhood team, Grimsby Town, and the old wooden Barrett Stand where I used to pay fortnightly homage. It always takes a while to understand another ground, to recognise that it has a history, characters and a whole socio-cultural baggage that you can never fully appreciate, mainly because you yourself have been brought up on a different model.

There is nothing you can do about this, but the older you get the more you are prepared, at the very least, to admit the possibility that another team might have a history as colourful as the one in your heart, and that it might have things of interest that yours never had. Nevertheless, the first sensations here at Recre are ones of solidarity. It's an instinct you pick up from having watched too much Fourth Division English football, for I can smell failure in the air, can see it etched on the faces of the crowd as I climb the stand. It's something in the way the people sit, hunched and resigned, as if they've come despite their better judgement. The euphoria of their 1978 promotion looks like a distant memory.

A steward beckons me into the *palco*, the box for the privileged – either a dignitary, official or journalist who can take his or her place in the highest part of the best stand and enjoy the spectacle without having to worry about the cascade of peanut-shells and cigarette butts that characterises the lot of the poor groundlings down below. The lowest order of the privileged classes, the journalists, are bunched together between three crumbling concrete walls at the top of the stand, some of them leaning over the main wall that separates them from the masses like horses nodding over a stable door.

I come in through the back and am introduced to the legendary Cotán Pinto. Avuncular, in his late fifties, he pops a biro behind an ear and stands up formally, eyeing me a little suspiciously. I try to reassure him: 'Please don't make a fuss. I don't want to disturb your work.' To which he replies with disarming frankness: 'Oh good. Then we'll talk at half-time.' His colleague to my right motions for me to sit down on a stool that they have presumably reserved for me, and I take out my note pad – to blend in and look the part.

The colleague introduces himself as being from the *Huelva Información* newspaper and tells me: 'Never mind the old fart. He's getting a bit long in the tooth now and he can only concentrate on one thing at a time – eh Cotán?' Whereupon the butt of this sarcasm begins to sketch a rough but skilful caricature of the man to my right, dressed in a skirt and sporting horns on his head – the sign of the cuckold in Spanish culture. 'Ha – go and fuck a fish!' the cuckold laughs. It appears I am in for an interesting 90 minutes.

It doesn't take long for Villareal to score. The mild optimism generated by a few flurries of rather aimless home attacks is soon crushed by a ridiculous goal, symptomatic of a team who are low on luck and confidence. The long-haired blond midfielder who had spent an hour in the hotel talking to his *amor* on the mobile will now have something of more substance to tell her at half-time. The Recre goalkeeper's attempt to punch away a corner results in a two-fisted waft at the Andalusian air, and a clumsy tumble over his own defender. As he struggles to his feet, Villareal's Lothario stubs his shot some five yards out, but the ball bobbles on a divot and evades all the Recre defenders' flailing attempts to stop it trickling goalwards. It ends up in the net amid a pile of bodies, and the blond lover-boy races to the dug-out, hair dancing on the breeze, as if he has just scored the sudden-death goal in the World Cup final.

There is a deathly hush in the stand, which makes the celebrating Villareal players look like disrespectful children playing at a funeral. The journalists, instead of trying to establish how the goal was scored, break into a chorus of foul-mouthed invective against the manager (he's from Bilbao – which explains it all) and shout across me in their attempts to apportion the blame to someone – the president, for having no real youth policy, the manager for being *un inocente* and so on. I shrug. As far as I can see, it's early days yet, and it's a game of two halves.

Looking around the ground from the *palco* it is difficult to connect the scene below with the goings-on of over 100 years ago. Recre are still wearing the same colours – blue and white stripes and white shorts, but they look curiously undernourished and smaller than the Villareal players, strutting around in their more confident yellow tops. There is a photograph in Llorden's book of the 1927 Recre team, by then playing in the Second Division of the regional Andalusian league and about to be promoted to the First. The players stand in an apologetic sort of way, their arms hanging by their sides. Only one of them has that confident crossed-arm posture you associate with team photos of today.

They are either small, or skinny, or both, and as my grandmother used to remark, 'they looked like a good meal would stiffen 'em'. The contrast with the photographs of the beastly Bilbao teams of the period holds some sociological significance. Huge strapping Giant Redwoods staring at the camera, fed on a diet of beans, fish and steak – the stuff of intimi-dating champions – itching to go out and kick their opponents to death. Down here they must have been fed on crumbs.

Socio-economically, Andalucía has improved dramatically, but not to the same extent as the north of Spain. Flying down from San Sebastián, Spain's second most expensive city after Madrid, the contrast is eloquent. Whereas in San Sebastián no one would be seen at a football match unless dressed in their best, here the 7,000 or so folks seem to be much less preoccupied with the labels on their clothes, as if they had more basic budgetary priorities.

In a pause in the game I ask Cotán if Recre's black central striker, Bodipo, is local. In the match programme, there is an interview with him, and I have been reading it while a Villareal player receives treatment. Besides, he seems a decent player. 'Nah – he's from Seville,' replies Cotán. 'Almost all the players are. There's no decent kids coming through now, and if they do, they go to Betis or Sevilla. The ones that come here have failed up there. So where are we going?' He points down to the ground, or Segunda B, as I take his gesture to mean.

Bodipo responds to various questions in the programme. The first one asks if he prefers beer or wine. 'Wine, from La Rioja,' he replies. An English player would probably have said 'mineral water'. In women he likes the qualities of 'humility and sincerity' and his favourite food is paella. On the next page there is a quiz on the history of the club consisting of five questions, all of which I can answer after an hour browsing through Llorden's book. Send the answers to *Afición Decana* (supporter's club) and the first ten correct entries will win you a colour poster of the Colombino Stadium.

I decide to resist the temptation. Besides, the club secretary has already given me a commemorative poster of the club and despite the initial coolness of the journalists, it is clear they are quietly chuffed at the fact that I've come to the game, even if they are trying hard to do their jobs and pay me minimal attention. Whenever Recre do something half decent, such as putting together three consecutive passes, they look back at me, gauging my reaction. I can tell that they want me to like their team, to identify with their cause.

At half-time the *Canal Sur* commentator bursts into the *palco* from behind and thrusts a microphone under my nose. The national radio circuit is doing the rounds of the Second Division half-time reports and instead of doing his usual bit, this journalist has decided to get a foreign perspective. To my own horror and surprise, cliches stream from my mouth with curious fluency, as if my tongue has been waiting all its life for this moment. I say politely that Recre were playing well up to the unfortunate goal and that in the second half, given some sweat and application, they could at least draw the game. I commit myself, under pressure, to a 2-1 result. The hacks around me nod appreciatively.

They look less appreciative as full-time approaches and Villareal make it 4-0. The cushions are beginning to spin down onto the pitch and my friend Craioveanu is playing havoc with the poor youngster drafted in to play left-back. Every time the Romanian gets the ball, Villareal seem to score. As the whistling and booing begin, I excuse myself and make my way down the central aisle to the fence at pitch level. The steward recognises me and lets me out on to the running-track. Over on the south side there is a curious banner that has attracted my attention and I want to get a picture of it. It is draped over the high fencing and it reads *Peña Mackay* (Mackay supporters club). According to Llorden's book, Dr McKay (the supporters have misspelt it) was the real father of the club, even more than Sundheim.

The game carries on to my left in the white glare of the floodlights. Craioveanu speeds down the touchline, unnervingly close to where I am walking, and knocks in a cross. The white ball whistles through the evening air and I can hear the players panting and swearing. The crowd noise is just a dull discontented murmur as I line up the photo of the huge white cloth banner. The members of the *Peña Mackay* notice me from behind the fence and begin to pose jokingly for a photograph. There is little else to occupy their attention, since their team has clearly thrown in the towel.

McKay, who did a term as club president between 1903 and 1906, joined up with Sundheim and the German Doetsch in the early 1870s after Sundheim had convinced the Bank of London to invest in the project. McKay came out as the on-site doctor, beginning his work in 1873 up in the Cerro Colorado. There were 152 'houses' to accommodate the workers, but conditions must have been tough up there back in August 1873 when the foundations of the plant were first laid. Two years later McKay was permanently resident in Huelva, looking after the better-heeled employees of the *barrio inglés* down the road from the Casa Colón.

Something of a sportsman himself, it was McKay who apparently organised (and played in) the initial encounters between the predominantly English workers of Rio Tinto and the Scots over at Tharsis. The Tharsis copper mines, smaller and less productive, were developed and working before the Rio Tinto plant, but the quantities of raw material were never such as to bring in their wake the infrastructure that was put into place to support the Rio Tinto complex which, by the turn of the century, was one of the major copper-producing plants in the world. Sundheim and his friends were no fools.

Their major problem, and that of the workers under their direction in those early years, was the amount of time that would lapse between ordering parts for the plant and their subsequent arrival. There were no faxes, internets or mobiles. But there were cloths, and there was string. The combination of these magical materials produced rudimentary footballs, and games were played between the employees of the two mines. There are no records of any games still extant, but it is known that McKay was a decent player, despite being in his early forties.

All the documents I have read refer to him as an Englishman, but the surname looks rather north of the border to me. It's tempting to conclude that the sporting contact between the two mines was brought about by McKay precisely because it put him in touch with his fellow Scots and probably extended his socialising possibilities a bit further – a few Burns' nights wouldn't have gone amiss up there in the barren wastes and swamps of the Rio Tinto. It's impossible to establish whether Sundheim played, but his German colleague apparently did.

These would probably have been the first games played on the soil of Spain, a year before Captain Adams set out on his eastward march and stopped to play with some local workers. Those workers would have been tutored in the arts of the game by sailors and staff of the English ships docked in port – but their colleagues up in the Cerro Colorado were probably locals from Huelva anyway, and the game had obviously begun to spread like a benevolent virus. The only question that remains is whether the date of August 1873 is really the date of the first flight of a ball through Spanish air.

Plácido Llorden speculates in his book that there were others before then, not only among the workers of the Tharsis mines but up in the Rio Tinto hills between 1863 and 1870 when one Joseph Lee Thomas, an English civil engineer, went back and forth from Blighty on the invitation of the Spanish government to establish whether or not the mines were worth exploiting. Lee Thomas must have been accompanied by fellow engineers and site surveyors. They are never named, but maybe it was they who were the first to kick the cloth ball through the warm Andalusian air.

But as we now know, the Huelva Recreation Club was formed 16 years after the foundations of the plant in Rio Tinto had been laid. By that time a considerable infrastructure had been built up, the pioneers of the venture had made themselves rich and a whole army of expatriates was seemingly buzzing in and around Huelva helping themselves to some of the pickings, organising elaborate booze-ups or trying to keep fit. Their relationship with the locals remains unclear, although if there was resentment at the fact that the English were bleeding that part of the land dry, it has never surfaced. Any such sentiments are entirely absent from the attitudes of all the Spanish chroniclers. On the contrary, they are all quite misty-eyed and reverential towards these invaders.

Indeed, they talk of the first 'official' game played on Spanish soil in terms of a national event, despite the fact that of the 21 players (the Seville side could only muster ten) gathered on that March morning in 1890, only two were Spanish. But that was the way things were, and it would be wrong to poke fun. Duclós (whose son went on to play for Seville) and Coto, both in the Huelva team, were the first of the line, the first to play in a representative side – and because they belonged to a club their participation was written down and recorded for posterity. Acts of faith are fine, but they are of little use to the more empirical demands of history.

On March 8, at five o'clock in the morning, 22 men set out by train from Huelva to Seville: 11 players, two referees (both English and on the club committee) and nine other members of the club along for the ride, as cheer-leaders or orange-peelers. Whatever the reasons of the nine for going along, it is recorded that each member of the 'expedition' would have to pay for the trip out of his own pocket. They were travelling on the invitation of a group of British expatriates who constituted the Seville Water Works, a company charged with the modernisation of the city's sewage system, not 'British employees of the Rio Tinto mines' as erroneously reported by some sources. The game was scheduled for 11am, at the Tablada Hippodrome. The newspaper *Los Sports* reported that there was a large (but unspecified) number of spectators:

> *Foot-ball – es un juego de pelota muy distraído y a la vez higiénico por el mucho que requiere. La particularidad de este juego consiste en que, en vez de botar la pelota con las manos y con las paletas, se bota con los pies, y, en casos apurados, con los hombros o con la cabeza.*

It's a paragraph worth reproducing in the original Spanish, out of respect for the fact that these were the first two sentences ever written about a competitive match on Spanish soil, organised by two distinct entities representing two distinct geographical locations. Translated, the unnamed journalist wrote that:

> Football is a very enjoyable and healthy ball game since it demands a lot of physical effort. The peculiarity of this game resides in the fact that instead of striking the ball with the hands or with bats it is struck instead by the feet and, in extreme cases, using the shoulders or the head.

The two line-ups are printed, although since we know that Wakelin played in goal in the club's previous game in Huelva against the ship, Alcock's name at the head of the list may not mean that he was the goalkeeper – the journalist obviously preferring to single out the captains first. The order of the other names seems to be random and the inclusion of only nine players and a substitute is baffling. However, the teams were recorded as the following:

Colonia inglesa sevillana	Huelva Recreation Club
Maccoll (capitán)	Alcock (capitán)
Logan	Yates
Strougler	Wakelin
Rikson	Duclós
Annodall	Coto
Mandy	Kirk
White	Daniels
Welton	Curtis
Craig	Gibbon
Un sustituto	
Dadley	Smith

Great names. Where have all the Alcocks and Gibbons gone, long time passing? It is interesting, given the favourable result for the 'English colony' in Seville, 2-0, that it took a further 17 years for the first team to be officially founded in that city – when it was, it was made up exclusively of wealthy land-owning Spaniards. The relationship between the expatriates of the water works and the people of Seville must have been a more professional, more distant one than that which had been built up in the smaller town of Huelva. The Seville players that day simply cannot have been in a situation where they were coming across many locals on a social or sporting basis. In Huelva, the Spanish presence in the club was hardly overwhelming, but it was there nonetheless, and it was obviously not merely token. Had it been thus, the game would never have taken off in Huelva.

Recreativo never made many waves, and by 1902, in the first national competition to invite teams from around the country, they were conspicuous by their absence. Seville might justifiably claim to have established themselves more quickly as a force in the game, but in terms of sheer population, that hardly comes as a great surprise. But back on March 8, 1890, Huelva Recreation Club had their big day out, lost to ten men, but contributed in some small way to the spread of the game in Spain.

The unarguable fact that if it hadn't happened in Huelva, it would have happened somewhere else, should not be allowed to diminish Recre's status as the *decano* of the Spanish game. It seems more interesting that the first two clubs to be founded, Recreativo and Palamós (1898), should not have gone on to establish themselves among the giants. The same is true of the English game, as if, in a more authentic interpretation of the spirit of sport, the founders had other things on their minds than the mere pursuit of world domination. Of course, a more mundane interpretation of this would be that neither Palamós (in Catalonia) nor Recreativo had the financial wherewithal to compete, once they were cast adrift from their original moorings. Without airports, motorways and high-speed trains, Huelva was a long way from anywhere. Barcelona, Real Madrid and Athletic Bilbao always had the money or, at the very least, the potential for obtaining it.

Those three were all represented at the aforementioned Coronation Cup in 1902, and it wasn't until 1906 that Huelva finally made it to the annual national cup competition in Madrid, where they reached the semi-finals, only to bow out 3-0 to the eventual winners, Madrid FC. By all accounts, Huelva played some great stuff, but were a bit lightweight up front. But apart from a dearth of strikers, the obvious difference between a club like Recreativo and, for example, Barcelona, was that Huelva had no political reason for forging ahead and forming an institution that could grow to be recognised as a representative body of its community. All football clubs perform this role to some extent, but not all need to generate and live off *morbo* in quite the same way as the three leaders of the Spanish scene came to do. Those who write that the tensions between Barcelona and Real Madrid only really surfaced after the Civil War, or that Basque nationalistic expression did not exist before Franco, should look again at the stormy relationships between these clubs almost from the off.

These particular thoroughbreds were already frothing at the mouth in the stalls, and once released began pushing and shoving all the way down the track. They will never reach the finishing line, of course, but along the way they have created sporting institutions that are safe bets when it comes to generating profits. People will flock to invest in expressions of regional nationalism (or implicit rejections of it, as in the case of Real Madrid) and the fact that these leviathans grew from clubs which were expressing the Hellenic concept of a more general sporting ethos should not blind us to the fact that they quickly transmuted into something more brazenly political.

Huelva had none of this to sustain them. They took part again in the 1907 tournament but won only a single point, against newcomers Salamanca, and withdrew the following year, despite the fact that the Madrid authorities were offering subsidies to travelling participants, to be paid out of the anticipated gate money. Six of the 11 players in Huelva's 1906 line up were Spanish. Though the British presence in the side is still significant, it is clear that the expatriate roots of the club were beginning to fall away. By 1909 the club was officially renamed Real (royal) Club Recreativo de Huelva, in recognition of King Alfonso XIII's acceptance of the position of honorary president (he only had to turn up to the odd game every five years). Whereas the presidency of the club as a fitness-cum-social centre had been exclusively British – Charles Adams from 1889 to 1902 and Alex McKay from 1903 to 1906 – thereafter the men at the helm were always Spanish.

Back at the game, I return from taking a photo of the *Peña Mackay* and the referee is about to put the Recre players out of their visible misery when another journalist approaches me, armed with a dictaphone, and begins to ask why I have come to the game, how the league compares with its English equivalent and how I had come to hear of Recreativo. As the game ends behind the small man's balding head, I tell him diplomatically that Recre would be fine in the First Division, though on what I have seen I secretly fancy Grimsby's chances against this lot. He asks me where I am staying, and wonders if he could meet me the next morning to extend the interview, to which I agree.

On the way back to the hotel, I stop off at the site of the Velódromo. It was built in 1892 entirely from English funds, but on land that belonged to the Rio Tinto Company, about 20 yards from the top of the street that marks the start of the *barrio inglés*, running parallel to the old railway line that connected the port with the mines. The club committee were anxious that the stadium should be completed to coincide with the 400th anniversary of Columbus's landing in the New World, and from its planning to its opening the whole project took a mere 14 months.

It boasted a cycle track around its perimeter (hence the name), as well as a tennis court, roller-skating area and gymnasium. Football was just another sport to be played there. Now some kids are playing five-a-side under dim yellow floodlights and three youths watch from a wall above, rolling a joint. The football area and the tennis courts are all tastefully shaded by palm trees, and I try to imagine the lie of the old pitch, from the sepia photos reproduced in Llorden's book. The ground was Recre's until 1956, when the town council built the Estadio Colombino and rented it to the club.

In the morning, the balding, friendly little man is waiting in the lobby at 9.30 sharp. I have emerged from the breakfast bar of the hotel with the local papers, one of which, he tells me keenly, contains his report and a short piece about me. I remark on the harsh tone of the reports of the game, as if the press has already written them off, and so early in the season. I point at the headline in *Huelva Información* that trumpets **Recre aplastado por un Villareal muy superior** (Recre crushed by vastly superior Villareal) to which my new friend replies enthusiastically that the headline is his, stabbing at it with his finger. I look to the bottom of the piece for his name – Juan Bautista Mojarro García.

'They were truly awful,' he adds, shaking his head and falling back into the sofa in the empty lounge. 'I have to report the truth, or else things will get worse,' at which point he whips out several books from a shopping bag and piles them up on the coffee-table between us. 'I'm a writer too,' he smiles. 'I would like you to have these,' he says, and with startling generosity hands me three of his novels. 'This one is the one I would really like you to read,' he says, and as if to ensure that this will happen he opens the cover of *Silencio y Soledades* (Silence and solitude) and signs it *'con amistad'* with that typical openness you get in the south of Spain, in stark contrast to the colder, more distant people where I live. He shows me the *breve* he has written about me, couched in the typically florid language of the south, as if my visit has been of immense historical significance: *'El historiador inglés, Philip Ball, presenció ayer el partido desde el palco con el fin de relucir el nombre del Recreativo...'* (The English historian, Philip Ball, watched the game from the *palco* yesterday with a view to rekindling the name of Recreativo...).

Before he goes, he urges me to read *Silencio y Soledades* and gives me his phone number so that I can tell him what I think. The book, he tells me, is about a woman who lives with her worker husband on one of the houses by the Rio Tinto mines in the Cerro Colorado, circa 1875. 'She has an affair,' Juan explains, 'and you can read a little of what it was like back then, for the guys who were playing football up there, with your English friends. It will help you with your book.' I thank him in that embarrassed English way that has neither the language nor the bodily gestures to cope with sudden acts of spontaneous kindness.

On the flight out of Seville I read the back cover of *Silencio y Soledades* and take in my friend's impressive literary credentials. The picture of him on the dust jacket is of about a decade past, given the relative abundance of hair and sharper chin-line, and from the potted biography I calculate his current age to be 54. Judging by their titles, the other books that he has written all seem to touch on similar themes – solitude, angst and loss – and yet he seemed such a chirpy fellow. Maybe it has something to do with living down there in Huelva, cut off from the mainstream, the swamps of Doñana to the east, a foreign land to the west, and to the north mile upon mile of bleak and arid flatlands, eventually punctuated by the fists of the Cerro Colorado.

It can't have been much fun up there, year after year, even for the locals who were at least accustomed to the unforgiving summers. No wonder they started playing football in the coolness of the afternoons, after the day shift. In the book, the protagonist Eva spends a lot of time looking longingly out of their 'prefab' to the south, wondering if she has made the right decision to come and live out there, wondering if life shouldn't promise just a little bit more.

Half an hour into the flight it's clear that Eva is going to try her luck with one of the English workers, or more probably vice-versa, and that it'll as likely as not end in tears. I scan the pages for a mention of football, of shirts thrown down as goalposts in the afternoon sun, but it seems as if Eva's Don Juan is to be one of the chaps who run a race around the plant every Friday afternoon after work, his hairy chest exposed to the fading sunlight and Eva's tired eyes.

Poor Recre, seemingly doomed by geography to spend the rest of their days looking backwards. At the end of the season, while Villareal were joining the elite, they finished second from bottom, though they were saved from relegation to the wasteland of *Segunda B* because Mérida and Logroñes failed to meet the federation's financial criteria. Recreativo's club song says it all really, a howl in the wind of a century that has largely passed them by. Apologies for some poetic licence in the translation, but it's the jaunty spirit of the piece that matters:

> *Himno del Recre*
> White and blue is the flag
> Of my seafaring Huelva
> In the Spanish fields the first to play the game!
> A hundred years, a hundred years, a hundred years is ours
> The colours of my Recre on the Crown of Royalty's name

Recre, Recre, Recre
Long live my Recre
Long live my team, my sporting club of old!
Recre, Recre, Recre
Long live my Recre
Long live Recreativo brave and bold!

Ole! My fighting Huelva
In our football first to shine
From the terracing we shout and beat our chest!
For we want to see our Recre
Yes, we want to see our Recre
In the Spanish fields competing with the best!

Recre, Recre, Recre
Long live my Recre...

The song was written in 1989 to commemorate the club's centenary. All clubs in Spain have a *himno*, as they religiously put it, and they all reveal something of the particular historical and cultural *raison d'être* of the institution. For Huelva – apart from the optimistic battle-cry of the last line – the subtext of the song is an inglorious past whose only real achievements have been longevity, royal patronage and, of course, the founding fathers bit.

But let us not begrudge them their 15 minutes of fame. Call me a loser, but I for one would much sooner be among 7,000 souls at Recreativo's old ground than sit through the spiritual death of the corporate Premier League experience. The biggest shame of the whole Huelva story is that fate could have dealt them a happier blow by handing them one of their two years in the top flight in their centenary year, rather than 1978. But the fact that they got there at all is cause enough to celebrate. It's a friendly little club who touchingly treated my visit as the best thing to happen to them that day, given the adverse events witnessed on the field. It's not every day in the world of football that strangers make you feel at home.

Happily, the new century has seen something of an upturn in the club's fortunes. By the end of 2000 a remarkably stingy defence had seen Huelva to fourth place in Segunda A, having conceded only six goals in the first 18 games of the season. Having been miraculously saved from relegation the previous season, they missed out on promotion by a point.

The next season they proved it was no fluke and returned to the top flight for only the second time, this time in a new stadium (Nuevo Estadio Colombino), inaugurated in November 2001 with a game against Newcastle United – a club which turned professional in 1889, the year of Recre's birth.

I went to see my old friends again in November 2002 at El Sadar, Osasuna's ground in Pamplona, and seemed to bring them some luck. As many had predicted, they were down at the bottom of the table, but Osasuna weren't doing much better. Recre's 1-0 win, secured with a penalty five minutes from the end, was their first victory in the top flight since June 2, 1979, when they beat Espanyol 3-1 at home. Outside the press area, after the game had finished, the players were still giving each other high-fives in an atmosphere of near ecstasy.

I approached the defender José Galán, the only player left from the 4-0 debacle at home to Villareal in 1999 and showed him the programme I had kept as a souvenir of that evening. He seemed slightly confused. 'Do you want me to sign it?' he asked. 'No, no,' I stuttered, slightly embarrassed. 'I just wanted you to know that you don't lose every time I come to watch you'. At this, he turned to a ruck of team-mates and shouted 'Hey! Get this guy some free tickets. He can come to every game!'

Oddly enough, the club must have heard him, because they did indeed get me a ticket for the King's Cup semi-final at the same ground, in March 2003. It was chucking it down, the crowd were hostile and the pitch resembled a paddling pool, but Recre battled back from 2-0 down to draw and win a place in the final for the first time ever. It was a wonderful game, and I felt strangely privileged to be there.

It would be nice if the future could extend a little more generosity to this unique little club, but at least their second whiff of the big time has given them cause to sing their song with genuine cause for optimism: Long live Recre, long live Recreativo brave and bold!

3. the quarrymen

Athletic Bilbao and the politics of the Basque Country

The Spanish are keen amateur historians and tend to have a good knowledge of the key events in their own history. Better than the British, certainly. The average man or woman in the street can usually be trusted to hold forth on the history of the country, or their region, until the cows come home. They're good on trivia too, and it's not just a certain type of man that can deliver the goods, but young children of both sexes, and their grannies.

In my first year in Spain, I was amazed to overhear a restaurant conversation at the table next to me between five elderly, well-dressed women, all talking animatedly about the Spanish First Division, its players and the over-cautious tactics of the national manager, Javier Clemente. On catching me smiling, one of them asked me what the problem was. Secure in the knowledge that I was unlikely to be taken to task on the grounds of political correctness (the phrase has only recently entered the language) I shrugged my shoulders and told her the truth – that I was surprised to hear them talking about football. She waved her hand in dismissal of my comment: 'What do you want us to talk about? Our husbands?' she cackled, and continued to hold forth on the rights and wrongs of the sweeper system.

Of course, the men are at it too. On the internet you can satisfy your statistical lust over the 'all-time table' of the Spanish First Division. Most Spaniards could have a good stab at picking the top 20 out of the 53 teams who have played at that level, and would have absolutely no problem with the order of the top five, which is:

1 Real Madrid
2 FC Barcelona
3 Atlético de Madrid
4 Athletic Bilbao
5 Valencia

The only possible surprise is that Atlético are third and Athletic Bilbao fourth, although the gap between them is narrow. When Atlético went down at the end of the 1999-2000 season they had amassed 2,438 points in their top-flight history, to Bilbao's 2,425. The Basques almost leapfrogged them, but Atlético returned in 2001 and are hanging on.

However, the factual knowledge floating around the country has failed to purge one myth that seems to have endured to the present day, namely the idea that Athletic Bilbao were the first club to be officially founded in Spain. They weren't even the second, but the myth is understandable given the prominence of the team in the years preceding the formation of the league in 1928, and the tendency of the natives of Bilbao, famed for their *chulería* (cocky self-importance), to propagate the idea.

The truth is that Bilbao beat Real Madrid and Barcelona by a whisker and that the emergence of these three teams around the turn of the century enabled other teams from those three regions to form and flourish. By the time the first professional league was formed in 1929, Catalonia was also represented by Español and Club Deportivo Europa, the region of Castile had produced Atlético Madrid, the Basques had Real Sociedad, Arenas and Real Unión to accompany Athletic. The only team of the pioneering ten outside the 'big three' regions was Racing Santander from Cantabria – and they were to finish bottom that first season.

José María Arrate, the wine merchant elected president of Athletic Bilbao in 1994, wrote in an introduction to the club's centenary book:

> Athletic Bilbao is more than a football club, it is a feeling – and as such its ways of operating often escape rational analysis. We see ourselves as unique in world football and this defines our identity. We do not say that we are either better or worse than others, merely different. We only wish for the sons of our soil to represent our club, and in so wishing we stand out as a sporting entity, not a business concept. We wish to mould our players into men, not just footballers, and each time that a player from the cantera makes his debut we feel we have realised an objective which is in harmony with the ideologies of our founders and forefathers.

Stirring stuff, and hardly the kind of sentiments that any old club can express, partly for fear of ridicule. Athletic are rarely ridiculed, however, partly because their history speaks for itself – they have never been out of the top division – and partly because they are one of those sides that always seems to fight to the last. Difficult to beat, tenacious, dogged... all those adjectives can be safely applied. Like Newcastle, Bilbao smells of football. If you were taken blindfolded into the city, unmasked, then asked to look around, you would know it was a place where the reserve team attracts crowds of 10,000 or more. There might not be anything specific you could point to as proof (apart from middle-aged chaps in ill-fitting replica shirts), but you would know because of something in the air, something in the way the people and the traffic move, something that tells you they are impatient for the weekend to come around. The hunger is both broad and deep. At the end of the 2002-03 season in the national women's league, 35,000 turned out for the final game that Athletic needed to win to lift the title. They didn't disappoint, beating Hispanis of Seville 5-0 to claim the trophy.

Although Bilbao now boasts the startling Guggenheim Museum, for many years it was a place town planners and architects preferred not to be associated with, its urban sprawl a nightmare of lumpen grey concrete, its roads choked with traffic and its rivers long since abandoned by anything resembling a fish. The reason for this was, of course, industry, and by the turn of the century Bilbao's iron was driving the Spanish economy and attracting 'immigrant' workers from all over the country.

A further consequence of this was that in the second half of the 19th century the city, handily placed on the Bay of Biscay, saw plenty of foreign visitors, most of them British, who were there to play various roles in Spain's industrial revolution. Sons of the Basque educated classes had also been hopping on ships bound for the British Isles to complete their studies in civil engineering and commerce, visits that coincided with the early decades of English football.

Nevertheless, as in Huelva, it appears to have been the workers who initially got things moving. Among them were miners from the north-east of England, brought over on short-term contracts, and shipyard workers from Southampton and Portsmouth who came to contribute to Bilbao's burgeoning shipbuilding industry. Although their first colours were blue and white stripes, Athletic eventually settled on red and white stripes, probably as a nod to both Sunderland and Southampton, although the theory is disputed (see chapter nine).

Until 1894, as the *bilbaínos* tell it anyway, the locals simply went along to the northern bank of the Nervión river and gawped at the British workers playing football. It remains unclear, from press cuttings of the time, whether this was because of the curious game they were playing or because they took off their shirts in summer – an unspeakably risqué act for the conservative Basque onlookers who were also interested, it would seem, in the fact that the players wore shorts just above the knee, God bless us.

Still, such unseemly behaviour could not prevent the first game taking place between a team of students just returned from Cambridge and the pick of these contract workers on May 3, 1894. The students had been hanging out together at a local gym called Zamacois, obviously the place to be seen in 1894 if you were young, spoke English and had a wealthy daddy. According to the newspaper *El Nervión*, the game, still written as the compound English noun 'foot-ball', kicked off at 10am in the area known as Lamiaco, and was won by the 'foreigners' by a difference of five goals. The paper quaintly omits to record the actual score, as if the importance somehow resided only in the 'difference'. Three weeks later came the inevitable return game. This time the pitch was roped off and the match was watched by a *número sustancial* of spectators who once again saw the locals lose by five goals, although someone suggested after the game that it was actually six.

The student who seems to have initiated that first game was one Juanito Astorquia, a young, middle-class merchant's son who had been studying in Manchester. One of the Zamacois gym crowd, it was he who headed the committee, nicknamed 'the magnificent seven', which founded the club in 1898, a year before Barcelona got in on the act. However, what they actually founded, four years after those first 'international' encounters, was named Bilbao Football Club, not Athletic Bilbao at all, and since there was no legal signing of this alleged act of founding, Athletic's celebrations of their centenary in 1998 begin to look a little dodgy, from a strictly historical perspective.

Most of the club's historians, in their less nationalistic moments, point to 1901 as the true founding year. On June 11, one Luis Márquez put quill to paper in order to ratify the election of various executive posts to the club, all decided upon within the more solid framework of an official meeting – agenda, minutes and all – the likes of which do not exist for the so-called 1898 foundation. When one adds to this the fact that it was only in 1901 that the deliberately anglicised name Athletic Bilbao began to appear, Bilbao's claims to being the first significant team in Spain look decidedly like an attempt to rob Barcelona of that particular crown.

The meeting in the Café García in 1901 seems indisputably to have been the real date of Athletic's birth – but say as much on the streets of Bilbao at your peril. Besides, it all boils down to whether you wish to define a founding date as a legalistic act or as a spontaneous occasion, for want of a better term. The issue is important because of its significance to the whole identity of the *pueblo*, and where it figures in relation to the rest of the country. If such facts are disputed by those outside of the community, they certainly are not contested within it.

Nor does anyone dispute the widely-touted idea that Athletic have only ever had Basques playing for them, a fact that is hard to square with the presence of one 'Alfredo' Mills as vice-captain elect in 1901. The official history of the club describes him rather lamely as *como de casa* (like a local) – a term of convenience it would appear, especially as a newspaper piece of the time claimed that Mills, by all accounts a fine player, spoke 'practically no Spanish at all', though he had been in the country for more than 20 years.

His grandson John, who now lives in Brazil, explained to me that his grandfather worked in a wireless relay office in Getxo, a suburb of Bilbao, and spent his working days entirely in the company of other expatriates. He is buried in Getxo cemetery, and, Spanish speakers or not, the family has remained faithful to the club, despite the years and the distance. Before they are out of nappies, all children born into the family, even the branch that settled in Madrid, are ritually dressed in Athletic shirts and photographed for the album. Alfredo's Brazilian great-grandson, on work experience from Liverpool University in 2003, had no trouble finding temporary employment in Athletic's marketing department. Family takes care of family.

After the Café García meeting, the first signs of *morbo* began to appear when the other team from Bilbao, Bilbao FC, still including six Brits, challenged Athletic to a game in 1901. It ended all square at 1-1, but Athletic finally recorded their first official win in the return, 3-2 on January 19, 1902. After the game, pockets of spectators jumped the ropes and began to play little games of 'foot-ball' in their respective corners. One reporter, J Ugalde, waxed prophetically on the pitch invasion in the following terms:

> While the aces drank their lemonades in the changing rooms, many of the spectators, numbed by the cold afternoon, played the game in imitation of those who had finished their noble exhibition. Who knows? Maybe one

day everyone here will play this game. It seems to be bringing folks together. It seems to arouse extraordinary curiosity.

It certainly brought the two *bilbaíno* clubs together. Their temporary fusion as Vizcaya (Biscay) was the occasion for the first foreign venture of any Spanish side, as far as is known, a trip to Bordeaux where they beat Burdigala 2-0. For the return game, in March 1902, 3,000 people turned up at Lamiaco to watch the Basques destroy the French side 7-0, an astonishing number of people for that time and, by all accounts, too many to be satisfactorily restrained by a few droopy ropes around the pitch. In May of the same year, Vizcaya won the Coronation Cup in Madrid and were greeted on their return by cheering locals lining the streets. No open-topped bus as yet, but the momentum was gathering. And, of course, the political import of all this was never too far away, lurking in the wings but ready to take centre stage whenever the occasion demanded.

The Basques' view of themselves as a political community waiting to be taken seriously was growing in a parallel street. The Partido Nacionalista Vasca (PNV) was founded in 1894 by Sabino de Arana, whose father had been exiled in France because of his Carlist sympathies. (Originally attached to followers of Carlos, the pretender to the Spanish throne on the death of his brother Ferdinand VII in 1833, Carlism became a byword for fanatically rightwing Catholic and pro-monarchist views.) Arana came to prominence by coining the term *Euskadi*, meaning 'collection of Basques' – a community which had been around since time immemorial but which had never got around to giving itself a name.

This increasingly self-conscious nationalism was worrying Madrid to the extent that Arana was briefly jailed in 1895, but the horse had already left the stables. Why it had done so seems to have been connected to the problem of the *maketos*, as they were called by their reluctant Basque hosts. These were the migrant Spanish workers who had moved north in their thousands and who began to be perceived as a threat to the survival of Basque society in its traditional form. Navarre, Alava and Gipuzcoa, the other three Basque regions, lacked the industrial middle-class that provided, and continues to provide, the PNV with much of its support in the coastal areas, and especially Vizcaya, the region around Bilbao.

The coincidence between the emergence of Athletic and the growing influence of the PNV in the early years of the 20th century cannot be overestimated, and the two institutions have walked hand in hand ever since. Athletic Bilbao's prominence in the 28 years up to the formation of a professional national league ensured that the political momentum of conservative Basque nationalism could prosper off the back of the sporting prowess of its representatives. This story was to be repeated in the 1950s in Catalonia, where Barcelona's dogged efforts to oppose the hegemony of the greatest of Real Madrid's sides encouraged the development of the CiU Party (Convergencia i Unión) under Jordi Pujol, the current president of Catalonia's Generalitat.

Athletic Bilbao's wonderful ground San Mamés, nicknamed *La Cátedral*, was built in 1913 after the club had won its fourth King's Cup in the first eight years of the competition. It only took seven months to build, but was certainly an ambitious architectural enterprise, rising up only 12 years after that meeting in the Café García. It was the first major purpose-built stadium in the land, planted with English grass to boot and honoured by the presence of King Alfonso XIII and his wife for its second official game, against an amateur London outfit, Shepherd's Bush.

The building of the stadium also represented an important business principle, only possible in a country where the *socios* (members) still effectively run the club. Spanish football is all about private enterprise, not plcs. In the second half of the century, some grounds would be constructed out of municipal funds, but with municipal strings attached. By and large, as we shall see in the cases of Barcelona and Madrid, the idea of financing the club through the investment of the broad membership (as opposed to a few rich directors) was to prove an enduring success, an original Spanish initiative which ensured that the club literally belonged to the community.

In 1904, Athletic's paid-up *socios* numbered only 34, but by 1913 the figure was up into the hundreds, enough to sustain the cost of building San Mamés. Each member contributed a part of the original estimated cost of 50,000 pesetas – an astronomical sum in those days. The final bill rose to 89,000, but no one seemed to worry too much. By that time it was clear that these individual stakes in the club would grow, and the stadium as pure collateral investment was unlikely to lose its value overnight. Coincidentally, 1913 was also the year in which the Spanish Football Federation would declare itself a legal entity.

The inaugural game in San Mamés had been played a fortnight before the King turned up, against Real Unión from the drab town of Irún on the Spanish Basque Country's eastern border. Real Unión were beginning to be a force in the game, as evidenced by their victory in the King's Cup that year, a win that was threatening Athletic's hegemony in the region, although the Club Ciclista de San Sebastián (later Real Sociedad) could claim to have begun that process when they won the competition in 1909. However, Real Unión got the big invite and were accorded the dubious privilege of conceding one of the most significant goals in Spanish history, namely the first goal to be scored at San Mamés by Rafael Moreno Aranzadi, better known as 'Pichichi'.

Pichichi proved to be a figure as famous as any bullfighter. The poet Federico García Lorca's lament for Ignacio Sánchez Mejías, killed in the ring in the 1920s at *Las Cinco de la tarde* (five o'clock in the afternoon), remains Spain's most famous poem, but the painting of Pichichi by the Basque artist Emilio Arteta is one of sport's better contributions to art. Moreno, the product of a working-class 'migrant' father and a Basque mother, lounges half provocatively, half anxiously on the white fencing of the old Jolaseta ground, his great swan neck inclined towards the object of his desire, his future wife. Her long, slim back is curved and taut with sexual tension and her eyes are discreetly turned from the artist, as if the attentions of the footballer are not quite in line with the etiquette of the times and the tryst should not be taking place, especially at half-time.

Before the 1998 World Cup, Julen Guerrero, Spanish squad member, Athletic midfielder and an object of desire in most Spanish households, was photographed in a similar pose with his girlfriend, the shot deliberately echoing Arteta's painting, except this time the couple were framed with the Guggenheim Museum as background. Guerrero's understandable awkwardness at the proceedings only served to emphasise the brilliance of the original.

Pichichi Moreno died in 1922 at the age of 29, victim of a sudden attack of typhus, and he was mourned in the manner of Rudolf Valentino. Four years later a bust was unveiled at San Mamés of the legendary striker, and opposing teams still pay homage by leaving a bouquet of flowers at its base. In 1953 the Spanish federation decided to inaugurate a trophy for the top scorers in both the First and Second Divisions and to call it *El trofeo Pichichi*. The tradition has stuck, and foreign journalists, surrounded by their Spanish counterparts in press boxes around the country are often to be heard asking for a translation – 'Who is this Pichichi?' – given the frequency with which the term is used. It's a bit like calling a similar trophy in England 'The Dixie'.

Since no footage of the player survives, it is difficult to separate the fact from the legend, although his goal-scoring record was quite phenomenal. Pichichi began a tradition at Bilbao of goalscoring centre-forwards who were to benefit (allegedly) from the club's allegiance to *la manera inglesa* (the English way), as taught to them by a succession of imported British managers and embarrassingly referred to as 'the old 1-2-3'. This meant three touches from goalkeeper to centre-forward, who would then of course unfailingly bang the leather mercilessly into the onion-bag.

The English connection with Bilbao is significant for various reasons, but chiefly because Spain's best team up to the outbreak of the Civil War in 1936 only believed in applying the philosophy of *la cantera* to players. By 1911 the word *cantera* was beginning to appear with some regularity in local football journalism, but the idea that only the sons of the Basque soil could wear the red and white stripes did not extend to the concept of management. The club referred to England as *la madre del fútbol* (the mother of football) and signed their first foreign manager in 1910, a Mr Shepherd (they were never referred to by their Christian names, presumably out of deference). Although he pleased the locals by wearing a bowler hat, Shepherd was to last a mere two months in the hot-seat, apparently due to homesickness.

Nevertheless, he left his mark on the game by introducing the training practice of hammering lines of short poles into the ground to be dribbled around. The quaint borrowing of *el dribling* into the Spanish lexicon seems to have occurred around then, the general feeling being that the English were still better at it than the Spanish, and that the importation of English managers would inevitably lead to the development of the magic art in Spain. The final echo of this Anglophilia only fell silent with the resignation of the *bilbaíno* Javier Clemente from the national coach's job in late 1998, although by then England had come to stand for something much less noble than skilful dribbling.

Clemente came to fame in the early 1980s when he led Athletic to two successive league titles, after serving them with distinction as a player. His teams were seen as effective but dour, perpetrators of the famous *bloque* with which the Basque teams have now become associated. The formation, playing two defensive midfielders as a shield to twin centre-backs and a sweeper, was *la manera inglesa* according to Clemente, and he claimed to be a slavish adherent. It has never been altogether clear from which English team Clemente had taken this system, but he never failed to swear allegiance to the 'mother' system.

This preference became even more marked when he was in charge of the national team and became notorious for his suspicion of flair, his inclusion of too many uncreative but solid workers and his tendency, as famously summed up by *Marca's* Julián Ruíz, to include in his squads players from Athletic who had played 'a couple of decent games' for their club. Juan Antonio Camacho was to restore a more 'Spanish' feel to the national team on taking over from Clemente, and the press were certainly more comfortable with him (despite his famous temper). However, on Camacho's resignation after the 2002 World Cup, Bilbao returned to the scene with the surprising appointment of Iñaki Saez, Clemente's old right-hand man and another Basque in thrall to English ways. When Saez was appointed, he announced his intention to combine the 'technique and intelligence' of the Spanish outlook with the 'commitment' of the English. Seems like they just won't go away.

Back in 1913, Athletic were also showing interest in the possibility of more exotic influences and at the end of that year invited Ferencvaros over for a friendly. Rather like their English friends 40 years later, the 5-2 defeat at the hands of the Hungarians seems only to have further consolidated the Basques' tendency towards hubris, and the game had to be abandoned 15 minutes before the end due to a pitch invasion by the locals, apparently incensed at the Hungarians' bully-boy tactics. Several visiting players suffered the deadly *paraguazo* treatment (being bashed on the head by an umbrella), all of which was forgotten later at a friendly supper put on by the hosts – although according to *El Nervión* the principal culprit stayed put in his hotel.

By 1914, the federation had decided to put a stop to the system of free applications to the King's Cup and inaugurated a series of regional tournaments, the winners of which would subsequently participate in the national cup. They called it, for the first time, the Spanish championship, and Athletic won it for the first three years under the tutelage of the next Englishman in line, a trained masseur by the name of Mr Barnes. No particular fan of the bowler, he introduced a more attacking style, but the tactical details seem lost in the mists of time, probably because he could count on our old friend Pichichi. He left in 1916 to return in 1920, the predecessor of the most famous of them all, the notorious Mr Pentland, who was appointed in 1923.

The arrival of Fred Pentland, who had played for Blackburn Rovers (among others) in the first decade of the century, coincided with the first clear signs of professionalism in the Spanish game. Pentland was interned in Germany for the whole of the First World War and seems to have spent most of his time training German officers in fitness and technique. In 1920 he managed the French football team at the Antwerp Olympics and then spent a year training Racing Santander, whereupon Athletic literally bought him from the Cantabrian club, offering him 1,000 pesetas a month – a decent sum in those days. Spain's achievements at the Olympics had inevitably led to more international games, and the *morbo* of success was beginning to open the purse-strings.

'Freddie' Pentland is almost as revered in the club's history as Pichichi, although it's difficult to decide whether it was due to inspired management or because he embodied to perfection the idea of the eccentric English gentleman. He was known simply as *bombín* (bowler hat) and several photographs taken at the time suggest that he was not so much eccentric as barking mad. Pentland's first act at his first training session with Athletic was to show the players how to tie their bootlaces correctly – 'get the simple things right and the rest will follow' was apparently his motto. Pentland smoked big cigars and wore his bowler, even in training, but his contribution to Spanish football is not to be scoffed at. He is remembered above all as an advocate of the short-passing game, as opposed to 'the old 1-2-3'.

Barcelona, halfway through the first league campaign of 1929, decided to adopt *lo de Pentland* (Pentland's way), and won the title with it. In turn, Barcelona's stature in the game from then on influenced others in adopting the 'ball into feet' approach. That this system was associated with an Englishman seems something of an irony, and truth to tell it was more likely that Pentland had left his native shores precisely because of his reluctance to play under the auspices of the big hoof. In 1923 Athletic won the cup playing the possession game, but after failing to win anything else for the next two years opened a debate over which system should be adopted. Pentland, perhaps sensing problems, moved on to Oviedo.

When he returned to Athletic in 1929, his dedication to the possession game paid off more handsomely and the Basques won the second and third official Spanish leagues, in 1929-30 and 1930-31. In the latter season they pummelled Barcelona by the extraordinary score of 12-1 in San Mamés, a result which remains the Catalans' worst-ever defeat. In Pentland's last season in Bilbao, 1932-33, Athletic finished runners-up to Real Madrid and had clearly assimilated the notion that a more patient game, so characteristic of modern Spanish football, was the way forward.

Strange to report then, that in the 21st century, the English, revered as the apparent exemplars of this approach, have still not truly mastered this aspect of the game. Pentland was clearly a maverick, a type never comfortably accepted in the British game, and he was not alone in finding a better reception abroad than at home for his approach – around the same time Jimmy Hogan, Arthur Rowe and others were inculcating the 'Scottish' passing game in Austria and Hungary, with similarly profound effects on the style of football those countries adopted.

Obviously *lo de Pentland* was not typically *lo de Inglaterra*, but it's nice that they thought it was. Those who recall the sublime aesthetic of Cruyff's Barcelona Dream Team of the early Nineties should always remember that it owed something to a tradition stretching back to Pentland. Paradoxically, however, it was shunned by the Athletic teams of the postwar period in favour of the aforementioned *bloque*, culminating in Clemente's successful but unattractive side of the Eighties, modelled on his own personal interpretation of the English way.

Pentland's idiosyncratic Spanish and his odd behaviour gave rise to a thousand anecdotes, many of which survive. The most famous phrase to be handed down to the present generations was the legendary: *¡Que poco te quera bombín. Sólo tres minutos!* (Only three minutes left for you, bowler hat!). These words were first shouted from the dug-out three minutes from the end of Athletic's legendary cup win in 1923 against the the Catalan club Europa, in Barcelona's old stadium Les Corts.

The players had already begun a tradition of whipping Pentland's hat off his head whenever they won a game, and ritually jumping up and down on it until it was no more. Pentland apparently never mastered the verb form *queda* (remains), substituting his own defective form *quera*, an error sympathetically copied by the Basque players and presumably one of the reasons why the phrase became so famous. Pentland had an open credit scheme with a prestigious London hatter and optimistically ordered 20 a year.

In 1959 the club brought him over from England for what they call here *un homenaje* (homage). San Mamés was packed to the rafters and Pentland, grey and frail, kicked off the game between Athletic and Chelsea after Javier Prado, the president at the time, had pinned the club's Distinguished Member medal on to his immaculate crombie. When Pentland died in 1962, in Dorset, Athletic held a ceremony at San Mamés which included an *aurresku* (high-kicking dance) in front of a small memorial. It's a solemn ritual and reserved only for a select band of people considered to have contributed significantly to the culture. An orator then read out the first part of Pentland's famous bowler-hat cry, 'How little time is left for you', in poetic reference to his death.

When Athletic finally built their centenary museum in 2001, an official from the club got in touch with me asking if I knew of the whereabouts in England of any of Pentland's family. They had no memorabilia of Pentland, and wondered if his surviving children might have some medals or trophies that could be displayed in the museum. After a number of bizarre twists and turns through English rural life, the barman of the golf club in the tiny Dorset village of Lytchett Matravers finally put me in touch with a friendly local who knew Pentland was buried in the local churchyard ('Pentland, eh? Used to be manager of Real Madrid, I think').

Establishing the whereabouts of Pentland's daughter was on the agenda for the next meeting of the parish council and I was supplied with her phone number. Susan Hilton, now in her seventies, was amazed and delighted to have been contacted, and was very happy to speak to Athletic. Born in Madrid when Pentland managed Atlético (not Real) after his last spell in Bilbao, she still spoke good Spanish. She supplied the club with several medals and photographs, all of which are now on display at San Mamés.

The reverence for Pentland supports the notion that the club embodies 'a feeling' and that it is 'different', as claimed by Arrate. I first saw a match in San Mamés in 1994, a UEFA Cup tie against Newcastle United. The atmosphere was unlike anything I have experienced before or since. If certain other key aspects of Athletic's self-image are based on shaky foundations, it cannot be disputed that the club is special. Outside the ground that night I saw acts of friendliness and goodwill that would have brought a lump to the throat of the hardest football cynic.

The Newcastle fans who had travelled down through France seemed bemused by it all. Expecting, as ever, to be beaten up or at best abused by their hosts, several of them recounted tales of astonishing kindness – one garage owner had refused to charge a group of them for replacing their coughing exhaust pipe, merely on the grounds that they were English, and had then taken them out and paid for several rounds of drinks. 'They just don't let you pay man!' was the chorus, spoken with a shaking head and tones of gratified disbelief. English journalists sent to the city to cover England's 1982 World Cup campaign had similar stories to tell. When the *Sun*'s reporter sent home a story referring to Bilbao as 'City of Hate', the other papers joined forces, ostracised the journalist in question and pointed out in a letter to the *Sun* that Bilbao was in fact the 'City of Hake', the fish forming one of the Vizcayan region's finest dishes, *merluza en salsa verde* (hake in green sauce).

The Geordies were naturally unaware of the Anglophile tendencies of their hosts and the early history of the club, inextricably tied in with England and free of all traces of *morbo*. If Real Madrid had been in town, it would, of course, have been a different story but, for all their fanaticism, Athletic's younger fans have never had a reputation for violence. The ground, smart though it is, is like some throwback to a happier, sepia-tinted football era. The terracing rises up sheer from the edge of the pitch and the players are boxed in on all sides by the baying hordes.

Even as you take your seat – an object bitterly resisted by the traditionalists – you seem to be transported back to the days of rattles, cloth caps, steaming hot mugs of tea, mud, rain, and a hard but appreciative working-class audience. Until 1997, when Barcelona finally overhauled them, Athletic had been Spain's cup side *non pareil*, with no fewer than 22 victories to their name. Throw in eight championships, the last in 1984, and it adds up to an impressive history. It is not only thanks to the parochial efforts of Clemente that Athletic have supplied more players for the national team than any other club, Real Madrid included.

Athletic have always had a reputation for cultivating great centre-forwards. In 1941, Telmo Zarraonaindia made his debut for the club, and over the next 13 seasons went on to score 294 goals in league and cup competitions, plus 20 for Spain in as many games. Understandably known as Zarra, given the impossible morphology of his surname, his 38 goals in the 1950-51 season still stand as a record, although it was equalled by the Mexican Hugo Sánchez in 1989-90. Sánchez took eight more games to reach the same tally, a fact that has kept Zarra on top of the all-time goalscorers' podium. Playing in an era of greater sophistication than that of Pichichi, Zarra is still considered the greatest home-grown forward of all time in Spain, although the crown does not necessarily go to the most prolific. Style counts for a lot in this country, but in terms of pure goalscoring, the man seems to have been something of a machine, aided and abetted by the midfielder José Luis López Panizo, also considered one of the greats.

The main thing that makes Athletic 'different', of course, is the awkward issue of Basque-only players, *la cantera*. In the late 1980s I interviewed the former general secretary of Real Sociedad, Javier Expósito, about the sudden change in their attitude towards the introduction of foreign players. They had just signed John Aldridge from Liverpool, the first time a non-Basque had played for the club. I asked why they had changed their policy. Expósito, a much-respected figure at the club, was . by then a couple of years off retirement, having served the club in various roles over 35 years. He eyed me suspiciously.

'What policy?' he frowned. 'The policy of not signing foreign players,' I offered, cautiously. 'We believe in the policy of the *cantera*,' he trotted out, adding: 'There has never been any policy of exclusion.' At this point I hesitated, drew breath and asked, as politely as possible, why the club had therefore signed Aldridge, while no Spanish league players had been considered. The implication of the question was not lost on him – namely that Spanish stock was unacceptable but that Aldridge was not – but he refused to rise to the bait. 'We just prefer to develop the *cantera*,' he repeated. And then, as if to end the game, he added: 'If you want to know why we're signing foreigners now, you'd better ask them over there', and he nodded his head in a westerly direction beyond his office wall, in a clear reference to Athletic Bilbao.

Athletic, of course, have retained their commitment to the cause, and the policy is a brave one, given the limited population (three million) from which decent players can emerge. Barcelona, with similar nationalistic sentiments propping up their history, have never adopted the practice, despite having a larger regional populace to quarry from. Given this fact, it is no surprise that Athletic's qualification for the Champions League in 1998 as runners-up to Barcelona was greeted with feverish delight in Bilbao. Several British broadsheet papers wrote pieces on the subject, praising the club for its insistence on home-bred players while the rest of Europe was greedily operating the foreign mercenary policy.

The *Sunday Telegraph* eulogised the club for finishing second above the vastly richer Real Madrid and suggested that they might be a model for the 'future purification' of football – a return to grass-roots, youth policy, local identification and so on. At one fell swoop Athletic were the darlings of the anti-federalists, suspicious as papers like the *Telegraph* have always been of the concept of one happy Europe, one currency, one central bureaucracy. Bilbao's success seemed to champion a different vision, a more traditional, conservative one.

By contrast, when Real Sociedad rose from the ashes of three poor seasons and almost won the league title five years later, their runners-up spot was treated in the foreign press as a surprise but not as a politico-cultural event. By that time, of course, 33 more foreign players had passed through their ranks. Their two top scorers were a Turk and a

Serb, and at the beginning of that same 2002-03 season they had even signed a Spanish player, Boris, from Oviedo. This in itself had raised a few eyebrows in the national press, but Sociedad still had more players in the starting line-up from their own regional *cantera* (as opposed to the Basque Country as a whole) than Athletic could boast. It is this question of the definition of the *cantera* that has caused so much friction between the two clubs in recent years.

From outside Spain, Athletic's policy looks romantic and rosy but, as with any fairy-tale garden, there are plenty of worms lurking just beneath the surface. For starters, the 'forefathers' whom the president Arrate invokes in his Biblical prose as justification for the club's defiant ways were probably of the same ilk as several of the political protagonists currently at the forefront of the rightwing nationalist PNV.

The leader throughout the Nineties, Xabier Arzalluz, delivered a notorious speech in 1996 in which he claimed that there were two levels of 'Basqueness'. Those second-generation immigrants whose parents had moved into the area from Spain in search of work were distinguished from the 'true' Basques, identifiable not only by mastery of their fiercely complex language but also by the extra bone to be found at the back of their skulls – anthropological proof of the ethnic distinctiveness of a pure race. The poor Spanish were implicitly dismissed as mongrels, a mixture of gypsies and idle north Africans snoozing away their worthless lives in the heat of the Andalusian sun.

Politically, there is little that people like Arzalluz can do about the dilution of pure Basqueness (as he sees it) through immigration. But in the subtext of President Arrate's article of faith one can perhaps read the real meaning of the club's Basque-only policy. It is as though football can do what politics cannot, and simply exclude those whom it wishes to exclude. The 'forefathers', despite needing immigrant workers to bring about their industrial revolution, inevitably ended up resenting their presence. How could they celebrate the good old days before the immigration, when all their neighbours still had that extra bone? Easy. Turn the emerging football club into a theatre of nationalist dreams.

Of course, it would be misleading to imply that Athletic have ever sought to exclude the *maketos* – descendants of 'immigrants' – from their ranks. The merest glance at the names of the players who have pulled on the red and white stripes in the past 100 years is sufficient to tell you that the progeny of the original immigrants have always been able to play for the club. Pichichi himself was a *maketo*. With such a limited population to choose from, further restrictions on the gene pool could hardly have made sense, in footballing terms. If there has ever been a historical bias towards taking on players of pure Basque descent, then it would have been incumbent upon the victims of such a policy to speak up. As far as is known, no one ever has. However, whether this inclusiveness has always gone down well with the hardline nationalists is more debatable. What the club has done, and what some at the club might have preferred to have done in the past, may not be the same thing.

Athletic's connection with the PNV is so intimate that they can even boast of having had the first president of the first legitimate Basque government (1936) as a player. José Antonio Aguirre, who led that ill-fated administration, played with Athletic with distinction in the early 1920s. He is in many ways more prominent in Basque nationalist history than the party's founder, Arana, for it was Aguirre whose term of office was to be so spectacularly cut short by the bombs of Guernica. The fact that he was an ex-player of Athletic has further fuelled the political engines of the Athletic story. All subsequent presidents of the club have belonged to the PNV. Had they not, they would never have got past the hustings.

One indisputable problem with Athletic is that they have traditionally been the richest team in the Basque country and are therefore still blinded by the pretension that all the best players in the region should come unto them. This is stretching the idea of the 'quarry' perhaps a little too far. Of the side that played in the Champions League, six were from Gipuzcoa, the province to the east of Bilbao that includes San Sebastian. Bilbao is the capital of Vizcaya, but prefers to ignore this distinction when robbing the other Basque teams of their best players. The controversial transfer of the young Joseba Etxeberría from Real Sociedad has already been mentioned. After Spain's triumph in the Under-18 World Cup in Nigeria in 1999, Athletic moved quickly for the team's best player, Pablo Orbaiz, then under contract to Atlético Osasuna of Pamplona. Athletic's most promising youngster for the 2002-03 season, Fran Yeste, was similarly a product of Osasuna's cantera. These were typical examples of the poaching that provokes resentment among the other Basque clubs.

Of these, the most unlikely to come to prominence in recent years was Alavés, from the Basque capital of Vitoria. They were promoted back to the top division in 1997, but are in a similar predicament to Osasuna. Their policy of inspired loan signings and a never-say-die spirit saw them captivate Europe in their UEFA Cup campaign of 2000-01. But of course, that put their players in the shop window and the best of them were snapped up. Relegation duly followed in 2003.

Real Sociedad, now a fairly well-off club themselves, would probably love to practise the same ideology as Athletic, but have generally found that impossible in the face of their cousin's constant raids on their own *cantera*, implied by the westward nod of the head of Expósito, back in his office in 1989. The fact that Real Sociedad took to signing foreigners, but not Spanish players, looked xenophobic, but since it was Athletic's behaviour that denied Sociedad the fruits of their region, one is forced to conclude that Bilbao's crime was the greater. Times would seem to be changing though, and Sociedad's success in 2003, coupled with Athletic's growing financial problems, seem to have shifted the balance between the two a little.

The whole business begins to look rather silly anyway if you examine the ethnic make-up of the two leading Basque sides carefully. In 1996 Real justified their signing of Oscar de Paula from Second Division Badajoz on the basis that, although he had been raised down south in Extremadura, he was actually born in Bilbao, where he had stayed approximately a month as a baby. Athletic's definition of what constitutes a Basque is even odder, given that three of their players in 2003 were born in La Rioja, the wine-growing region to the south of the Basque Country and definitely 'Spain', while Ismael Urzaiz, their international centre-forward, is from southern Navarre.

Although Navarre is one of the seven traditional Basque provinces (the other three being in France), it has had a very different political history from Vizcaya, Guipuzcoa and Alava, and the further south you travel, the fewer people you find who would take kindly to being described as Basque. The five-times Tour de France winner Miguel Indurain hailed from the same area, but resisted the many attempts the Basques made to claim him as one their own.

Indeed, if you look dispassionately at how many of Athletic's first-teamers have really come roaring up from the quarry over the past century to play on the soil of Bilbao's imagined lands, the spiritual chimes of Athletic's ethnic crusade start to sound distinctly out of tune. Which is not to say, of course, that the idea of a team full of local boys is a bad one. The problem with Athletic's version of the dream is that is has never been an entirely honest one.

Nevertheless, it would be churlish to end on a negative note about such an interesting club. The young supporters who pay fortnightly homage at the *Catedral* probably have little knowledge of or interest in the policies of the PNV, and while they are inevitably influenced by those who would insist that only Athletic Bilbao can really represent the true spirit of Spanish football, 90 minutes in San Mamés might almost convince you that they're right.

Athletic and Real Sociedad are still forces to be reckoned with in Spanish football, while Alavés and Osasuna have had their moments. In 2000, Osasuna were promoted back to the top division, meaning that for the first time ever the four would be together among the élite. The other two Basque sides who have formed part of the region's productive footballing reputation, Real Unión and Arenas de Getxo, are now modest clubs playing in the Regional Preferente, a series of feeder leagues to the regionalised Segunda B and national Segunda A. They would struggle to compete with the better teams from the Conference. Attendances are poor and most of the players are cast-offs from the ranks of the bigger teams in the region.

But Real Unión and Arenas left one indelible stamp on the history of the game in Spain, in the old national cup competition, just before it was replaced by the professional league proper. Real Unión, from the border town of Irún, narrowly defeated Arenas, from the middle-class outskirts of Bilbao, in a game which remains the only truly national final disputed by two Basque sides. Athletic and Real Sociedad, for all their rivalry, have never managed to do what these two more obscure clubs achieved in Zaragoza back in 1927. The fact serves as a reminder that Athletic did not have it all their own way back then. The development of the professional game owed a lot to clubs like these.

Irún, like most border towns, is not a particularly attractive spot, but its strategic importance as a crossing into France always meant there was work to be found, at least before European Union legislation brought the barriers down and left a third of the workforce on the dole. At the beginning of the 20th century, Spanish 'immigrant' workers, French Basques and the original local population had combined to swell the town into a mixed community large enough to accommodate two football teams, Irún Sporting Club and Racing Club de Irún. In 1915, the two sides decided to become Real Unión after eight years of fairly tepid local rivalry.

Racing Club had already won the cup in 1913, beating Athletic 1-0 in a replayed final, but only because that same year had seen a temporary schism in the fledgling national structure, brought about by a split between those clubs who wished to form what they called *La Unión de Clubes* and those, like Racing and Athletic, who had stayed faithful to *La*

Federación. Real Sociedad and Barcelona played out a rival final (won by the latter), but the following year the federation remodelled itself in order to reunite the warring factions.

In 1918 Real Unión won their first cup, beating Real Madrid 2-0, a feat they were to repeat in 1924 when they defeated the glamour boys from the capital, 1-0, down the road in San Sebastián. As already mentioned, the frontier club was one of the pioneering ten who were chosen to take part in the first national league competition in 1929, achieving the dubious distinction of being the first club in the history of the Spanish league to concede a goal – scored after five minutes by the Español forward 'Pitus' Prat. Most present-day Unión supporters know of this unfortunate fact, a hurtful piece of trivia whose pain might be soothed if they knew how ironic it might seem to English speakers that the first official professional goal in Spain was scored by a fellow called Prat.

Real Unión were relegated in 1932, never to return to the heights of the top division. Arenas de Getxo finished fifth that same year, but finally went down in 1934, also destined never to return. The disappearance of these teams from the public eye of the top division was nevertheless redressed by the simultaneous emergence of both Alavés and Osasuna, thus reinforcing the Basque presence in a league which by 1934 had been extended to include 12 clubs.

Getxo, formed in 1909 as Arenas Club in a deliberate attempt to create some local rivalry for Athletic, were from a middle-class district to the north-east of Bilbao, then a separate town, now a posher part of the urban spread of Greater Bilbao. When in 1914 the Barcelona of Bru and Alcantará turned up for a series of three friendlies against Arenas, the Catalans lost every game. Two years later Arenas won the northern championship, a regional tournament which included all the established Basque sides. This gave them access for the first time to the national Spanish Cup competition on which they immediately left their mark, reaching the final in Barcelona before losing to Real Madrid 2-1 after extra time. In 1919 they won it, beating a powerful Barcelona side by the extraordinary score of 5-2, again after extra time.

The ability of Arenas to establish themselves on the national circuit so swiftly after their foundation is further proof, if any were needed, of the uncanny ability of the Basques to reap good footballers from their fertile soil. In 1925, the Barcelona of Samitier and Platko were to get their revenge in the final down in Seville, but Arenas' last defiant gesture of the century that would eventually consign them to obscurity came with that narrow defeat to Real Unión in 1927.

There is something curiously poetic in this event, not only as an exclusively Basque final but also because it represented the final sigh of amateurism in Spain, killed off for good the following year on the formation of the country's first national league structure. The two sides were both invited to participate, of course, but they were unlikely to last long in the face of the growing financial pressures brought to bear. Nevertheless, Arenas finished third in 1929-30 and managed to fend off their wealthier cousins from Bilbao until 1932, when their star Cilaurren made the short but inevitable trip over to San Mamés, beginning a trend that was to seriously limit the club's horizons for ever more.

In the early years of the new century, Basque football continues to thrive despite internal wrangling and occasional gnashing of teeth over the vexed issue of the *cantera*. Needless to say, a few more trophies in the cupboard would not go amiss, but for the time being the biggest clubs on the Spanish circuit will continue to regard a visit up north as one to be feared, and quite rightly too.

4. *sunshine and shadow*

The ambiguous truth about Barcelona

In his book *Football Against the Enemy* Simon Kuper memorably remarks: 'FC Barcelona's motto is "More than a club" and next to them Manchester United look like Rochdale.' He goes on to note that Barça run an art competition so prestigious that Dalí once submitted an entry, the Pope is member No 108,000 and the club's museum is the best attended in the city, pulling in more visitors than the Picasso Museum. Most football supporters from Sidcup to Sydney now know these facts and could also tell you that Barça is the 'flagship' for Catalan nationalism. They might even add that the Dream Team that won the European Cup in 1992 was much dreamier than any other team in the history of the game and that even the toilets at the Camp Nou smell of roses.

Barcelona became more than a bit imperious and overbearing towards the end of 1990s, sometimes going so over the top in their self-worship that you began to sympathise with the *madrileños*, looked down upon as an inferior race incapable of producing anything innovative or interesting, in art, business or football. But however much the constant recounting of Barcelona's majestic assets grates, it cannot be denied that there is indeed nothing quite like this institution anywhere on earth, with its turbulent and fascinating history that signposts the twisting political roads of 20th century Spain.

Barcelona were not the first official team to be formed in Catalonia. That particular mantle is worn by Palamós CF, founded in the summer of 1898 as Palamós Foot-Ball Club on the Costa Brava, a year before their bigger cousins came into being. The club was formed, like all the others, by a gentleman who had been abroad studying (in England) and who had come back twitching for a game. The side that Gaspar Matas got together is proudly described in their official history as 'a team made up exclusively of locals' – a sentiment that would be echoed the following year on the foundation of another club, Español, as a calculated snub to the foreigners who had set up FC Barcelona.

Thanks to the club's massive popularity, much of what has been written about Barcelona is so uncritical that it has created an unhealthy climate of literary lap-dogism, which in the end does the phenomenon no favours.Outside Madrid and the walls of RCD Espanyol, the club is extraordinarily popular. Even in the highly politicised streets of the Basque country, kids walk around in replica Barça shirts in the confident knowledge that no one will take them to task, whereas the wearing of a replica Real Madrid shirt would be courting ostracism, at best. Certain regions of Spain, particularly those that were loyal to the Nationalists in the Civil War, such as Asturias or Castilla-León, still harbour a good deal of residual affection for Real Madrid, but in most parts Barcelona are remarkably well liked, despite their high-profile success, riches and more than occasional tendency towards insufferable pomp and circumstance. In terms of popularity, at least, they are certainly nothing like Manchester United.

After the 1992 Olympics, the city of Barcelona seemed to become a symbol for the go-getting Nineties, a busy hive of fashion, creativity and the smiley side of the work-ethic badge; a city and a region fairly foaming with self-confidence, frothing at the mouth with self-importance. Europe's youth flocked to it as once they must have flocked to Paris in search of the zeitgeist. Dalí, Gaudí, Miró... you name it, they were Catalans. Picasso was from Málaga, but everybody thinks he was from Barcelona. They even claim Christopher Columbus as one of their own.

They have their own language and nearly everyone speaks it with much less political self-consciousness than do the Basques their own tortuous tongue. Barça websites (though not the official one) mostly offer you their pages in Catalan and English only, not as a snub, but more as an unconscious reflection of the fact that Spanish plays little part in their lives. There are no Catalan terrorist organisations. Catalan nationalism is more about holding Madrid to as much ransom as possible, while its seats in the Spanish parliament determine the balance of power in the country as a whole.

Central government can never push things too far any more. Upset the Catalans and you risk losing office. Calls for independence are not canny enough for the people of this region. They have plenty of autonomy, thank you, and know better than the Basques how to exploit it. Besides, in the last decade of the 20th century, their football team, their 'flagship', consistently rubbed Madrid's nose into the dirt. Real Madrid's relief at Barça's failure to progress beyond the group stages of the 1998-99 Champions League was understandable. If they had won it, they would have done so in their centenary year in their own stadium – a confluence of romance and poetry so powerful that its vibes would surely have eclipsed Madrid's pretensions to world domination for at least the next millennium. In fact, the winds shifted again, this time in favour of Madrid, with a new flurry of Champions League successes and their own centenary celebrations to douse the dying embers of Barça's own big party in 1999.

Barcelona is indeed more than a football club, not only figuratively but literally. Like several other Spanish clubs who have copied the model, it is a *polideportivo* (multi-sport) institution which succeeds in symbolically incorporating the whole community by extending the football base into other sports, namely basketball, handball and hockey. The former two are both successful spectator sports in Spain, and hockey is on the up. The teams involved in these sports are subsidised by the football section and wear the same colours.

Madrid may have been spared the ghastly sight of Barça winning the Champions League final in the Camp Nou, but they were nevertheless obliged to suffer the copious trumpet-blowing that emanated from Catalonia at the end of that centenary season when all four Barcelona teams were proclaimed national champions of their respective sports – a phenomenal achievement, from which the Catalanist press mercilessly squeezed as much political and cultural juice as possible.

This was, of course, only to be expected, and in a sense the *madridistas* would have been disappointed if their foe to the east had not played according to the long-established rules of *morbo*. But it must have been galling, nevertheless, to have contemplated what seemed at the time to be something approaching empirical proof that the Catalans are indeed something of a master-race, a region of self-confident and self-congratulatory winners.

Of course, all giants have feet of clay, and one mitigating factor in all of this for the anti-Barça lobby is that the football, basketball and handball teams boasted precious few drops of Catalan blood in their ranks. On the football field, Barcelona were more or less the Dutch national team. Even their second strip was changed to orange to make the players feel at home. Such a situation would be unthinkable for a club like Athletic Bilbao, and although Real Madrid themselves are hardly famed for excluding foreigners from their ranks, even they would flinch from transforming their particular flagship into such a foreign body, to the perceived detriment of the local *cantera*.

But this has never been, and probably never will be, a matter for shame or regret in Barcelona. It is nowhere to be found in the dictates of their sporting constitution, but the Catalans pride themselves on their lack of parochialism, on their cosmopolitan air, on their time-honoured practice of looking outward, of absorbing influences and of transforming them into their own eclectic dynamic. The motto for the club's centenary was *El centenari de tots* (Everyone's centenary) whose deliberate ambiguity might have meant that it was for the whole of the Catalan community, the Catalanist community (that is, the more nationalist elements), Spain or the whole world. Whatever it meant, it embodied a subtle message of inclusiveness while simultaneously managing to invite outsiders to take an admiring look.

Time and time again footballers have arrived from foreign shores and rapidly been 'Catalanised' – which is not to say that they have necessarily learned the language, but rather that they have absorbed the peculiar *tarannà* (way of being) of the region which they have almost invariably found attractive. To borrow a term from sociology, most have found few problems in 'acculturating' themselves to the manners and mannerisms of their hosts, and have ended up becoming honorary Catalans. Even the notoriously ill-adapting British have not been immune to this phenomenon, from Vic Buckingham (manager from 1969 to 1971) through to Gary Lineker, Steve Archibald and Terry Venables, who got off on the right foot at the Camp Nou by addressing the crowd in halting Catalan at his first training session. The painfully reserved Mark Hughes, on the other hand, was one exception.

Johan Cruyff himself never learned Catalan, but insisted on having his son christened Jordi (after the local patron saint, better known as St George in England) in 1974 – a time when the use of Catalan names was still prohibited by the constitution. Cruyff has since suggested it was merely the sound of the name that he liked, but to the local population, still officially silenced under the dying regime of Franco, the christening seemed like a radical and much appreciated gesture. The added fact that the authorities had initially refused to stamp the registration papers (his son was born on Dutch soil) but had finally capitulated to Cruyff's bullying insistence made him an even bigger hero in their eyes. To this day, Cruyff can do no wrong in the eyes of most Barcelona fans, and he has the freedom of the city.

The Catalans, unlike Real Madrid, prefer their heroes to be political creatures, and Cruyff was merely the most famous of a long line. The Hungarian Ladislao (Laszlo) Kubala, one of the club's stars in the Fifties, and later national team manager for many years, lived in the city until his death in 2002. Hristo Stoichkov, the tetchy Bulgarian forward and hub of the Dream Team, now considers himself Catalan and has pledged to settle in the city on his retirement. The founder and father of the club, the Swiss Hans Kamper, changed his name to Joan Gamper, Joan being a typical male name of the region. Suffice to say that the substantial Dutch contingent, controversial when the team began the 1998-99 campaign badly, eventually seemed to be absorbed in the time-honoured fashion, all seduced by Barcelona's confidence and swagger, by the all-encompassing embrace of its broad church.

There have been exceptions, notably Diego Maradona and Ronaldo, but neither man had reached anything approaching true maturity during their spell at the club. The behaviour and attitude of both suggested they knew from the start that their stay was to be temporary, their agents and entourage calculating they would benefit more if their clients effected a brief but spectacular visit. Maradona spent too much time in Argentina and Ronaldo too much in discussions over his next contract to ever really appreciate Barcelona's offerings to the full. Neither is remembered with much affection.

Nonetheless, there are those who would dispute this interpretation of the welcoming nature of Catalanism. For them the church is too broad, particularly where its definition seems to depend too much on a direct link with the peculiar institution that is FC Barcelona. In October 1900, less than a year after the foundation of Barça, another, very different football club was formed. Español appeared on the same northern side of the city, in the Sarrià district, with the explicit purpose of representing Barcelona's 'immigrant' population, a largely working-class constituency. The club was initially called Sociedad Española de Football and was founded by Ángel Rodríguez, a student of engineering at Barcelona University. He had seen Kamper playing with his English friends and decided to form a team made up exclusively of locals, which at first meant his friends from the university faculty.

Students back then were almost exclusively middle-class, of course, and Rodríguez himself was the son of the rector. But the founding message of the club nevertheless pointed clearly towards a different audience: 'We create this club to compete with the foreigners of FC Barcelona.' The word 'Español' in the original name was hugely provocative, given the sensitive political climate of the time. In 1898 Spain had lost its last significant colonies, Cuba and the Philippines, in a disastrous war with the United States. In Barcelona the effect was to sharpen antagonism towards Madrid, particularly among the industrialists who blamed the central government for losing their profitable colonial markets. In 1901 the conservative Catalanist party, the Lliga Regionalista, won four of Barcelona's seven seats in the national election, the first significant mark of Catalanism in Spain's politics.

Rodríguez was clearly using the cosmopolitan persuasion of the early Barça for his own ends, but his little wind-up ensured that for the next hundred years the club he formed would for ever be associated with the political right of Catalonia, simply by making the rather brazen equation of 'local' and 'Spanish' – hardly a link that was likely to appeal to the Catalan heartlands.

The club did well from the start, and those who suggest that their history is one of almost total failure forget that within two years of their foundation they were playing in the first King's Cup. They subsequently took part in all the competitions up to the founding of the league proper, making the final in 1909, 1911 and 1915 – as many times as Barça. Indeed, they defeated 'the foreigners' 3-1 in 1909 on their way to the final, which they lost to San Sebastián. By 1930 they were good enough to inflict on Real Madrid their heaviest ever defeat (8-1), and their early development seems to have been sufficient to attract a fan base which did not endorse the idea that FC Barcelona represented the city and the region. In 1916 they gave a debut to a 16-year-old who was to become the most famous of all Spanish goalkeepers, Ricardo Zamora. It hardly helped the relationship between the two clubs that Zamora was transferred to Barça three years later.

In 1918, after the US president Woodrow Wilson made his famous speech on the rights of nations to self-determination, the campaign for home rule in Catalonia gathered strength. A large petition in favour of independence remained conspicuously untouched by Real Club Deportivo Español, as they had by then become known, who instead started up a counter-petition against autonomy. The wording of their petition was the work of the *Peña Ibérica* who had been formed as a vigilante thug group to harass the secessionists.

The *Brigadas Blanquiazules* (blue and white brigades), with their deliberately militaristic connotations, still exist, priding themselves on their neatly designed swastikas. Despite the fact that during the 1990s the club tried to distance itself from its far right associations, one wonders how many of its core supporters would still agree with the counter-petition's introductory text: 'Our foundation is for ... the affirmation of the principle of national unity in all aspects of Spanish society.'

Just to show their loyalty to the cause of 'national unity', the *Peña*

Ibérica joined up with the Falangists in 1933 and fought alongside them in the Civil War. Soon after the war Español won one of their only two trophies of the 20th century, beating Real Madrid 3-2 in the 1940 final of the Generalísimo's Cup. They lost to Valencia in the 1941 final, but it should come as no surprise that their brief golden era coincided with the period in which their city neighbours were still trying to play the game with a ball and chain attached to one foot, their best players exiled, their president a *madridista* stooge, their tongue banned and their every attempt to reconstitute the club viewed as a political act.

It says a lot for Barcelona's spirit that they came back from the ashes of the war to win the cup in 1942, beating Athletic Bilbao 4-3 in an epic final. As mentioned in the opening chapter, Franco apologists have sought to portray this final, between the two flagships of the secessionist movements the dictator tried to suppress, as evidence of the subtlety of his leadership. The theory maintains that Franco preferred the two clubs, especially Barcelona, to rise again, because their recuperation would ensure the continuation of the *morbo* factor over which he and his forces exerted manipulative control. It would smooth the way to making Real Madrid the emblem of their own dominance. Whether or not this is true, the Barça side of the Fifties is still reckoned to have been their best ever, overshadowed only by the European exploits of a Di Stéfano-led Madrid.

Franco could not have counted upon the fact that the late Forties were to see an economic revival in Catalonia, attracting large-scale immigration from the south, particularly Andalucía. But it was Barça who became the magnet for the working-classes that Español had origi-nally hoped to recruit. After the war they were there in much greater numbers, and the need to settle in, to acculturate to the Catalan way, became a priority for people whose very identity was in question. To support Español, whose temporary powers were already diminishing by the end of the Forties, may not have looked like such a useful option.

This explains why at the end of the century Barça had 112,000 members while Espanyol, in what was their centenary year, had 16,000 – no more than they could boast in 1950. In the winter of 1996, during a conference on multilingual education in Barcelona, I was intrigued by the presence, day after day, of a small group of protesters outside the conference centre, huddled around a brazier. As I took one of their leaflets, I noticed that the man who handed it to me wore an RCD Español badge on his jacket. The literature he gave me was complaining about the fact that an international conference such as the one I was attending should have had the gall to advertise its presence outside the conference hall using only Catalan and English. This was, the leaflet complained (in Spanish of course), a clear affront to the Spanish language and a typical example of how Catalanism was going too far in its attempts to promote Catalan to the detriment of Spanish. The Catalanists were the new fascists, they were implying, and the leaflet bemoaned the fact that their children were being deliberately deprived of the language of Cervantes in their schooling.

I was more interested in the fact that at least one of them was an Español supporter. It was as though this first or second generation immigrant, as he must have been, articulate, well-dressed and clearly blue-collar, had levered himself into a socio-economic position which no longer required him to bleat along with the other arrivistes at the Camp Nou. He told me firmly that he was Catalan and proud of it, but that he could not tolerate this new 'inverted fascism', as he put it. He was probably as representative of the anti-Barça lobby as it was possible to get, with a rightwing vision of Catalonia that he was less prepared to tell me about – not that I asked him. Two years previously his club had changed its name to 'Espanyol', in a rather belated attempt, one feels, to advertise its own version of being Catalan. Over in the Camp Nou they were unlikely to have been impressed.

What would Hans Kamper have made of it all? By the time of his death in 1930, he had seen, and been on the receiving end of, plenty of *morbo*. Kamper was 22 when he turned up in Barcelona in 1899, having left his native Switzerland to help set up some sugar trading companies in west Africa, presumably with daddy's backing. Why he never got there has never been satisfactorily explained, but when the ship left for more exotic locations, young Hans stayed to try his luck among the Catalans. He got a job almost at once, as an accountant for a tram company with which an uncle had connections.

Hans had already had a hand in setting up FC Zürich, and the enterprising young buck was quickly into his stride in his new surroundings, hanging out in various city gyms looking for fellow football enthusiasts. Having settled on the Solé gym as the most propitious for his purposes, Kamper managed to persuade the owner, Jaime Vila, to allow him to gather together a group of young sporty types for the purpose of playing football. The other members of the gym, mostly well-off locals, had not taken up his offers to form a football team, probably because they thought it beneath them. So he wrote a letter to the paper.

As Jimmy Burns points out in his book *Barça – A People's Passion*, the mainstream Catalan bourgeoisie considered the sight of men in short trousers 'morally reprehensible', and if they practised sport at all it was 'to ride horses, shoot or play tennis – in long trousers'. What's more, the working-classes were revolting, in both senses. Ten days before FC Barcelona were officially formed, the mayor of the city resigned in protest at the spiralling new taxes imposed by central government in Madrid, a duty particularly resented in light of the fact that Barcelona's burgeoning economy was beginning to prop up the country, along with the furnaces of another troublesome city, Bilbao.

The movement *Tancament de Caixes* (literally 'locking up of the strong-boxes') was provocative enough for Madrid to declare a virtual state of war on Catalonia – a 'pay up or else' approach, whose main effect was to stir up militancy in the unions and the factories. The owner classes were not so happy either, but could afford, for the time being, to sit back and watch. Football seems to have been regarded as the game of the great unwashed, assuming that the bourgeoisie were aware of it at all. It was only foreigners like Kamper and a few other small groups, mostly English, who could cut through the snobbery, exempt from the alleged social undesirability of the fledgling game.

Barcelona celebrated their centenary in some style throughout 1999, but the climax of the event was held back until October 22, 100 years to the day since Kamper's note to the newspaper *Deportes*:

Sports Notices
Our friend and companion Hans Kamper... former Swiss [football] champion, being keen on organising some football games in the city asks anyone who feels enthusiastic enough about the sport to present themselves at the offices of this newspaper any Tuesday or Friday evening between the hours of 9 and 11pm.

The eight-line notice in the paper's sports section has become football's most famous announcement. The swift response to his clarion call was sufficient to enable Kamper to hold a founding meeting a month later, on November 29, in the Solé gym. Present were those who had read *Deportes* a month earlier and who had gone along the very next evening to see what it was all about – another Swiss, three Englishmen and two Catalans. Kamper asked for a vote, and one Walter Wild was handed the honour of the first presidency. Wild was a friend of the Witty family, Anglo-Catalan shipping merchants who held positions of some significance in the city's business circles and whose interest in the early years of the club was vital in getting the sport as a whole more accepted in the places that mattered, places where purse strings opened and more radical, middle-class Catalan militancy could get in on the act.

But in those early days of the club, politics was not an issue. As typical late Victorian British merchants, the Wittys would have been more concerned with steering clear of any activities that might have complicated their business dealings. As former pupils of the public school Merchant Taylors', they would have been brought up to believe in the virtues of participation over mere victory, of the value of healthy minds in healthy bodies and of the rounding of the human personality through sporting prowess – all a bit too Corinthian for the likes of the Catalans, and probably for Kamper too.

The Witty brothers, Arthur and Ernest, despite spending many years in Barcelona, never got much further than heavily accented Spanish, whereas Kamper's son claimed he never remembered his father speaking anything other than Catalan, even at home. By the time the club was five years old, the Wittys were beginning to distance themselves, while Kamper was rapidly turning native. By 1925 his process was so complete that he was kicked out of the country for six months by the authoritarian government of Primo de Rivera. By contrast, Arthur Witty, shortly before his death, declared in an interview that he hated the way Barça had politicised their act, with all its aggressive and partisan consequences.

Ernest Witty did useful things for the club, like ordering decent leather balls, good kit and referees' whistles through his shipping company, but the most important legacy left by the brothers was the famous *azulgrana* colours of the club, first sported in late 1900 during a game between Barcelona and another outfit of locals called Hispania. No one seems able to translate the colour *azulgrana* satisfactorily, even though the contemporary press often refer to Barça under this name. *Azul* is blue and *grana* is actually cochineal, but you've seen the shirts, so never mind the semantics. Perhaps 'blue and maroon' will do.

Arthur Witty's son claimed, in an interview for Jimmy Burns's book, that the famous colours were the same as the colours of the Merchant Taylors' school teams and that Arthur had been responsible for suggesting they should become the colours of their newly formed club. It's a plausible theory, although the more common one is that Kamper himself had decided on the colours, basing them on the shirts worn by

FC Zürich. Zürich did indeed wear these colours (more or less), but according to an alternative theory of the Anglo-Catalan author Toni Strubell, the colours hark back to the French Revolution and the colours adopted by Robespierre and the *sans culottes* of the First Republic.

Zürich appear to have made a conscious decision to adopt these colours because of their historical significance and, of course, red and blue are still on the French flag today. This theory undoubtedly goes down well with the Catalanistas, since it represents yet another raspberry blown in the direction of Madrid. It's just as well no one told Franco about the possible *Liberté, Egalité* connotations of the *azulgrana* shirts. In all events, there is no particular consensus over the origins of Barça's colours, a state of affairs that suits most people fine.

By 1911, while Barcelona were sporting the cross of St Jordi with the red and yellow stripes of Catalonia in their badge, Español were using the royal crown and calling themselves Real Club de Fútbol. The politicising of the rivalry was thus well under way. In the 1909-10 season, during a regional cup game between the two clubs, the Barcelona players walked off at half-time in protest at the referee's decision to disallow a Barcelona goal for alleged handball. But in truth he was reacting to the fact that several hundred Español fans had invaded the pitch threatening to lynch him if the goal, which would have put Barça 2-1 in the lead, was allowed to stand.

Shades of 1924, when Pepe Samitier, Barça's first real star, was sent off, provoking a mass showering of coins onto the pitch of Les Corts, the club's first major stadium. The game was cancelled and ordered to be replayed behind closed doors by the military authorities, an unwise decision which led to mass battles between the opposing supporters outside the gates as the game trundled silently on inside. Les Corts was inaugurated in 1922 with a capacity of 20,000, a tangible testimony to the fact that Español – still playing more or less behind ropes – were falling rapidly into the shadow of Barça's growing popularity. The ground was opened with the unlikeliest of fixtures, a Catalan XI v St Mirren, and two years later the dictator Miguel Primo de Rivera and his cronies looked sideways as Spain took on Austria in the stadium.

In 1923 the La Riva family, wealthy textile industrialists, bought Español some land deliberately close to Les Corts and built a stadium known as Can Rabia (White House), later to be known as Sarrià. In similar fashion to their appearance on the heels of Barcelona in 1900, they were still a step behind. From then on, the story of FC Barcelona is one of spectacular lurches between *sol* and *sombra*, light and shadow, joy and despair. There has never been a period in Barça's history when it could be said that they were merely treading water. The mid-table of life has not been their calling – the major reason, it hardly needs to be said, for the popularity and fame that has fluttered round their light since the dawning of the Franco years. There are those who might dispute this interpretation of their history, pointing to the fact that the Thirties and the Sixties were relatively fallow periods – but there were good reasons for these periods of relative non-achievement, and it can hardly be sustained that during those years the dog had lost its teeth.

In pure footballing terms, two of the darkest blots on their history are the aforementioned 11-1 defeat in 1943 at the hands of Real Madrid and the 12-1 reversal up in Bilbao in 1930, against an Athletic side at the height of their powers. You won't find much mention of these results in the centenary exhibition, although the former crops up as an example of Madrid's fiendishness. No such excuse can be offered as a mitigating circumstance for the latter debacle, although it is true that the team were without the injured Samitier that day. The fact that Barça finished a mere point behind the champions Bilbao that same season makes the score even more extraordinary, and, according to the press reports of the game, it could have been more.

Barça had, of course, won the initial league in 1929, but they would have to wait until 1945 to win their next. The blots in between, excepting that disastrous trip up to the Basque country, were almost all of a political nature. Perhaps the most significant occurred in 1925 and anticipated the problems to come. It does seem as though some Rubicon was crossed that day, June 14, 1925, some public recognition that things would never be the same again, and that Barcelona had defined itself irrevocably as a community of bolshie traitors, the kidnappers of the dream of a united Spain.

The occasion was a benefit match at Les Corts in aid of the *Orfeó Català*, a choral society that had played a significant role in the Catalanist cultural revival since the late 19th century. Primo de Rivera had already begun to put the boot in before the game, closing down local government and banning the public use of the regional language, as Franco was to do 15 years later. He let the game go ahead – against a side called Jupiter – but refused to allow any tribute to the *Orfeó*, probably because the society had itself been set up as a tribute to Anselm Clave, a 19th century Catalan nationalist and an important cultural figure in the region.

To annoy Rivera, the founder of the *Orfeó* turned up for the game, along with several prominent Catalan political heavyweights. The Wittys, still around, had invited a band of the Royal Marines to play at half-time, from a Royal Navy vessel which happened to be moored in the city harbour for the week. Showing a fine disregard for the bewildering intricacies of foreign politics, the poor chaps thought it would be a nice gesture to the packed stands to belt out the Spanish national anthem, as a thank-you for the invitation.

As the derisory whistling began to build into a crescendo, the confused band stopped playing. The well-documented fact that no Englishman can stand a silence of more than five seconds is never better illustrated than on that day, as the band immediately struck up *God Save the King*, at which, much to their relief, the crowd burst into enthusiastic applause. The Catalans may have thought it was a joke, or even a gesture of solidarity from their English visitors that the band had followed the first five bars of the hated Spanish anthem with a nod to their own royal family, but when the news reached Madrid, no one was laughing.

A military edict fined the Barcelona directors for allowing the anti-Spanish farce to take place. The authorities implied that it had been a conspiracy, but the idea that the Wittys had invited the Marines along to take the mickey seems more than a bit far-fetched. Still, paranoia can go a long way, and Barcelona's activities both as a club and a team were proscribed for a six-month period. Gamper was 'invited' to leave Spain, which he did, fearing for his family's safety. The very fact that Les Corts was packed that day was evidence not of a widespread musical sensibility in the population so much as a collective sense of political opportunism and a simple love of the game of football, for the 1920s marked the first golden age of the club, the *sol* before the *sombra* of the decade to come.

Three players, all of them curious and singular characters, were responsible for this happy period; Paulino Alcántara, Ricardo Zamora and Pepe Samitier. The former was born of Spanish parents in the Philippines but was brought up in Barcelona. Between 1912 and 1927 he scored 356 goals, making him the highest scorer in the club's history. A sickly young child, Alcántara was nevertheless spotted by Kamper and a colleague and hurried into the first team at the age of 15, a debut that yielded an auspicious hat-trick. After a couple of years flitting between the first-team and the *filial* – the Spanish term for youth team and a concept created by Kamper – Alcántara's parents returned to the Philippines and took their son with them.

There he continued his studies in medicine, played for a team called

Bohemians (top scorer of course) and travelled to Tokyo to represent the Philippines in the Asian Games – at table-tennis. Meanwhile, Barcelona, having lost out on two regional Catalan championships, had decided they wanted their Renaissance boy back in the fold. Alcántara's parents refused to allow him to return, but in 1917 he contracted malaria and informed his parents that he would not take the medicine prescribed unless they allowed him to go back.

In 1920, he was picked to play for Spain in the Olympics in Belgium but was forced to stay at home in order to take his final medical exams. Dr Alcántara finally made his international debut two years later, scoring both goals against Belgium. He carried on for another five years, eventually hanging up his boots to become a GP. Of the three stars of the golden period, he comes over as the least controversial, the one least touched and affected by stardom. In many ways he was responsible for the conversion of Barça from an amateur club of fitness fanatics to the professional bearer of the flag. Once there was a hero, a focal point in human form, there was no turning back. In 1910, largely due to Kamper's doggedness, the club had 510 members. By 1921 it had 10,000. It also had Samitier and Zamora.

According to the veteran Real Madrid defender Jacinto Quincoces, in an interview with *Epoca* in 1978, Ricardo Zamora was more famous in his day than Greta Garbo, and better looking. He was certainly a better goalkeeper. Zamora's name still adorns the annual trophy awarded to the season's best goalkeeper in Spain, as Pichichi's does the top scorer's version. Zamora *El Divino* (the divine) along with Samitier *El Mago* (the wizard) represented Spain's first twin versions of the superstar syndrome, appearing as they did at a time when the game was turning professional and the players at the bigger clubs were beginning to earn reasonable sums.

Zamora began at Español in 1916, went to Barcelona in 1919, where he spent his golden years, then returned to his beloved Español in the late Twenties before ending up, like Samitier, in Real Madrid's colours. As with so many figures from the dark ages of football, it is difficult to separate the truth from the misty-eyed recollections, but everyone seems to insist that Zamora was the greatest, better than Yashin, Zoff, Shilton and any others you care to mention.

When people ask whether the Finneys and the Matthews would have survived and shone in the modern game, the arguments usually centre around the fact that the radically different physical attributes demanded from the modern player make comparisons almost impossibe. With goalkeepers, one suspects things have changed rather less. Large hairy-arsed forwards still bear down on goal, unleashing thunderbolts that take the net with them, just as they did in the old days. Back then, though, the ball was heavier, the forwards could assault you in any way they chose and defending was not such a dedicated and sophisticated art as it is now. Goalkeepers, if anything, had to be better in the old days – which suggests Zamora was every bit as good as they say he was.

He was certainly hard to miss. Enormous of build and charismatic by nature, he took to wearing a cloth cap and white polo-neck jumper on the field, a look copied by several of his contemporaries. Zamora, like Samitier, always managed to give the papers something to write about, and sported himself as a society dandy throughout the Twenties. His favourite tipple was cognac, and he smoked three packs of cigarettes a day. Returning from the 1920 Olympics he bought several crates of Havana cigars and stuffed them under his train seat, hoping to get away with importing an amount well in excess of that allowed. He was caught smoking one in his compartment at the border by a customs officer, who enquired as to the contents of the large crates below his seat. Arrested and forced to spend the night behind bars, he had to pay a 500 peseta fine and give up all his beloved contraband to the local police.

Controversy continued to shadow him and he was suspended for a year after Barcelona's 1922 championship season when he lied to the tax authorities about the signing-on fee he had received in a deal that was meant to take him back to Español. He was succeeded by the Hungarian Ferenc Platko, another legendary keeper and in many ways a more popular one. Zamora's eagerness to move back to Español seemed to arise both from implicit anti-Catalan sentiments and an eye for a quick buck, also apparent when on his transfer to Real Madrid in 1930 he picked up 40,000 of the 150,000-peseta transfer fee.

Six years later he was still laughing, when it was he who foiled Barcelona in the last cup final before the Civil War, played in Valencia. With Barça 2-1 down and pressing towards the end of the game, Zamora pulled off a stupendous save from José Escolá. There is no film of it, but there is a photo, taken at close quarters by the side of the post to which Zamora had dived. The weather had been sunny for weeks and the pitch was very dry. Escolá hit the ball hard and low, aiming for the inside of the post. Half of the stadium rose to acclaim the goal, upon which Zamora's dive sent up a plume of dust, obscuring the scene. When the dust cleared, Zamora was standing there impassively, the ball in his hands.

Several months later, Zamora was smoking his three packs and drinking his cognac in the cafes of Nice, having been through several extraordinary experiences on the outbreak of the Civil War. In July, the pro-Nationalist paper *ABC* reported seeing Zamora's bullet-riddled body in a roadside ditch in Madrid's Moncloa district. The reports of his death provoked a huge commotion. In 1934 he had been given a medal of the Order of the Republic by his namesake, President Niceto Zamora – a ceremony that conferred on him more of a pinkish demeanour than he probably would have wished, given his connections with Español and his previous indifference to the Barça cause. It's said that on receiving news of the swearing-in of the Republic in 1934, Stalin glanced at the dispatch and asked the messenger: 'This President Zamora. Wasn't he a famous goalkeeper?'

Zamora's death at the hands of Nationalist forces was therefore plausible, but *ABC* and several radio broadcasters whose colours were being hastily nailed to the masts preferred to broadcast the news that Zamora was another heroic victim of the 'Reds', causing an outbreak of memorial services, especially in those communities that had swung behind Franco. While these were taking place, a group of Republican militiamen, unamused by the reports and knowing of Zamora's where-abouts, arrested him and took him to the Modelo prison, a dangerous place for anyone who had made a virtue out of playing for Español.

However, instead of being executed, he was given a ball by the guards and taken out into the yard for a game, so that they could say that they had played with the legendary keeper. Over several tension-filled days, which would make a fine subject for someone with an eye for a film script, Zamora kept his potential executors at bay with tales of his playing days and an endless series of penalty competitions. When he finally slipped out, in disguise, he was driven up to the French border and on to Nice, where he met Samitier and signed up for the local side.

In December 1938 he was back on the other side of the frontier, in San Sebastián, to play for Spain against Real Sociedad in a benefit for Francoist soldiers. Zamora's presence in the side was naturally exploited to the full by the Francoists as propaganda – the great one had returned to give, as it were, public endorsement to the regime. No Barcelona player was in the side, of course. Most of them were in exile anyway. Real Sociedad do not like to be reminded of this awkward little episode in their history, although of course they would claim, with some justifi-cation, that they had little choice but to take part.

Two weeks later, the first edition of *Marca* was published from a press in San Sebastián. The cover page featured a Teutonic-looking gentleman with blond hair, his right arm raised in fascist salute under the heading **Right arm raised to the sportsmen of Spain!** No wonder, given the importance of this event to the Fascists, that Franco later awarded Zamora the Great Cross of the Order of Cisneros in the Fifties – since his presence back then represented a clear endorsement from a famous and popular man. Curiously, when I sent a series of questions (from San Sebastián) to *Marca* about this era, they refused to co-operate.

Samitier, in many ways the true star of Barça during the defining Twenties, was also detained by a faction of the anarchist militia during the war, but was also released and allowed to escape to France, although the circumstances are still relatively unclear. Presumably he had decided not to tell them that Franco was his hero, a fact that sits uncomfortably with the status he still enjoys within the club, which even survived his defection to the ranks of Real Madrid in the Thirties.

Alcántara may have been a star in terms of his goalscoring, but Pepe Samitier, 'El Sami', was the main focus of attention once Zamora had flown back to his blue and white nest. In the Barcelona museum at the Camp Nou you can see his first contract with the club in which it is written that he will receive a luminous watch and a three-piece suit as signing-on bonuses. Like Zamora, Samitier made his debut in 1919, at the age of 17. Young, working-class and wet behind the ears, he was nevertheless by 1925 the highest paid player at the club and thus by default the country's highest earner.

Barcelona's move to professionalise their playing staff that year met with a protest in the semi-finals of the cup, when Atlético Madrid walked on to the pitch and unveiled an appeal for the clubs habitually involved in the competition to remain amateur. At the beginning of the second half, Platko and the German defender Emil Walter brought on a counter argument, hastily penned during the break, which defended the right of foreign players like themselves to earn a decent living from the game. Barça won 2-0 and by 1929 Atlético Madrid had themselves shed their amateur status.

When professionalism became the norm after the inception of the league, there were no controls on the amount players could earn, which meant Samitier's status as the league's top outfield player guaranteed his position as top earner. By then his friendship with another working-class icon, the Argentinian tango singer Carlos Gardel, meant he had to be earning a decent sum to fuel his taste for night-clubbing – a habit that seems to have been tolerated by a timorous but appreciative board of directors, who were once famously photographed looking the other way as Samitier and his troupe of night-birds passed them early one morning down the Ramblas.

Samitier is important in the annals of European football because the accounts of his playing style suggest that he was among the first players to orchestrate the game from the back. Until then, the linchpins of the teams had been centre-forwards in the bruising Basque style, a model whose end-product always depended on the ability of the forward-lines to fight their own battles, win their own balls and navigate their own routes to goal. Samitier, the first 'midfield general' to emerge at the top of Spanish football, seems to have played in a position combining the roles of what the Spanish would now call the *pivote* (central midfielder) and the sweeper. The oddest thing about Samitier is that while he was accused in some circles of being a *leñero* (chopper, hacker), despite his relatively slight physical appearance, he was also a prolific goal scorer, second only to Alcántara at the time. His famous *langosta* (lobster) kicks were the template for the later *chilena* or bicycle-kick, most famously practised in later years by Denis Law and Hugo Sánchez.

Gardel's other Catalan friends, political figures and radical artists who could hardly have been natural companions for someone with Samitier's views, nevertheless took him under their wing, at least publicly. But Gardel died in an air-crash in Colombia in 1935, and when the Civil War came it was the Nationalists who enlisted Samitier's image to their cause. By 1938, *Marca* were using his escape from the 'Reds' as proof that he was always a true Spaniard at heart, publishing in their first edition a breathless account of his allegedly daredevil escape to France and temporary exile. In fact, he left on a French warship, and seems to have been spared any swabbing duties. While playing for Nice with Zamora, he seems to have got rather too close for comfort to the wife of the club's president, and could be seen most mornings taking her poodles for a walk. Nice almost won the league title that year (1937), losing out to Bordeaux. By then Samitier was considered something of an old butcher, having taken out the Bordeaux forward Nallet in a game towards the end of the season with a tackle that would have graced the repertoire of many a fearful name to follow him.

When he died in 1972 there was mass mourning and something akin to a state funeral in Barcelona, a rather ironic send-off given that he was probably much matier with the Real Madrid fraternity in his later years and made no secret of his admiration for Franco. As Jimmy Burns has suggested, at the time of his death Barcelona needed to celebrate

Samitier as 'a symbol of the club's greatness', given that they were going through a particularly rough time and Johan Cruyff was still over in Holland.

As with Kubala, who ended up in controversial circumstances at Español, there are those who would still like to know more about Samitier's real views on the club that has decided, despite the misgivings, to immortalise him. Kubala, similarly, has been forgiven his trip across the Diagonal to the Avenida de Sarrià in 1963 – a trip that had nothing to do with politics and everything to do with maintaining a certain lifestyle. Be all the doubts as they may, Samitier's period with Barcelona, from 1919 to 1933, yielded five King's Cups, Spain's first official league title and 12 Catalan championships.

After the glint of the gold came the inevitable shadows, and the biggest and most traumatic stain on the shirt of FC Barcelona was the death of their president, Josep Sunyol, murdered by Falangist troops in August 1936. His murder and its subsequent cover-up through and beyond the Franco years has become one of the defining motifs of Catalanism. It also represents the most irrefutable evidence that football and politics are darkly intertwined in Spain – in some ways the history of 20th century Spain can be read in the martyrdom of a football club.

In the same way as the poet Lorca's murder at the hands of the Guardia Civil was used as evidence that the fascist right was a movement that could only flex its muscles through acts of thuggery, so Sunyol's death is now seen as the truly defining moment of the club, the desecration of an ideology in bud, of cultural separatism, independence, the right to autonomy. It proved that even then, Barça was more than a club, and this sense of historical continuity affords some comfort to the current bearers of the flag, the season ticket holders who can buy the right to participate in and continue their heartfelt tradition of deepest *morbo*.

Sunyol, a qualified lawyer, was the kind of man the Nationalist fraternity most feared and despised. He was the founder of the left-leaning newspaper *La Rambla* during the dictatorship of Primo de Rivera and held various minor political posts in Barcelona in the 1930s. He came from a long line of Catalan political militants who would have seen a place on Barça's governing board as a good opportunity for starting a political career, which is precisely what Sunyol did in 1928, at the age of 30.

Sunyol got in because his family were wealthy and had impeccable cultural and political credentials, but even before moving into football circles he had gone a step further than most of his family had ever done, joining *Acció Català*, a leftwing Catalan movement with an anarchist-flavoured philosophy.

Anarchism had maintained a significant following in Barcelona since the 1870s, and the crash of 1929 and subsequent depression gave it added credibility. The collapse of stocks and shares around the word was brought uncomfortably close to home by Gamper's suicide in 1930, devastated by the overnight disappearance of his entire savings. Sunyol continued to operate under a dictatorship hostile to all things Catalan, and once the regime fell in 1930, he began to use *La Rambla* to articulate his vision of the fusion of football and politics in Catalonia, a synergy that he felt would eventually secure democracy and self-determination for the region.

Few have ever questioned whether Sunyol was actually interested in football, or whether he just saw it as a means to an end. His articles in *La Rambla* were hardly classics of football reporting, briefly mentioning results and team matters before launching off into political rhetoric under the slogan 'Sport and Citizenship'. Whatever the truth, he was elected president of FC Barcelona in 1935 at a time when there were so many leftwing factions parading the streets that his vision of a politico-sporting utopia had long since been forgotten, suffocated by the myriad conflicting ideologies bubbling to the surface.

The tense and chaotic situation had led to a declining interest in the potential role of FC Barcelona to influence events, a state of affairs Sunyol was apparently attempting to reverse that fatal August day in 1936 when he rather foolishly (bravely for some) drove up into the Guadarrama mountains outside Madrid to make contact with Republicans still holding their own against the Nationalist forces in areas south of the capital. His exact motive remains a mystery. Julián García-Candau even suggests in his book on Real and Barça that Sunyol was on his way to offer an ex-Oviedo player, caught up in the conflict, a contract to play for Barça when hostilities died down.

Sunyol found himself on the wrong road in an area controlled by Falangist troops. The opposing forces in the Civil War took few prisoners, and it seems he was gunned down there and then. Whether or not his killers knew who he was when they shot him, they certainly would have found out soon afterwards. Sunyol officially disappeared and his body was only exhumed in the 1990s through the efforts of Toni Strubell and other journalists and academics, who got together to force the reluctant Barcelona president Josep Lluís Núñez to recognise and publicise the 60th anniversary of his death, the 50th having been completely ignored by the club. Núñez, never a great hit with the Catalanist lobby, was desperate throughout his 20-year reign to avoid being labelled politically. Any initiative on his part towards Sunyol would have been seen as a fairly radical act, and might have disturbed some of his business associates.

In the photograph of *Els Amics de Josep Sunyol* (The Friends of Josep Sunyol) laying the commemorative wreath, the surname 'Suñol', written in Spanish without the Catalan 'y', can be seen on the memorial stone. Sunyol's only surviving son had distanced himself from the ceremony and threatened to publish an article stating that the site did not belong to his father but to some other 'Sunyol', if the group insisted on using the Catalan spelling. After the Civil War, when the Sunyol family recovered much of its appropriated wealth, a part of the family branched to the far right and never came back. The murdered Sunyol may have become a symbol of Catalan nationalism, but that did not prevent him being posthumously subjected to the curious twists of late 20th century Catalan politics.

In the week before the celebration of the 60th anniversary, the Friends of Sunyol stuck up posters around the city with the message 'How to kill a president'. When Strubell met Núñez a week later, the president told him, apparently in all seriousness, that he had not emerged from his house for three days after seeing one of the posters.

It seems quite right and proper that Barcelona, through the efforts of some of its supporters, should have purged themselves of the 50-year silence surrounding Sunyol, but they should no longer feel any great need to push the martyrdom line any further. Sunyol's name should have appeared in 1976, the year after Franco's death, not in 1996, and for that the club has only itself to blame.

The ambiguity of Barcelona's politics continued under the successor to Núñez , Joan Gaspart. Although he preferred the fact to go unnoticed, Gaspart was a paid-up member of the Partido Popular – a party that is rarely the flavour of the month with the nationalists and which has its roots in the old Alianza Popular, a rightwing party associated with post-Franco sympathisers. The simple notion of Barça as the 'flagship' of Catalan nationalism looks again to be distinctly suspect.

Barça emerged rampant from the war years, like a phoenix on ampheta-mines. Renamed Barcelona Club de Fútbol by the dictatorship, they won the league in 1945 (under Samitier), 1948 and 1949. They also triumphed in 1952 and 1953, by which time they had Kubala, the Hungarian maestro who many view as the club's greatest ever player, despite his fondness for the bottle and his susceptibility to injury. But in 1953 Di Stéfano arrived in Madrid and of the next 16 championships, Madrid won 12, not to mention the odd European Cup.

Of course, those who refer to the Fifties as a period of failure at Barcelona are speaking in strictly relative terms. Between 1954 and 1958 the Catalans finished second three times and third twice, though in the same period Madrid were champions four times, with only Bilbao in 1956 interrupting the sequence. But success finally came in 1959, coinciding with the arrival of the Argentinian manager Helenio Herrera. Herrera's boldest move was to dispense with Kubala, gradually easing him out while signing two other influential Hungarians, Sandor Kocsis and Zoltan Czibor. The young Luis Suárez, brought over from Galicia, was seen by Herrera as the natural successor to Kubala, and he followed his mentor to Internazionale three years later.

Lazsi Kubala is, in many ways, as big a figure in the history of the Spanish game as Di Stéfano, though there remains a feeling that he somehow failed as player, that his drinking, womanising and injury problems helped Madrid to rule the roost during most of the Fifties. But Di Stéfano liked him, and was visibly shaken when he stepped off the plane from Glasgow after the Champions League final in May 2002 to be told that his old sparring partner had died that same morning – the day after Madrid's 'ninth'.

Kubala's arrival in Barcelona has been the subject of many a tale, but the truth seems to be that he was genuinely unaware of where he was going and for whom he was signing. Samitier, having seen him play in Madrid in 1950 for the touring exiles Hungaria, decided to move in before Real Madrid and brought him by train to the Catalan club. Kubala, allegedly in an alcoholic daze, remarked to Samitier that he had seen a sign on which he swore he had read the word 'Barcelona', and wasn't he supposed to be signing for Real Madrid? Samitier just told him to go back to sleep. If, as has been alleged, Samitier really was a 'double agent' in the Di Stéfano deal three years later, then maybe it was because he lived to regret his role in providing Barça with Kubala.

He certainly regretted the arrival of Herrera towards the end of the decade, and moved to work openly for Real Madrid, claiming that the master of *catenaccio* was 'inhuman'. Kubala himself outlasted Herrera and played his last game for the club in 1961, then stayed on first as youth trainer and then briefly as manager before departing to Español in understandably acrimonious circumstances. Until Suárez, who stayed all too briefly, and then Cruyff, Barcelona probably felt that Kubala was the man who should have brought them world prominence, and yet all they got was a gutful of Real Madrid.

Herrera, whose parents had fled poverty in Andalusia for Argentina and Morocco, was certainly cosmopolitan enough for Barcelona, but his reputation as a footballing dictator and as the ultimate advocate of defensive cynicism hardly fits the club's free and easy style. Yet in the midst of Madrid's glory years he brought Barcelona success that would elude them for more than a decade after he left. In 1958-59, Herrera's first season, they won the double. The following season, two days after pipping Madrid for the league title on goals scored, they met them in the European Cup semi-final.

Unfortunately for Barcelona, but luckily for the citizens of Glasgow, they failed dismally to put the brakes on what would turn out to be Real's greatest show of their whole roller-coaster ride – the sublime 7-3 destruction of Eintracht Frankfurt at Hampden. To get to that final, Madrid beat Barça 3-1 both in the Bernabéu and the Camp Nou, results which stuck badly in the craw of the community and which finally put paid to Herrera. He was sacked two days later by the president Miró-Sans, desperately looking for a way to hang on to his fading power.

The next season the clubs were drawn together again in the first round of the European Cup and Barça went on to win 4-3 on aggregate in controversial circumstances. In the first game in Madrid, a 2-2 draw, referee Arthur Ellis gave the Catalans a penalty after ignoring his linesman's flag for offside against the Brazilian Evaristo, who was then fouled. Barcelona won the second leg 2-1 at the Camp Nou, but not before another Englishman, Reg Leafe, had disallowed no fewer than four goals. The tie warrants a tiny, reluctant square of print in the *Historia del Fútbol Español* published by the rightwing magazine *Epoca* in 1994, amid a sea of triumphalist pages celebrating Madrid's consecutive run of European Cups.

The game even came to confirm people's suspicions about the so-called cartel of Spanish referees who allegedly favoured Madrid during the Fifties and Sixties. The two Englishmen, so the reasoning goes, could not have been bought off so easily by Franco's cronies and instead their decisions favoured Barcelona, if anyone. Unfortunately, no one was helping Barça in the final, and with a slowed-down version of Kubala attempting to run the midfield, they went down to a little-known Benfica side 3-2 in Berne. Still, Barça were the first team ever to knock

Madrid out of the competition and had at least put a temporary end to their colossal strides across Europe.

The 1960s were to prove one of Barcelona's greyest decades, which even the retirement of Di Stéfano failed to lighten. Real Madrid and their neighbours Atlético exerted a total monopoly on league titles during the period, and Barcelona had their noses well and truly pushed out. It was as if the failure against Benfica were to mark the whole decade, a period made doubly painful by Herrera's subsequent successes at Inter.

Good, solid home-made players came through the ranks, like Josep Fuste and Charly Rexach, but this may have been due at least in part to the new president Enrique Llaudet's priority of balancing the books – since he had to bear the brunt of the escalating costs of the new Camp Nou. A new star to rekindle the flames of the early Fifties did not form a part of his shopping list. There were also rumbles from below that he was a Francoist, and that he had no heart for 'the cause'.

Llaudet presided over the Fairs Cup win in 1966 against Zaragoza but was gone by 1968, when the club managed to put a temporary smile on their supporters' lengthening faces by defeating Real Madrid 1-0 in the King's Cup final in the Bernabéu, 32 years after the two had last met in a final. Franco himself handed over the cup and looked less than chuffed at having to do it. The wife of General Vega, sitting with Franco in the directors' box, apparently turned to Barça's new (and more Catalanist) president Narcis de Carreras and remarked how pleasant it was that his team had won, since Barcelona too was 'Spanish'.

They won the cup again in 1971, but would have to wait until the 1973-74 season and the arrival of Johan Cruyff for their next league title. From then on, the club grew in size and self-importance, aided by the imposing Camp Nou, built in the mid-Fifties. Their fame, fortune and almost universal recognition as the biggest club on the planet – at least before David Beckham turned them down – could not be attributed, however, to an overflowing cup of success, since it was another 12 years before they lifted the next league title, a year after Maradona's departure. Despite three Fairs Cups and two Cup-Winners Cups, their attempts to rival Real in the biggest prize of the lot, the European Cup, had never got further than another losing final, the 1986 penalty shoot-out debacle against Steaua Bucharest in Seville, under Terry Venables.

It would seem, therefore, that the reason for the Pope's decision to join the bandwagon, along with millions of others, was the arrival of the so-called Dream Team, the side that won four consecutive championships between 1991 and 1994 and which saw off Sampdoria at Wembley in the

1992 European Cup final – the same year as the Barcelona Olympics, Freddie Mercury and a general sensation in the air that it was impossible to go for more than a few hours at a time without hearing Barcelona mentioned in some context or another.

El Dream Team, as the Spanish press decided to call it, after the US basketball team which cruised through the Olympic tournament, was a rather worrying conceit for several reasons, chief among them the fact that its appearance in capital letters seemed to be suggesting that not only was it the best Barça team of all time, it was the best team ever to have emerged on planet Earth, full stop. Since no one ever bothered to explain what the phrase was supposed to mean, it can only be concluded that a conspiracy of ambiguity has since conferred an inappropriate greatness on that team (and manager) of the early Nineties. In a deliberate linguistic nod to the concept, Real Madrid's all-star side of he early 21st century was dubbed *El Floren team*, after the canny president responsible for setting it up, Florentino Perez.

Johan Cruyff still lives in Barcelona and takes his member's seat at most home games, deliberately allowing himself to be an occasional focus for disaffected fans, particularly those who had questioned the modus operandi of President Núñez. Núñez, an awkward little man with an unfortunate expression that seemed locked into a permanent sneer, had been festering in the post since 1978 and had survived players' rebellions, dozens of votes of no-confidence, petulant star players and Cruyff's periodic attempts to dislodge him from his throne – the last coming in 1999, during a homage to the Dream Team at the Camp Nou, where Cruyff, hand in hand with *Marca*, unleashed attacks on Núñez in the week before the game.

Cruyff presumably thought he might bring about a *coup d'état* on the night, but all he did was strengthen Núñez's resolve to stay put until he himself could choose to go. He finally resigned at the end of the trophyless 1999-2000 season, saying he was tired of being unappreciated. At the farewell press conference he surrounded himself with the 138 trophies won during his 22-year period: 27 from football, 25 from basketball, 50 from handball and 36 from hockey. He could instead have mounted a large finger on the screen behind his podium, but the journalists present got the message.

Núñez has been given little credit for the assembly of the Dream Team, while Cruyff's association with it means he is now rated as one of the all-time great managers, along with his undisputed place in the pantheon of all-time great players. Cruyff himself, never one to waste too much energy on a self-effacing gesture, is hardly likely to challenge the description, but the evidence of his managerial genius needs to be sifted through rather more carefully than it ever has been by the Spanish press and the more nostalgic among Barça's supporters.

Cruyff was certainly no fool when it came to spotting a good player, or at least one whom he felt could be taught to play according to his philosophy. Like Herrera many years before him, Cruyff was able to walk into the gaze of 120,000 people and tell them that he was the boss, that he would brook no interference, no questioning. Núñez was put firmly in his place, a state of play that he was quite happy to accept, as long as the results were good and the cash was flowing in. Only later would he realise that his employee was eyeing his throne, and had been doing so from the very beginning.

When Cruyff was appointed manager he turned the place upside down, bringing in the Basques José María Bakero and Aitor Beguiristáin from Real Sociedad, then Andoni Goikoetxea. From abroad came Ronald Koeman from PSV, Michael Laudrup from Juventus and 'madman' Hristo Stoichkov from CSKA Sofia in 1990. With the exception of Koeman, none of these signings seemed particularly world-shattering at the time, but each player went on to perform perfectly within the framework Cruyff erected for them. Laudrup, a quiet and modest man, spoke at length about Cruyff after retiring to take up his wine interests. He told a Danish newspaper that he left Barça because in the end 'I couldn't stand him any more' but that Cruyff was nevertheless 'a real coach. He had original ideas, and he could communicate them.' Cruyff had an uncanny ability to see where a player would perform best, even when the player himself had never contemplated it.

In his first week at the club, he turned up unannounced at the 'Mini' stadium, a venue just down the road from the Camp Nou used by the youth and B teams. Just before half-time he wandered into the dug-out and asked Charly Rexach, the youth team manager at the time, the name of the young skinny lad playing on the right side of midfield. 'Guardiola – good lad' came the reply. Cruyff ignored the comment and told Rexach to move him into the middle for the second half, to play as the *pivote*, a difficult position to adapt to and one not used by many teams in Spain at that time. 'Pep' Guardiola adjusted immediately, as Cruyff had suspected he would, and when he moved up into the first-team in 1990 he became the true fulcrum of the Dream Team.

Born in Santpedor in the Catalan heartlands, Guardiola also satisfied the need for a local focus among the legions of foreigners and Basques. Although he was not the only Catalan in Barcelona's ranks, he was the only one who wrapped himself (literally) in the flag after important victories, delivered his after-match comments in Catalan, signed petitions in favour of a breakaway Catalan national side and toured schools in the region encouraging the students to read Miquel Martí i Poll's poetry during Catalan literacy campaigns. Out on the pitch, Koeman and Bakero snapped and barked at the heels of anyone who strayed into his zone, for he was a delicate player whose canny art needed protection.

Cruyff got it right with Stoichkov too, finding in him the focused, aggressive front man with the 'fast and nasty' profile that Julio Salinas, the club's main striker, could never quite live up to. Stoichkov had distinguished himself the previous year by marching into the triumphant opposition's changing-rooms after the Bulgarian cup final and smashing the trophy to pieces on the wall as the players celebrated in the bath, an act for which he was all but chased out of the country.

For a while in the early Nineties he seemed unstoppable, outrageously fast and lethal in the box, when he wasn't sitting out a suspension for abusing a referee or kicking a lump out of an opponent. He even chased a poor hare around the perimeter track at Camp Nou in a frothing rage after it had been released onto the pitch by Atlético Madrid fans just as he was cutting in from the right wing and pulling back his left leg to curl in what would have been his third goal of the night. The hare, blinded by the floodlights, ran across Stoichkov's path and made him stumble. The Bulgarian was almost the only one who failed to see the funny side.

At times Barcelona's football reached heights that adjectives cannot really scale. Everyone in Spain who was remotely interested in football found themselves glued to the television every time Barça were on – which was almost every week. The delights seemed endless – the subtlety of the almost telepathic communication between Laudrup and Beguiristain, Goikoetxea's runs on the right flank, Koeman's shooting, Guardiola's razor-sharp passing, Stoichkov's aggressive and bony grace.

They were fantastic to watch, but a dream team? None of the squad could defend – a footballing attribute which Cruyff seemed to view as an inferior preoccupation of managers who feared the opposition. Barça's high-risk strategy won them friends and influenced people because it made for spectacle. The managers who succeeded Cruyff have had to face the weight of expectation created by this side, not just in terms of success but in terms of sheer bravado. Bobby Robson was lucky in that he had a young and frisky Ronaldo running riot for him the season after the Dutchman's departure, but Louis van Gaal's more pragmatic style had the Catalans reaching for their handkerchiefs despite the continuing influx of trophies.

The Dream Team were also ridiculously lucky. The last three of their four consecutive titles were all won on the last day of the season thanks to failures by their rivals rather than their own brilliance. Twice Real Madrid lost in Tenerife to hand the title to their bitter rivals. In 1992 they led 2-0 at half-time, but contrived to lose 3-2. The Galician referee, the suggestively named García de Lorca, was, according to the following Monday's edition of *Marca*, 'bent'. *Plus ça change.*

The next season Madrid again lost it, rather than Barça winning it. I was there that night in the Heliodoro Rodríguez, in the grim industrial outskirts of Santa Cruz. It was a hot windless night and the acrid stench of the petrol refineries hung in the bowl of the packed stadium. You knew Madrid were going to lose the minute they stepped out on to the pitch. They looked scared. Tenerife had a better side that year, and the open hostility of the islanders towards the aristocrats from the capital seemed to get to them straight away.

The next day, the lugubrious Joan Gaspart, then Barça's vice-president, unwisely proclaimed that Tenerife's 2-0 win was just reward for the money his club's directors had offered them to beat Real Madrid, despite the fact that the three points had also won them a place in the UEFA Cup – surely motivation enough. All hell broke loose and there was even talk of a police investigation, but Núñez and Gaspart were technically correct in pointing out that they had done nothing illegal. Three titles on the trot, and counting.

The fourth was to be won in even more incredible circumstances on a day that has etched itself into the collective folk memory of Spanish football. This time Deportivo de La Coruña looked set to take their first-ever title. The Galicians had led all season, and despite Barça's grimly determined chase, Depor still led by a point as the final Sunday arrived. They had a home game against a distinctly average Valencia side, while Barça were at home to Sevilla, whom they slaughtered 5-2. Up in the rainy north-west Deportivo had to win, but had still not found a way through when, in the 89th minute, Francisco Camarasa tripped the Galicians' full-back Nando as he ran into the area and the referee pointed to the spot.

Miroslav Djukic, the Serbian defender, stepped up for his moment of immortality, the poor wretch looking as if he would rather be anywhere else. Bebeto, the usual penalty-taker, had allegedly felt the heat and got out of the kitchen, passing the buck to his team-mate. Djukic poked the ball forward, it rolled pathetically into the Valencia keeper's arms, and the title was Barça's again.

Their Double in 1998 and the league title in their centenary year were to prove the final acts of a decade of prominence and achievement. After the resignation of Nuñez, his henchman Gaspart ascended the throne. He never looked like a good choice, seeming to represent the opposite of that most treasured of Catalan virtues, *seny* (shrewdness). Once he was freed of the shackles that his deputy status had imposed on him for 20 years, he embarked on a vulgar display of power that alienated practically all who had pledged to serve under him.

As his power began to wane and successive resignations from the board threatened to undermine his position in the turbulent summer of 2002, he made the bizarre decision to re-employ Louis van Gaal. The pudding-faced Dutchman had won a couple of league titles in his first spell at Barça in the late Nineties, but the public had never taken to him – sure proof that the Camp Nou likes its representatives to be of a certain type. Van Gaal never seemed to understand, or want to understand, the Catalan thing. It held no interest for him, and his prickly reactions to criticism, his awful Spanish and his famously defensive phrase when hounded by the press, '*Tu – siempre negatiffo!*' (You – you're always negative!) – with the word '*negativo*' appallingly pronounced – made him an easy target for the caricaturists.

The city had breathed a collective sigh of relief when he left, and so was understandably perplexed when informed of his return almost three years later. Of course, he failed even to last out the season. Not long after Van Gaal's second acrimonious departure Gaspart was gone too, finally bowing to public pressure after he had become the most vilified man in the community. After a home defeat against Betis he stood defiantly in the presidential box as practically the whole stadium waved a collective handkerchief at him – the display known as a *pañolada* and a sign that your time is up.

It was an astonishingly theatrical performance, memorable for its hubris, but also typical of Gaspart's failings. He was too fond of being the protagonist, too willing to capture the headlines for whatever reasons. His time at the helm was an unhappy one for the club, three years without a trophy and a final season in which qualification for even the UEFA Cup looked a distant prospect.

Gaspart's departure was followed by the equally odd election of Joan Laporta, catapulted to the top of the candidates' list by his (unfulfilled)

109

promise to bring David Beckham to the club in the summer of 2003. Although Laporta was one of the founders of the *Elefant Blau,* a supporters' group formed in protest at the sacking of Cruyff, his election promised little in the way of immediate improvement, financial or otherwise. Beckham's snub was a measure of how low the club's status had sunk during the Gaspart years, a period that had seen the turbulence at the top mirrored by poor performances on the field. High-earning players such as Patrick Kluivert and Marc Overmars were regularly accused of not giving their all, and at times it seemed that just about everything had gone wrong since the moment Luis Figo had been persuaded to leave for Madrid.

It was no secret that Figo was none too keen on Gaspart, and his controversial decision to leave has always looked like a Portuguese version of *seny.* Real Madrid have not looked back since, but the times can change again. Barça have made a habit of coming back, and the sheer will that drives the community should see them eventually rectify the errors of the century so far.

No telling of the Barcelona tale can be considered complete without some mention of their supporters, divided into members, season ticket holders, those who turn up at the turnstiles when the fancy takes them, and the *penyes.* The latter is a phenomenon invented by Barça in the mid-1940s, when the club was in dire straits and in need of a supportive structure – both financial and spiritual – in the face of the hostility of the dictatorship. The original *Penya Solera* was founded in 1944 by a collection of ex-players (Samitier among them) and prominent members as a sort of social club-cum-supporters club which arranged weekly meetings in various sympathetic city bars to thrash out social initiatives, money-making schemes and in many cases just to have a good time with like-minded obsessives.

Now the club has over 1,200 *penyes* distributed all over the world and the concept has been adopted by other clubs throughout Spain. The word doesn't quite translate to 'supporters' club' because each *peña* has a different name and a slightly different set of customs, depending on the reasons for its foundation. The phenomenon is unique to Spain and compensates for its relative lack of programme and fanzine culture. Each player in a major Spanish side now has a *peña* named after him, and will usually turn up for the inaugural supper. When the same player leaves the club the *peña* often carries on regardless, until its members either tire of one another or are advised by their doctors to stop drinking.

Of course, the sheer number of Barça's *penyes* means there are a thousand tales of how they acquired their names, of which only some are comprehensible to the outsider. The *Penya 0-5* refers provocatively to Barça's finest hour in the Bernabéu, in 1974, the *Penya Minuto 111* refers to Koeman's extra-time strike in the European Cup final against Sampdoria at Wembley, while the *Jordi Culé* – a joining together of the patron saint with the club's curious nickname of 'arsehole' – surely represents one of the oddest epithets in football culture. The name, which more accurately translated means 'Those known for their arses', dates back to the early days of the Carrer de la Indústria stadium. The first seating was in a part of the stadium where the back 'wall' was made up of horizontal iron girders. From the outside, all you could see was row upon row of bums.

The *penyes* quickly came to play an important role for Barça, not only providing a social focus where people could get together for a bit of drinking and some illicit Catalan chat, but also for their financial clout. By 1953, the plans outlined for the construction of the Camp Nou were drawn up by the first association of *penyes* who pledged to finance the scheme, rather as the Athletic Bilbao members had done more than 40 years earlier for the building of San Mamés.

The difference here was that the *penyes* were not a group of wealthy locals, but included members from all walks of life. As a result, the subsequent construction of the stadium put the club very much into its supporters' hands, so that today the club's directors cannot really act without the backing of the official *penyes'* association. No other club in Spain is quite like this, even those which have a hundred or more of these curious orders. One interesting consequence is that the club, almost uniquely, has not required a sponsor to sully their shirt with some gaudy logo, although at the time of writing this policy did not seem likely to last much longer. It is certainly evidence of their determination to keep the club's image independent.

One of the more notorious of the Barça *penyes* is the one that calls itself *Boixos Nois* and which uses a bulldog as its logo. Founded in the early 1980s, its members are skinheads of the intransigent nationalist variety, although it would seem that this was not the original idea of the founders. Inevitably, the group has become a focus for anti-Madrid sentiment and a challenge to their notorious *Ultras Sur* thugs. Wonderful then to report that at the inaugural meeting of the *penya* the name 'Crazy Boys' was proposed and written down in the statutes as '*Boixos Nois*'. Only the next day did one of the founders realise they had misspelt the first word of the name, since 'crazy' in Catalan is *'bojos'*. *Boixos* means 'boxwood'.

So the hardest youths in the city are now known as 'Boxwood boys' because the founders who convened an emergency meeting to discuss the problem decided that the misspelt name was even crazier than the one intended, and decided to stick with it. Watch out – the boxwood boys are coming.

5. *white noise*

Madrid and the legacy of Franco

When someone mentions Barcelona, I see a city, hustle and bustle, Las Ramblas and wide thoroughfares. When someone mentions Madrid, I see white. The same thing happens with Leeds, a club which loomed large in my childhood. Leeds – clinical, white and invulnerable, lording it over all and sundry. And Real Madrid, or as we pronounced it in the playground 'reel' Madrid, whom nobody ever defeated, who seemed to have won the European Cup every year for half a century and who were probably better even than Leeds. I formulated the theory very early in life that if you were bold enough to wear such unattractive colours as all-white you were bound to be successful. Our rival school team's colours were also all-white, and they were winners too. A splash of colour was interesting, but it denoted a loser – as if the caprice of colour suggested a lack of single-mindedness. Indeed, when Don Revie took over at Leeds in the early 1960s he changed their kit from blue and gold to all white, modelling his new charges on the Spanish giants.

When Real Madrid lose, I still feel slightly uncomfortable, as if the natural order of things has been challenged and the apocalypse is just around the corner. Their supporters, judging by their perennially ill-humoured reactions to defeat, must feel the same. Spain's most successful club is almost neurotically fixated on winning, on hammering home the idea that nothing else matters – this being the essence of *madridismo*. For those who adopt this attitude, teams like Barcelona, who insist that their team represents 'more than a club', are merely rummaging about in the rubble of their own defeatism, looking for extra-mural scraps to cover up the truth of their (relative) non-achievement. It's a harsh way of looking at things, but when you've been rubber-stamped as the team of the 20th century by FIFA, on the solid basis of 29 league titles, nine European Cups, 12 Spanish Cups, two UEFA Cups and a couple of World Club titles thrown in for good measure, you can begin to understand the pretension.

As proof of this utter lack of sentiment, Real are the only club to have sacked their manager (Jupp Heynckes) a mere four weeks after he guided them to victory in the Champions League. At the end of the 2002-03 season the avuncular Vicente Del Bosque was similarly dispatched, after presiding over the club's 29th league title. He was informed that his services were no longer required (after 30 years' involvement with the club) in an upstairs room of the hotel in which the rest of the squad were tucking into their celebratory supper, exactly 26 hours after winning the league. Although it was clear that Del Bosque – and the players, who genuinely liked him – were upset, things were simply rolling on. Kings die or are exiled, and others take their place – *y punto* (and full-stop) as the Spanish say.

Nevertheless, there have been periods in Real Madrid's history when such ruthlessness has tended to exacerbate the internal problems of a club whose vaulting ambition has always ensured that a state of 'crisis' is never too far away. In the 1990s the crisis seemed to be permanent, with the club's over-paid 'Ferrari Boys' rumoured to be swapping insults, wives and fast cars more enthusiastically than they were performing on the pitch. A parallel crisis gripped Madrid at the top, where the club's former president Lorenzo Sanz was under investigation over his property dealings, the debts were mounting to frightening levels and the memory of Cruyff's 'Dream Team' was all too fresh.

The capital's clubs seem cursed with dodgy presidents. Jesús Gil, Spain's most famous man after Julio Iglesias, was eventually forced out of Atlético Madrid in 2003 after being accused of decades of serious book-cooking, and the eccentric businessman Ruíz Mateos, tiring of being in the financial firing-line at Madrid's 'third club', Rayo Vallecano, decided to hand the job to his wife four years earlier.

But out on the pitch, Real Madrid and defeat make uneasy bedfellows. There is a chant, which began in the Sixties and survives to this day, which alludes to this phenomenon: *Así, así, así gana el Madrid* (That's how Madrid always win). It refers to the alleged tendency of Spanish referees to award Real rather too many penalties, especially in the Bernabéu. Until 1975, the chant carried the clear implication that if the referees had not been bought they still feared the consequences of not awarding favours to Franco's favourite team. After the dictator's death, the suggestion was that Madrid still flew his flag, that the club was still happy to represent a centralist, more authoritarian type of Spain.

To what extent this is true, just as to what extent Barcelona are merely the 'flagship' of a different vision of Spain, requires some analysis. As with the Catalans, the story of Real Madrid is a rich one, and it would be unfair to dismiss it merely as one of fascism and favouritism – a line pushed by so many authors too easily besotted by the romance of Spain's regional struggles. Also too easily forgotten is the role of Atlético Madrid, which deserves more than a passing mention. Not only do they lie third in the all-time Spanish league table, but they won more league titles than their illustrious neighbours during the first 25 years of the competition, until Alfredo Di Stéfano came along and changed the face of Spanish football for ever.

Real Madrid is not a leftwing club. As ever, such a sweeping generalisation will exclude many ordinary fans, but that does not mean that the observation is an inaccurate one. The Bernabéu stadium is situated on the Castellana, an expensive district which boasts banks, museums and ministries. As Simon Inglis points out: 'No other football club in the world can boast such an esteemed address.' The fact that they play where they do underlines Real's status as 'an integral part of the national fabric', like having Wembley on Park Lane. Which is not to say that their 80,000 members are all monied reactionaries from the upper-middle classes dreaming of the return of a military government. Though you do come across some interesting types.

Driving back from a conference in Granada in late 1999 with some Basque colleagues, I stopped for a coffee break north of Madrid, on some bleak stretch of the Sierra de Guadarrama. The large, gloomy roadside café was almost empty as we ordered our *cortados*, standing up at the bar. It was a Sunday afternoon and there had been some games the previous night, chief among them the Basque derby at San Mamés between Athletic Bilbao and Real Sociedad, but I hadn't had a chance to watch the TV or read the papers. A copy of the football tabloid *As*, *Marca*'s Madrid-based cousin, was lying on the bar.

The headline ¡*Vergüenza!* (Shame!) attracted my attention. Opening the paper I was stunned to read that Real Madrid has been slaughtered at home, 5-1 by Zaragoza. I held up the paper so that my colleagues could see the score. Before I could turn the page to look for the Basque result a hard-bitten old gent on the other side of the bar – the only other occupant of the establishment save the barman – jabbed a finger in the direction of the paper I was holding and launched into a rant: '¡*Estos son maricones!*' (They're all poofters!) '¡*Eso no hubiera pasado en tiempos de Franco, os juro!*' (This would never have happened in Franco's time, I can tell you!).

The phrase must have popped up many a time in the heartlands since 1975, but the old boy hadn't quite counted on his audience on this occasion. The fact that nobody nodded in immediate solidarity quickly registered, prompting the almost inevitable '¿Así sois Vascos?' (So you're Basques?) and a few silent nods from my colleagues. 'You drew,' he added, as if to show he meant no harm. It's a comment that only a *madrileño* could make, having presumably assumed that as Basque brothers there couldn't possibly be any rivalry between Athletic and Real Sociedad – as if the distinction between the two clubs were unimportant, as indeed it probably was to him.

Back in the car, it occurred to me that the little scene had been like some short but telling sketch on the politics and sport of postwar Spain. In a matter of seconds there had been easily enough material for a whole book. The man, in referring to the good old years, had clearly signalled his political persuasion and had had the temerity to suggest, since he was on home soil, that a side like Zaragoza simply wouldn't have got away with it back in the good old days, when the trains ran on time, women behaved like women, the Commies never came out from under their beds and Real Madrid won most of their matches, especially at the Bernabéu.

All of which, of course, had been the source of many a problem for the colleagues I was travelling with that day – all good citizens now, but who grew up unable to speak their native tongue in public, and who had had no organ through which to channel their complaints about things like Real Madrid being awarded too many penalties. The old man in the bar was from a different planet, with a whole set of ideas and attitudes massively at variance to the people he was addressing. The scene could not have occurred in Britain. British sport has its hot spots but, Glasgow apart, the last hundred years have in no way conjured up such a volatile internal scene.

Real Madrid were founded in March 1902, the last of the 'big three' to appear on the scene. Whisper it on the terraces of the Bernabéu, but their first president was a Catalan, Juan Padrós Riubó – or 'Rubio' as he came to be known, the Spanish spelling effectively hiding the origins of the surname. With his brother Carlos he ran a cloth business on Madrid's Calle Alcalá. One source refers to the shop as a fashionable women's boutique called *El Capricho* (Whimsy). More manly histories prefer the cloth story, and in this version the shop is called *El Encanto* (Charm). They were very much second-generation *madrileños*, but their Catalan origins are not often mentioned in potted histories of the club.

When there is no choice but to mention it, as in the rash of publications which accompanied the centenary in 2002, the line is an interesting one. The author Luis Prados de la Plaza claims in his book *Real Madrid: Centenario* that the Catalan origins of the club are proof of Madrid's universality and open-doors policy. He suggests that it mirrored the city's cosmopolitan traditions, and the welcome mat that it has always laid down on its outskirts.

The team itself was a continuation of the curiously named club Football Sky, founded in 1895 as a sporting pastime for students at the *Institución Libre de Enseñanza* (Open Teaching College) who had been together at Oxford and Cambridge from 1891 to 1894. One Luis Bermejillo was the man behind the team and the name, but more importantly his secretary and treasurer friend was the Conde (Count) de La Quinta de La Enrajada, recently returned from the games fields at Oxford and heir to an aristocratic line that was involved in horse breeding and racing. That connection ensured that the first official competition in Spain in 1902 took place at the capital's Hippodrome, owned by the Count's family.

Madrid's origins were thus far from humble. The Sky name was never given the official stamp and by 1900 a split occurred, with Sky changing their name (understandably) to New Foot-ball Club – a fact less significant than the emergence of a new team, presided over by one Juan Palacios, called Español de Madrid. By 1902, when the tournament to celebrate King Alfonso's coronation took place, Madrid FC was the name Palacios gave to the team he entered, the Catalan Juan Padrós having been voted in as first president. Just to confuse matters more, Español de Madrid also continued to exist, and re-emerged in 1910 as semi-finalists in the Cup but, to all intents and purposes, Madrid FC was the institution that finally became Real Madrid in 1920, when Alfonso XIII accepted the invitation of royal patronage.

Although the record books reflect kindly on the early years of Madrid FC, who managed the first consecutive run of titles in the history of Spanish football from 1905 to 1908, the reality of those early tournaments suggests that one should not get too carried away. In 1905, only three teams bothered to turn up for the King's tournament in Madrid (Madrid, San Sebastián and Bilbao), the hosts beating the latter 1-0 in the final and receiving a gold medal each from their president, Padrós. In 1908 there were just two, Madrid and Vigo Sporting.

By 1912, things had got a little more serious. Santiago Bernabéu, the man who would tower over all Real Madrid did in the postwar period, made his debut as a player, having helped to construct with his own hands the club's first real stadium – the small Campo O'Donnell near an old rubbish dump on the corner of Calle O'Donnell and Narvaéz (the site is now a Disney theme park).

There was a wooden stand that held about 200 and a series of perimeter fences, not even high enough to stop the ball bouncing down Narvaéz if a shot cleared the bar at one end. By then Real Madrid had 450 members but, curiously for a club always associated with royalty and aristocracy, it took until 1924 before they got themselves a decent ground, the famous Chamartín stadium, which was inaugurated with a match against the FA Cup holders, Newcastle. Real won 3-2.

The ground, designed this time by an architect (an ex-player called Castell) and built by professional workmen, almost disappeared during the Civil War when its wooden stands were broken up for fuel, but the site was to be more or less the same as the one where Bernabéu finally and modestly named the present-day stadium after himself. Indeed, older *madrileños* often still refer to the ground as Chamartín, though probably more due to the nearby Metro station of the same name than out of any disrespect towards Saint Bernabéu.

Two years later the club 'came out' professionally by purchasing the Basque José María Peña from Arenas de Getxo for 6,000 pesetas. Having thus prepared themselves for professional league action, they were pipped at the post for the first title by Barcelona in 1929, and only managed fifth place – out of ten – the next season. As in the later case of Alfredo Di Stéfano, where the arrival of one player ushered in a period of success, the purchase of Ricardo Zamora for an astronomical 150,000 pesetas for the 1930-31 campaign, plus the arrival of Quincoces, Ciriaco and Olivares for another 60,000, brought the title to the capital for the first time the following season. They went through that 1931-32 campaign undefeated, conceding a mere 15 goals, and as a bonus signed Samitier from Barcelona in sensational circumstances. Just before the Civil War, Real were runners-up three seasons in a row, sealing a period of growing success and prestige.

However, it is of course the Franco period which made Real Madrid not only the most successful club in Spain (indeed, in Europe) but also the most controversial. Despite the claims of both supporters and opponents, Franco's role in Real Madrid's success has probably been exaggerated. The club are tiresomely referred to now as 'Franco's pet team', rather as if he was given to wearing a white shirt (instead of a black one) on presidential occasions. Franco certainly benefited from Real Madrid, but the club only got a few tidbits in return. This may not go down too well with those who wish to see Real Madrid's hegemony as the symbol of the successful, centralised Spain that Franco sought. In fact, football is a more appropriate metaphor for his failure to realise that vision, confounded as he was by all the rooms in his mansion and by all of those who failed to see his point.

Franco ran an efficient police-state, but he was too shrewd to have kidded himself that he had united the country in any way. In *My Private Conversations with Franco*, his cousin, also Francisco, wrote that after the Cup final in 1958, when Athletic Bilbao beat a tired Madrid 2-0, Franco told him he had been 'very impressed' by the enthusiasm of the Basques and their 'desire for victory', and that the crowd had been 'surprisingly impartial' given the nature of the meeting. He sounds like a Roman Emperor, oddly touched by the resolve of the Christians when faced by the lions. Of course, Real had just won their third consecutive European Cup and Franco could afford to be generous to the sons of those he had invited the Luftwaffe to murder 20 years before. But by 1958, the dictator had every reason to be extremely pleased with Real's contribution, given the circumstances he found himself in.

Spain's 'neutrality' in the Second World War, always written between inverted commas, saved Franco's dictatorship from immediate defeat, but condemned Spain to a longer and slower agony. Franco was initially keen to play a more active role in alliance with the Nazis, but Hitler feared that Spain – divided, economically backward and exhausted by war – would be a liability for the Axis. And as Germany's military position worsened, Franco's decision to stay out of the war was made easier. His neutrality, and the rapid onset of the Cold War from 1945, saved Spain from invasion by the Allies. Nevertheless, by implicitly supporting Hitler, Franco condemned his country to missing out on the fruits of the Marshall Plan after the war.

By 1956, the year of Real Madrid's first European Cup, won in Paris against Stade de Reims in the inaugural year of the competition, Spain's economy was in ruins and its rural population living in desperate poverty. By the summer of 1960, things were looking a lot better. Franco had finally allowed a pair of Opus Dei whizz-kids to begin to straighten out the economy, although it wasn't until the coming of mass foreign tourism that many parts of the country began to edge towards anything like prosperity. Real Madrid had won their fifth consecutive European title in a stunning display in Glasgow and the regime was looking a lot safer than in 1955, when the privations caused by the Allies' lack of aid had begun to stir the first signs of popular unrest.

Real Madrid's outrageous run of success acted as an invaluable ambassador for the country, lending it a sheen that hid a more prosaic and even grim reality. Franco had seen that football could be used to sway public opinion during the hard times and spread an image abroad of a nation of stylish achievers worthy of being allowed back into the international fold. Instead of the Dream Team, think of the Regime Team. Back in 1955, after their victory in the Copa Latina, Franco had decorated the whole Real Madrid team with the Imperial Order of the Yoke and Arrows, the symbol of his movement. The following year, the ex-player and then president, Santiago Bernabéu, picked up the Grand Cross of Civil Merit and the players the further honour of the Gold Medal of the City – before they had even won the European Cup! Perhaps Franco knew something that no one else did.

Certainly the fact that Bernabéu had been instrumental in setting up the tournament could hardly have failed to endear him to the dictator, especially five years later, when Madrid and Spain suddenly conjured up images of a great football club, instead of a politically repressive and financially rickety country. This international projection through football coincided with an easing of Spain's commercial and diplomatic isolation, proof of which was the agreement in 1958 to allow the US to set up military bases on Spanish soil.

By rights, Franco should have been a Ferrol supporter, having been born and brought up in the Galician town, but he was never one to hark back too much to his roots. He would always turn up for the Cup final and for the occasional game at Real, but there is no evidence to suggest that he was really a big fan of the game. According to the memoirs of Raimundo Saporta, public relations chief at the club during the regime, Franco never betrayed any emotion whatsoever during a game, never moving a muscle even when his favourite player, the speedy winger Francisco Gento, scored a goal or supplied Di Stéfano with a telling cross. It must have been tough on him to have to hand over the Generalísimo's Cup to Barcelona, something which he had to do several times – but he usually managed a smile.

In the early years of the regime, the players of both finalists in the cup were obliged to raise their hands in the fascist salute while the national anthem was played – no particular problem for Español and Real Madrid in 1940, but not so easy for Athletic Bilbao and Barça in the 1942 final. By the early Fifties, despite their determination not to be fazed by the

Marshall Plan policy, Franco and his acolytes had eased up on their demands for public displays of ideological solidarity and the players merely had to suffer a pre-match handshake with the minister for sport, the infamous General Moscardó.

That Franco benefited from Real's success abroad is indisputable. Exactly what the club received in return is a much more difficult question. Were any concrete favours handed out to them, either in the form of money or bent refs – or was it more a case of the existence of a general ruling climate in the country which favoured Castilian success and Catalan failure? Football is so politicised in Spain that it is virtually impossible to answer such a question from a local perspective. Ask a Basque or a Catalan and they would simply laugh at you in an 'Is the Pope a Catholic?' sort of way. But the evidence for the neutral observer is not so clear. For a start, Real Madrid won virtually nothing between 1932 and 1954 apart from three Cups, a statistic which sits uneasily with the favouritism theory. The 11-1 debacle against an intimidated Barcelona in 1943 should have been rubbed off the records, but it was rare that such barefaced hostility was practised, or that Madrid recouped those kind of dividends.

If there really is anything to pull out from under the table it probably resides in the axis of influence established during the war, when the former player Santiago Bernabéu became president of the club. Apart from his distinguished football career, Bernabéu had been decorated in the Civil War for services to the Nationalist cause, and he was to become the great Satan in Catalan eyes. It was he, not Franco, who pronounced the famous phrase that 'Football has done a service for the country' in 1969. He was alluding to the oft-quoted theory that Franco's regime only lasted as long as it did because the long-suffering Spanish public had become so besotted with the game and all its attendant *morbo* that they let the dictator get on with his dictating – a historical curiosity, according to those commentators who have observed, quite correctly, that the Spanish mentality is basically anti-authoritarian.

But there is more to it than that. A major book like Jimmy Burns's *Barça – A People's Passion*, which should really have been entitled *Barça good, Madrid bad*, unquestioningly toes the old conspiratorial line about bent refs and a systematic policy to keep Madrid at the top of the pile. It falls for exactly the trick Franco began to pull in the Fifties, when he realised that although you could keep 'em down, you couldn't wipe 'em out. He knew very well that the *morbo* that was heated up in the Fifties between Real and Barça would allow the Catalanists the illusion that through football they had a 'focus for political expression', giving them the chance to stick two fingers up at him every fortnight.

To the faithful who gathered at Les Corts and later at the Camp Nou it may well have seemed that their support was a revolutionary way of expressing their independence, but to Franco it was surely all a bit more amusing than the Catalans will ever admit, besotted as they are by their own creative triumphalism. Barça's so-called threat to the regime was really not very threatening at all. The bull had been well and truly neutered. Of course, in their canny way, the Catalans have since risen up and put themselves in the driving seat of the economy, but it was the appearance of ETA in the early Seventies that really had the fascists sweating. It was ETA who killed off their last chance of extending the Franco years beyond the dictator's death, not the yah-boo stuff that was rising from the terraces of the Camp Nou.

Another enduring myth about Madrid, happily propagated by writers such as Burns, is that Barcelona was the only city in Spain to have suffered during the Civil War. In fact, Madrid too held out until the very end of the war, and was hardly a Nationalist hothouse. It was very much on the losing side in the war. The city suffered three years of bombardment and starvation, but was not occupied until the war was over, and the workers' militias were equally active there as in the more romanticised centres, such as Barcelona.

And while Barcelona, as we saw in the previous chapter, have recently resuscitated the memory of their wartime president, Josep Sunyol, it is still a little-known fact that at the end of the war, Real Madrid's Republican president, Rafael Sánchez Guerra, refused to flee the city as it was about to fall into Franco's hands, and suffered torture and imprisonment. Later he was to slip away into exile in Paris, where he was to play an important role in the government-in-exile. The club's vice-president, Gonzalo Aguirre, was arrested then murdered in prison, as was the club treasurer, Valero Rivera.

Real Madrid's own official publications are also guilty of avoiding the awkward bits, for example, completely ignoring the existence of Antonio Ortega, an obscure character who seems to have taken over as president between 1937 and 1938. All records of the club faithfully list Sánchez Guerra as president between 1935 and 1939, but there seems to have been a period in which he handed the reins to his communist friend, Ortega. In fact, brave though Sánchez Guerra was, it would appear that he had little active involvement in the club during the war, and that Ortega took over from another republican, Juan José Vallejo.

Ortega was a colonel in the leftist militias and helped to defend Madrid in the early days of the war. Arrested at the end of the conflict, his final fate is unknown – but he was Real Madrid's president, and a hero of the fallen republic. Some people in Catalonia have taken the trouble to unearth the cover-up regarding Sunyol, but no one cares about Ortega. There are plenty of people who would prefer things to stay that way, of course, but rehabilitating lost figures such as Ortega would certainly help the club cast off some of the neo-fascist accusations made by so many of those who still equate *madridismo* with devil-worship.

For many, the real devil at the heart of Franco's Spain was Santiago Bernabéu. A company lawyer by training, he assumed the presidency of Real Madrid in 1944 and immediately set about putting an adminis-trative team in place that would ensure the eventual rise of the club to unprecedented heights. Bernabéu's ascent to the throne marked a political change at the club. At the start of the Civil War he had been forced to flee to Paris after having been shopped by several of the club's republican committee members. He never forgot what he regarded as an act of back-stabbing, and by 1944 he was, to all intents and purposes, on a political crusade of his own, launched through the conduit of a sport that he understood much better than Franco.

Before long he took on Saporta as PR chief, bringing him over from the world of basketball where he had made a name for himself as a tough negotiator and a winner of friends in high places. Saporta was to play a crucial role in the signing of Di Stéfano, surely the key event in the club's history. Bernabéu also employed Antonio Calderón, a doctor from Seville whose official job was to communicate Bernabéu's various dictums to the players and the ancillary staff, but who in reality was signed because of his past, having been a league referee and president of the Andalusian Football Federation. Calderón had various generals of the regime in his pocket, and understood, according to the conspiracy theorists, how to manipulate the shady world of the referees' associa-tions. Meanwhile, Saporta worked his charm on the journalists who mattered and on the national radio network, and made equally important forays into the world of Madrid's banking fraternity.

After only a year in his post Bernabéu set about financing the complete reconstruction of the Chamartín Stadium, eventually to be named after him in 1955. Buying up five hectares of prime real estate on the Castellana was no cheap business, but Bernabéu was already a drinking buddy of the director of the Banco Exterior and was a personal friend of

Adolfo Suárez, later to become the country's prime minister. The combination ensured that the purchase of the land and the subsequent financing of the stadium were mortgaged on extremely favourable terms. Bernabéu himself broke the first ground, the site was blessed by a priest and Real took themselves off to Atlético's Metropolitano ground for a couple of seasons until the new stadium could be inaugurated in 1947, ten years before Barça played their first game in the Camp Nou.

When the Banco Exterior outlived its usefulness, Saporta moved the club's finances to the Banco Mercantil e Industrial, and later, curiously enough, to the Banco Popular, run by a family of Catalans whose main player, Domingo Valls Taberner, was a member of Barça's board. Maybe Saporta thought he could even buy off the enemy. Bernabéu's PR man became close to Franco, to the royal family and just about anyone that mattered. And the person who mattered most, back in 1953, was a 27-year-old Argentinian forward, who had illicitly joined Millonarios of Bogotá from River Plate. Financed by local barons, the Colombian club had imported its own dream team in order to raise the profile of their country and to further boost its already considerable bank accounts.

Alfredo Di Stéfano was one of the South American stars to get the call, and was in the team that toured Spain in March 1952. When Millonarios visited Madrid to play in a mini-tournament to commemorate their 50th year, Bernabéu and Saporta were both there. What they saw on that first night of the tournament had them immediately dreaming of world conquest. Di Stéfano, even in the relatively relaxed context of a tour match, was clearly several notches above anything they had previously seen, scoring twice in a 2-2 draw with the Swedish side Norrköping. Unfortunately for them, Barça's 'chief scout', Samitier, was there too, and thus began one of football's great thrillers, or scandals – depending, as ever, on the colours you wear.

Bobby Charlton described Di Stéfano as the 'brainiest' player he ever saw, which may have been a way of saying that he did not consider him to be the greatest. However, if Pelé is usually accorded that distinction, Di Stéfano as often as not comes in second. The statistics are impressive – so much so that there are good arguments for putting him at the very top of the list. Helenio Herrera was one who believed that Di Stéfano was the greatest of all time.

During 11 seasons with Real he won eight league titles, five of which saw him take the Pichichi trophy. He won five European Cups and scored 49 goals in all European campaigns. His overall total in the Spanish league of 228 is third behind Zarraonaindia and Hugo Sánchez, but he played fewer games than either of them. His total with Real Madrid is no fewer than 418, including cup competitions. He even scored 19 more in the league after he had left Madrid – inevitably to play for Español, perennial welcomers of fading greats.

As if this were not impressive enough, he managed more than 200 during his stay in Colombia and 23 for the Spanish national side, a figure only exceeded by Emilio Butragueño, Fernando Hierro and Raúl – but since Di Stéfano was only cleared to play for Spain in 1957, the four lost years would surely have put him at the top of that list too. In all official matches, his total exceeds the 800 mark, and some put it as high as 893. None of the other greats, apart from Stanley Matthews, kept going so long and so well. Pelé, Maradona and Cruyff all peaked earlier, whereas Di Stéfano kept the show going until he was 40.

Di Stéfano never played in a World Cup, thanks to a variety of unfortunate circumstances. In 1950 and 1954 Argentina did not enter, partly because the loss of players such as Di Stéfano to foreign leagues made them wary of putting the national team on display. In 1958, by which time he was qualified for Spain, his new country failed to make the finals. In 1962 he was injured. Had Di Stéfano had the chance to shine on that one stage that was denied to him, the popular view of Pelé as the world's greatest might be more frequently challenged.

Like Pelé, Di Stéfano was not really a striker. However, the description of the Argentine as a 'midfielder', as if this adds more lustre still to his goalscoring feats, seems a little misleading. In truth he was capable of doing anything and playing anywhere, and did not limit himself to one zone of the pitch or to one simple role. When the fancy took him, he chased back and defended, dropped deep to work the ball forward from midfield, moved out wide or went foraging in the box. What footage there is of him bears testament to his speed and unerring balance on the ball, head and body upright, calculating the next move. He scored with his head, with both feet, inside the box and from outside. No one has ever said as much, but he was probably a decent goalkeeper too. All in all, he was obviously a magnificent player, a fact not lost on those who saw him that night in the Bernabéu in 1952.

His subsequent transfer from Colombia to Spain is a very complicated story whose most intimate details would bore even the most fastidious historian, but some of it is worth recounting for the light it sheds on the issue of whether Franco's regime truly did Real any big favours. In this case, it would seem that it did.

Di Stéfano clearly represented to Bernabéu the piece of the jigsaw that made the rest of the picture much clearer. The idea that the player might team up with Kubala at Barcelona (as he was to do later for the national team) represented a nightmarish scenario to a man whose vision of Spain was very much in step with Franco's. The stadium he master-minded was an attempt to simultaneously boost the club's status and fix Madrid as the real 'centre of Spain', in sporting and cultural terms. It worked. Ten years later Barcelona unveiled an even bigger Camp Nou, but by then Real Madrid were the best team in the world.

Barça made the first move for Di Stéfano and entrusted their negotia-tions with River Plate (still Di Stéfano's official employers) to a Catalan nationalist lawyer, Ramón Trías Fargas, a man who knew South America well and who had the appropriate political credentials – his father, a doctor, had been exiled after the Civil War. Trías Fargas later claimed that the government in Madrid had bugged his phone when he was setting up the positive initial contacts with River Plate in Argentina.

Barcelona then brought in Samitier to 'help' with the negotiations, a move which has since proved to be the first brick in the building of the conspiracy theory. Samitier, judging by some of the photos of that period, had by this time shaken off any last remaining vestiges of his working-class background, and was more than happy to play the role of the sauve and handsome club diplomat, travelling to South America in his sharpest suits to secure the services of Di Stéfano. Besides, it meant he could get back in touch with some of his old tango mates with whom he had hung out in his playing days in the Thirties when Gardel was still alive.

He brought in a Catalan-Colombian friend of his, Joan Busquets, allegedly to help speed up the negotiations. But Busquets was a director of Millonarios' rivals Santa Fe and there seems to have already been some bad blood between him and the men who were financing Di Stéfano's team. When Millonarios refused a deliberately paltry offer from Busquets, Di Stéfano packed his bags and travelled with his family to Barcelona – River Plate having given their consent conditional on the agreement of Millonarios. Of course, because of Busquets, Millonarios withheld any such consent. Besides, Di Stéfano owed the Colombians $5,000.

Marti Carretó, Barça's president, was consequently handed the task of appeasing the Colombians. Trías Fargas has implied that Carretó was a government stooge, under orders (or threats) to maintain a hostile relationship between the Barça negotiators and the South Americans so that they would never consent to the transfer. Carretó did indeed seem to be offering them peanuts, which they predictably rejected. Meanwhile, Di Stéfano turned out for Barcelona – a little known fact – in a couple of friendlies on the Costa Brava, and was, on the surface at least, settling into the task of becoming an honorary Catalan.

It may be stretching the conspiracy theory a little too far, but it is said that he played poorly in the two games, and that Barcelona were no longer so convinced he was the man to partner Kubala. There are also those who claim that Samitier, paid secretly by Real Madrid as a 'double agent', had told him to play poorly, because it was he who was really behind the scheme to get Di Stéfano over to Madrid, with some initial help from Carretó. The plot thickens.

Real Madrid's Saporta never admitted or denied it, but it is said that while the negotiations were continuing, he would travel incognito to Barcelona and, dressed in suitably long coat and dark glasses, accompany Di Stéfano to several of Barcelona's best eateries with the purpose of convincing him that his future lay in the capital. It is not implausible that such entreaties might have had an effect. Di Stéfano, despite all the plaudits he received as a player, has never been talked of as a man who inspired much affection in his team-mates. As an old man, he certainly comes over as brusque, and those who remember him when he was younger agree he was never one to suffer fools gladly. In truth, he had walked out on River Plate, and then did the same to his Colombian employers, leaving the next club to pay off his debts for him. It looks as though Di Stéfano was always principally out to get the best for himself, whatever the consequences.

Both Barça and Madrid could afford to pay him well, but the crucial fact in Madrid's favour, above and beyond the political intrigue, seems to have been Saporta's suggestion that with Kubala already established as Barça's darling, the town would not be big enough for the two of them – and he may have been right. The two players were always friendly, and eventually played together for Spain, but Di Stéfano was a player who clearly needed to run the show. So, unfortunately, was Kubala.

The disagreements between Fargas, Carretó and Samitier were ruthlessly exploited (if not actively initiated) by Madrid. The Spanish federation, headed by Moscardó, in a move which hardly smacked of coincidence, suddenly passed a law banning the purchase of foreign players. Samitier had already handed over four million pesetas to River Plate in 1953 and had signed a contract with them, while Saporta paid Millonarios 1.5 million pesetas for Madrid's right to own Di Stéfano until 1954, by which date he was under contract to return to Argentina.

Saporta thus removed the Colombian obstacle from the path, but FIFA had given their blessing to Samitier's deal. The only way to prevent this was to pass a law which effectively blocked Di Stéfano's official unveiling by the Catalans, just in case the other elements of the plot failed to prosper.

The move worked a treat. Carretó travelled to Madrid to talk to Bernabéu, and in an implicit admission of defeat agreed to release the player and transfer him – to Juventus! Bernabéu is said to have agreed, but no sooner was Carretó back in his office in Barcelona than General Moscardó was on the phone, brokering a deal whereby Barça and Real would share the player for the next four years, a year at one club and the next year at the other, starting, of course, with Real Madrid.

The reception from the Catalan press, muzzled as it was, was incredibly hostile to the deal, and Carretó, because he had signed on the dotted line, was forced to resign. The interim management board that succeeded him, pending the election of a successor, tore up the agreement and handed Di Stéfano over to Madrid, in return for a compensation payment equivalent to the money they had already paid River Plate for his legal release. For 5.5 million pesetas Real Madrid had their man, and the second half of the 20th century in Spain was destined to wear a distinctly all-white look. Two weeks later, Di Stéfano scored four as Real Madrid destroyed Barça 5-0 in the Bernabéu. The subsequent friendly relations between Samitier and Bernabéu, despite the latter's well-documented dislike for all things *azulgrana*, is, as they say, a troublesome matter.

Of course, however great a player is, he rarely prospers in isolation. Along with Di Stéfano came Francisco Gento, signed from Santander in 1953. Five years later they were joined by Ferenc Puskas, by which time 'the regime team' had already won three of their consecutive European Cups, and four of the five titles disputed since Di Stéfano's arrival.

Gento, *La Galerna* (the gale), was a youngster playing for Santander's B team when a flu virus saw him promoted to the first team for the arrival of Real Madrid. Such was his performance that Madrid signed him three days later. Unlike the present atmosphere at Madrid, where a player has to perform wonders immediately or be cast out to the wilderness, Gento was given time to prosper after a first season in which he excelled only in fits and starts. Bernabéu stuck by him, largely on Di Stéfano's insistence, and the next season saw Gento really click. He soldiered on until 1971, bowing out after the Cup-Winners Cup final

An unsmiling Franco hands over the Generalísimo's Cup – modestly renamed after himself – to the Barcelona captain José António Zaldúa after the 1968 final. The Catalans beat Real Madrid 1-0, thanks to an own goal, in the first final between the two sides since the Civil War. *Popperfoto*

Fred Pentland, flanked by Chelsea's Jimmy Greaves and Ron Tindall, kicks off Athletic Bilbao's friendly in his honour at San Mamés, December 8, 1959. The eccentric Pentland built Bilbao's great passing side of the early 1930s and cemented the club's close ties to England. *Sr Elorza/Athletic Bilbao*

The British influence lives on. Recreativo de Huelva's *peña* commemorates Dr Alexander McKay, football missionary in 1870s Andalucía and one of the moving spirits behind the first club in Spain.
Phil Ball

Spaniards no, but foreigners yes. Real Sociedad give a big Basque welcome to Dalian Atkinson, John Aldridge and Kevin Richardson, their first foreign arrivals in 1989 and 1990. *Marca*

'I just clouted it and it went in.' Jesús Zamora's last-minute goal in Gijón secures the championship for Real Sociedad in 1981 – the first time since Franco's death it had been won by a non-Madrid team. The picture subsequently became a popular addition to the bars of San Sebastián. *Marca*

Reasserting Basque identity after Franco. José Iribar of Bilbao (left) and Real Sociedad's Ignacio Kortabarría display the Basque flag at the Atocha stadium, San Sebastián, December 1976. *As*

Ricardo Zamora's famous save in the dust of Valencia's Mestalla stadium denies José Escolá to help Real Madrid beat Barcelona 2-1 in the 1936 King's Cup final, just months before the outbreak of the Civil War. The goalkeeper, once a Barça icon, narrowly survived the conflict to be decorated by Franco. *As*

Pepe Samitier, raffish star of Twenties Barcelona, but a friend of Bernabéu in the Fifties and a key figure in Di Stéfano's move to Real Madrid. *Museu FC Barcelona, President Núñez, Colleció Fútbol Art, Pablo Ornaque*

The Friends of Josep Sunyol gather at the memorial to mark the death of the Barcelona president during the Civil War. Toni Strubell is third from the left. Note the spelling 'Suñol' on the headstone, at the insistence of Sunyol's son. *Jesús Fernández Blay*

Barcelona, tormented by Real Madrid's European Cup triumphs for so long, finally win their own at Wembley in 1992. Goalscorer Ronald Koeman (left) and Hristo Stoichkov celebrate the 1-0 extra-time win over Sampdoria. *Colorsport*

Ferenc Puskas strokes home a penalty, one of his four goals in Real Madrid's 7-3 thrashing of Eintracht Frankfurt in the 1960 European Cup final at Hampden Park. *Empics/Topham*

Once a cheat, always a cheat?
Emilio Guruceta, the controversial
referee accused of foul play by
Barcelona in 1970 – and
Nottingham Forest in 1984. *EFE*

Homage to some of the world's top clubs at
Sevilla's Sánchez Pizjuán stadium. But Athletic
Bilbao fans would prefer it if they could spell
the name of their team correctly.
Simon Inglis

The conundrum of Atlético Madrid. Born in Bilbao (with the colours to prove it),
based in Madrid, sponsored by Marbella. Jesús Gil, centre, laps up their 1996 Double,
masterminded by Raddy Antic, far left. Following relegation and a spell in jail for their
irrepressible president, Atlético fans finally turned against Gil, though his resignation
in 2003 still did not cut all ties to the club. *Empics*

Spain's greatest homegrown star, Luis Suárez (front row, centre), celebrates with the national team after winning the 1964 European Nations Cup – their first, and so far only, international tournament win. The symbolism of a victory over the Soviet Union in the final was exploited to the full by a triumphant Franco. *Offside/L'Equipe*

And the goal that got them there. A header by Marcelino (on the ground) deceives Lev Yashin seven minutes from time to complete Spain's 2-1 victory at the Bernabéu. *EFE*

Gerry Armstrong fires past Luis Arconada to give Northern Ireland a 1-0 win in Spain's nightmarish 1982 World Cup on home soil. Note Arconada's supposedly unpatriotic white socks.
Colorsport

Two that got away from Barcelona. Alfredo Di Stéfano welcomes David Beckham to the Bernabéu.
Empics

Dark horses thwarted again. José Antonio Camacho tries to restrain his players at the end of the acrimonious quarter-final of the 2002 World Cup, lost on penalties against the hosts South Korea after two Spanish goals were contentiously disallowed. *Getty Images*

defeat against Chelsea, Real's last European final for a decade. Gento is still rated as the fastest player ever to have trodden Spanish soil. An orthodox left-winger, he could score goals himself, but was there primarily to supply Di Stéfano. Gento was the only player to figure in all of Real's six European Cups won between 1955 and 1966.

Puskas, the other member of the trinity, was already 31 when he signed for Madrid in 1958. His presence seemed to revive Di Stéfano, who, at the same age, might have been considered near the end of his career. 'The little cannon' as the press called him (Di Stéfano, less euphemistically, referred to him as 'the big gut') was also brought to Madrid courtesy of Saporta. After the bloody suppression of the Hungarian uprising by Soviet troops in 1956, Puskas and the rest of the Honved squad had toured Europe and South America, uncertain whether to return to the chaos of Budapest. One game, in November 1956, was a 5-5 draw against a Madrid Select XI (organised by Franco's wife, according to Puskas) which was watched by Bernabéu.

Several of the Honved players were persuaded to return to their country, but Puskas declined and moved to Austria and then to Italy. Bernabéu, sensing further possibilities of extending his team's success, sent two Hungarians to Bologna to sound him out: Nemes, an ex-Real player and Österreicher, Honved's former financial secretary. Because Puskas had refused to perform for the new Honved, back in the national fold, he had been banned from playing in Europe by UEFA. His eventual transfer was greatly facilitated by the fact that the purchasers were Real Madrid. Saporta, it seems, with one visit to the organisation, charmed them (or paid them) into lifting the suspension. Puskas signed up and made his debut in the 1958-59 season.

Again, the figures say it all. Apart from forming an instant footballing relationship with Di Stéfano, Puskas scored 240 goals in 260 appearances – not bad for an ageing player with a beer gut. After three months together on the field, the two of them ran riot against Las Palmas in January 1959, both scoring hat-tricks in a 10-1 win. It seemed that the town was big enough for the both of them, probably because Puskas was a mild sort of chap who cared less about the limelight and more about simply pinging the ball around with his astonishingly accurate and powerful left foot. Barcelona, for a change, had not even contemplated signing him, but if it had occurred to them, so say the conspiracy theorists, they would not have had the *enchufe* (influence – literally 'plug') to persuade the UEFA barons to lift the sanction.

Kubala and Di Stéfano finally coincided at Español, but with Kubala as manager and Di Stéfano, at 37, playing out his final days. The fixture list contrived it so that the Argentine made his debut against Real Madrid, for whom Puskas was still playing. Madrid won and Di Stéfano failed to score. The game was not without its *morbo*. Di Stéfano had left Madrid under something of a cloud, having rejected Bernabéu's offer of a place on the technical staff. He preferred to play on for another year (there are those who suggest it was a question of money), a decision that led Bernabéu to ban him from the club, declaring that the Argentine could never return while the president was alive.

Puskas carried on less controversially until 1967, when he finally retired, at the age of 40, giving way to the next great generation of players, the youthful *ye-ye* team of Sanchís, Pirri, Amancio, Serena and of course Gento. The nickname *ye-ye* – a transliteration of 'yeah, yeah' from the Beatles' *She Loves You* – was meant to symbolise the youthfulness of the team, but now of course fixes it unmistakably in one decade. The Sixties were simply a *madrileño* wipe-out. From 1960 to 1970 the title stayed in the capital – eight times in the Bernabéu and twice over at Atlético's Manzanares. Valencia put a stop to it in 1971 (with Di Stéfano as coach) but two consecutive runs of league wins for Real Madrid in the Sixties, one of five and the other of three, began a new obsession in Spanish football with *ligas consecutivas*. Madrid had another five-year run in the Eighties, a record of dominance which explains why Barcelona have since made so much of the Dream Team's four-year run in the Nineties.

One of the few interruptions to Madrid's serene progress through the Sixties, apart from the eternal rumblings of bought referees, came on a summer tour of Venezuela in 1963. In the early hours of the morning of August 24, Di Stéfano was taken at gunpoint from his hotel room in Caracas by the NLAF (National Liberation Army Front) in an attempt to get some publicity for their cause. The story hit the headlines of almost all the major papers of two continents the following day, and the wailing and gnashing of teeth was such that the Venezuelan government began to get their tanks ready for a show of strength on the street. In a grainy black and white shot taken by his captors, Di Stéfano is glancing sideways at the camera in a black T-shirt, brow furrowed, his expression betraying his tension.

The photo was released by the NLAF for the Venezuelan press, with an accompanying explanation of the 'interview' between the dissident group's commander, Máximo Canales, and Di Stéfano. Canales explains to him that the Venezuelan government is corrupt, and that only a new revolutionary dawn can clear out the sickness and usher in a time of 'health and healing'. Di Stéfano was undoubtedly fascinated, but the trick certainly worked for the NLAF in terms of publicity, even if they failed to bring about revolution.

Di Stéfano was released two days later on the Avenida de La Liberación – presumably a little joke by his captors – and after much rejoicing he managed to turn out for the last game of the tournament against São Paulo. Canales is now a fashionable painter in Venezuela and has said he would like to invite Di Stéfano for dinner the next time he's in town. When asked about the invite in 1999, Di Stéfano told *El País* he had always felt honour-bound to refuse, but that he recognised his captors were only trying 'to make things better' – a rare political aside by the Argentine, however mild.

In the same interview, Di Stéfano declared that he had never felt in any danger, and then alluded to the fact that no one had put forward the theory at the time that the whole thing had been *arreglada* (set up) – by which he presumably meant that one of the other teams in the tournament preferred him kidnapped rather than out on the pitch. The fact that he was 36 at the time has probably also ensured that no one has ever suggested that Barcelona were behind it, in revenge for the original kidnap in 1953. But perhaps Di Stéfano should check with Canales if they ever have that dinner.

So Madrid made it, after all. Whether you believe there was a systematic policy in place to first obtain then perpetuate their pre-eminence seems to depend on which side of the political fence you have decided to settle. Barcelona, for sure, were cheated of the official sight of Di Stéfano in their colours, and this may well have been the crucial turning point in the history of Spanish football. But then again, Di Stéfano might have failed to blossom there. Football's history is full of teams who should, on paper, have carried all before them, but who failed to gel. Madrid did, and the second half of the century belonged mainly to them.

Barça's miserable record of three league titles between 1960 and 1985 is cited as further evidence that the referees were against them. There were six domestic cups, a couple of UEFA Cups and Cup-Winners Cups apiece during that time, but these are presented as further proof of the fact that they were being kept away from the one that really mattered, the league, and its passport to the one European tournament that brought true prestige in its wake. There is some evidence that this was more than paranoia, though, as ever, it is circumstantial and disputed.

In the Seventies, a league referee, Antonio Camacho, controversially declared that Barcelona would never win the title while José Plaza, a *madridista* through and through, was president of the National Committee of Referees. The comment was made a couple of years after another of Spanish football's key incidents – the infamous Guruceta episode. Emilio Guruceta was a young, inexperienced referee from San Sebastián who probably should not have been chosen to officiate in the second leg of the 1970 Cup quarter-final tie between Barcelona and Real Madrid in the Camp Nou. Both teams were out of the running in the league (it remains the only year since 1951 when neither finished in the top three) and the game had thus taken on more *morbo* than usual.

Real had won the first leg 2-0, but by the end of the first half in Barcelona they were trailing 1-0 to a Rexach goal and were looking decidedly wobbly until Guruceta awarded them a more than dubious penalty. Manolo Velázquez seemed to have been brought down well outside the box but Guruceta, yards behind the play, pointed straight to the spot. Thus began the famous Guruceta affair, a long-running controversy as to whether the young but cocky referee had succumbed to temptation and been bought off by someone in the pay of Real Madrid. Madrid scored, of course, and went on to beat Valencia in the final, but not before they had to run the gauntlet of near-rioting Barça fans. Rexach and several other players walked off the pitch in disgust at the penalty decision, only to be persuaded to return by manager Vic Buckingham for the sake of defusing a potentially ugly situation.

With two minutes left to play, part of the crowd invaded the pitch and Guruceta and his two assistants turned tail and ran towards the dressing-rooms – an unedifying sight, especially to the authorities who still viewed any public disturbances in Barcelona as akin to hostile political acts. Guruceta was suspended by the federation for six games, not for bias, but for allowing the game to get out of hand. If Madrid really had bought him off, so the theory goes, they would have done so in the knowledge that a Basque would be less likely to raise suspicions than, say, an Asturian or an Andalusian, regions traditionally more sympathetic to the capital. Guruceta went on to be a *polémico* referee, Spanish shorthand for people who actively seek the limelight. This is not in dispute, but the idea that he was bribed certainly is.

Footage of the foul on Velázquez suggests that Guruceta got it at least half right, albeit from 30 yards' distance. The tackle by the Barça defender Joaquim Rife appears to take place marginally outside the box, but in time-honoured fashion the Madrid forward manages to hurl himself far enough forward to end up in the area. Rife's tackle is probably not even a foul. He connects with the ball but follows through too far with his right leg, enabling his opponent to make it look illegal. But the incident is far from clear-cut, especially at ground level, with the sort of pressure Guruceta must have been under that night, regardless of whether or not a bag of cash was being filled for him over in Madrid. It is certainly insufficiently clear-cut to warrant the storm of righteous indignation that still surrounds the incident in Barcelona.

To a whole generation, the Guruceta game represents incontrovertible evidence that Madrid could pay off the refs if they so chose. Two months later, Guruceta was driving an expensive BMW around San Sebastián. He also set up a business in the south of Spain, manufacturing and selling sports shoes. All of this further contributed to the 'fact' that he had been bought, since no other referee in the league at the time could boast such material assets. Such evidence is unconvincing. Guruceta came from a well-known and respected family of athletes and sporting figures in San Sebastián, who were solidly middle-class. Dabbling in business and buying a BMW hardly seems so unusual. Would he really have spent his under-the-table fees so blatantly anyway?

In 1987, Guruceta was killed in a car crash while driving (a BMW, as it happens) in torrential rain to referee a cup tie in Pamplona, against Real Madrid. That seemed to be the end of the matter. However, seven years later came a further twist. A Belgian intermediary admitted that the Anderlecht president Constant Vanden Stock had bribed the referee for the second leg of the club's 1984 UEFA Cup semi-final against Nottingham Forest. Forest, 2-0 up from the first leg, lost 3-0, but not before they had had a goal disallowed and two decent penalty appeals turned down, while the Belgian club converted a spotkick of their own. The referee, it hardly needs to be added, was Emilio Guruceta.

According to Vanden Stock, Guruceta was given a 'loan' of one million Belgian francs (then around £15,000) the day after the game because he had implied to a club official that he was in financial difficulties. The pay-off is undisputed and it would appear that the intermediaries who helped to fix the game brought it to light either because they were blackmailing the club (Anderlecht's version) or because they themselves had begun to fear for their lives. No one seems to have questioned whether Guruceta's death itself should have been investigated more carefully.

Once a cheat, always a cheat? There is no way of knowing for sure. My own view is that there is no proof that Madrid ever paid anyone, although a chance encounter with one of the linesmen who officiated at the

Barcelona v Real game served to muddy the waters further. The linesman, who now owns a tailor's shop, asked not to be named, although he knows full well that records of his identity exist. I could easily have searched the length of Spain looking for informed witnesses and found no one, but instead stumbled across a prime player during a televised game in a subterranean room of a San Sebastián hotel. The city lights had suddenly gone out, leaving us all rooted to our seats in the darkness. A friend who was with me had mentioned during the first half that the vociferous chap to our right was a former referee. In the dark silence I decided to start up a conversation and innocently inquired whether he had known Guruceta.

'*Sí,*' came the hesitant reply.

'So what do you think of the 1970 incident then?' I asked, as casually as possible.

'I kept my flag down,' he replied, pausing for effect in the darkness.

One or two people coughed. I asked him if he'd like to come upstairs to the lobby and have a drink, but his reply was not what I was expecting.

'So who the hell are you, big boy? Magazines have offered me thousands to talk, but I've turned them all down. It's all in the past now. Why should I talk to you?'

I replied that I was merely interested and I heard him stand up and feel his way along the wall. He obviously fancied a drink. My friend and I groped along our side, finally coinciding with a thin, grey-haired little man at the bottom of the stairs. Up in the bar, with some light from the road outside, I could see he was already a bit tipsy. I bought him a beer and he expertly deflected my questions for the next ten minutes, eventually justifying his ambiguous stance by claiming that 'Guru' had been his friend and that dead men could not defend themselves from libel.

'We had to spend that night in the police station in Barcelona, for our own protection. It was a laugh. We were the three most famous people in Spain. Guru didn't want that. He just wanted to be a respected ref.'

I mentioned the BMW.

'Yeah, I was a bit surprised about that, but look, I'm not saying anything. You can draw your own conclusions. And in case you ask, I didn't buy a new car the next week.' Since he was getting louder and louder, I intimated that I was leaving. As I did so, he muttered under his breath: '*¿Le jodieron, sabes? Y no hizo nada.*' (They got him, you know. And he didn't do anything.)

No matter how many times I drop into the tailor's on the pretext of yet another tin of safety pins, he refuses to elaborate on what he said, indeed, denies ever saying it. He may have been drunk that night, but he was far from incapable. Was he suggesting Guruceta had been removed from the scene by the Anderlecht heavies? Did anyone check the brake cables after the crash on that rainy night?

It remains an open case, but not one that I personally care to take sides on. It seems to me that Guruceta's guilt in the Belgian case does not automatically imply culpability in the other. That being so, it is incumbent on big clubs like Barça to cut out the whining. If anyone has ever suffered persistently from bad, as opposed to bent, refereeing, it is the smaller clubs in the Spanish league who have never had the clout to do anything about the pressures to which referees are generally subjected. Perhaps Oliver Stone should take up the story and give us his interpretation.

Whatever official help Real Madrid might have had, it certainly came to an end with Franco's death in 1975 and the rapid dismantling of his regime. Though not exactly weak during the Seventies, when they won five titles, Real Madrid were no longer 'the regime team'. It took almost another ten years after the old dictator's demise for Real to develop a powerful new variation of their old image.

Di Stéfano came back as manager in 1982, a year after Real had lost the European Cup final 1-0 to Alan Kennedy's little chip in Paris. He was gone by the end of 1984, but not before he had promoted the next significant group of young players to the first-team, the famous *Quinta del Buitre*. This rather curious phrase is one of the most resonant of all the little titles and sayings that the Spanish are so fond of using to capture the essence of a certain period, especially in football. The *quinta* oversaw the development of *madridismo*, the modern legend to go with the *epoca dorada* (golden era) of the Fifties and the *ye-ye* team of the Sixties. It turned up just at the right moment, restoring Madrid to the centre of things by complementing the period now known as *El Movimiento* – an era of musical and cultural dynamism that (briefly) managed to draw people's attention away from Barcelona and back to the capital. Because it restored Madrid's self-confidence, the phrase has become strangely magical for Real supporters.

La Quinta del Buitre translates as 'the vulture squad' and requires some explaining. The scavenger in question was Emilio Butragueño, Real's centre-forward up until the mid-Nineties, when he was replaced by the equally revered Raúl. The word *quinta* is borrowed from military parlance, and refers to the call-up for national service. The *quinta* is the group of chaps thrown together during this spud-peeling year, who often remain in contact afterwards. In football terms, it referred to the significant fact that Madrid could at last boast that one of its great periods stemmed from its own roots, since all five of the original *quinta* were promoted from the reserve side, Castilla, and they were all *madrileños* apart from Miguel Pardeza – the least important figure of the five. As much as the team of the European triumphs is still revered, the names that most resonate are foreign – Di Stéfano, Puskas, Didi, Raymond Kopa, Santamaría – and neither Del Sol nor Gento was from Madrid.

The first two to get the call-up were the defender Manuel Sanchís and the midfielder Martín Vásquez, away at Murcia in 1984. John Toshack, on the final day of his first spell as manager of the club in 1991, said of Sanchís that he was 'the worst person it has ever been my misfortune to meet', referring acidly to the power that the *quinta* had by then established in the dressing-room of the Bernabéu, in the presidential corridors and in the national side. Unfortunately for Toshack, Sanchís was still there when he returned in 1999, brought back from Turkey by a president searching for a hard man to sort out the swollen egos.

Pardeza, originally from Huelva, was the third to appear, but the fourth, Butragueño, was the one who lent his name to the group and who deservedly went on to claim his place in the pantheon of Madrid's all-time greats. Di Stéfano sent him on in February 1984 away at Cádiz, with Real 2-0 down at half-time. By the end they had won 3-2, two of the goals having come from the boots of the young substitute, while an ageing Carlos Santillana, watching from the bench, must have realised that his distinguished career was about to come to an end. Butragueño quickly struck up an explosive relationship with Hugo Sánchez, the flamboyant Mexican bought from neighbours Atlético. That was one among various reasons for the title returning to Madrid in the summer of 1986, by which time the last member of the *quinta* was established in the first-team – José González, a right-sided attacking midfielder otherwise known as Michel.

Michel, now a respected commentator on Spain's TVE1, was always destined to be the most controversial of the group. In 1984, having seen his young mates promoted to the first-team while he had to continue sweating it out with the B team, he allegedly confronted Di Stéfano one morning outside the training-ground. Di Stéfano, not one to suffer disrespect lightly, even in his playing days, replied: 'You can play when your balls have dropped.' But with the team under new management in

1985 he was up into the first team, and went on to a distinguished career with both club and country.

When Javier Clemente took over as national team manager in 1992, his opening strategy was clearly to break up the *quinta*, not because he thought they were no longer up to the job but because he wanted to limit their influence and build a team in his image, not theirs. Michel, intelligent, articulate and very much the leader, never forgave him, and spent much of the late Nineties attacking Clemente's strategies from the safety of the television gantries. It all added to the legend.

Butragueño himself was one of the most curious-looking players ever to turn professional, with a boyish Peter Pan face, curly fair hair and a slight frame that made him look more like an angelic schoolboy than a ruthless striker. But ruthless he was, if only in the goalscoring sense. He never hurt a fly, was rarely booked, and his ability was based more on avoiding physical contact than dishing it out. He became a master of the art of 'one touch and go', bringing supporting midfielders into the attack by the subtlety of his immediate lay-offs, then ghosting into space in the area and scoring typically unspectacular goals – little chips, flicks, side-footed, deliberately muted efforts that became his trademark.

He is best remembered internationally for the four goals he put past Denmark in Mexico in 1986, when Spain suddenly destroyed a side that were looking as though they might even be capable of winning the tournament, 5-1. Butragueño was lethal, punishing the Danish back line time and again for its unfeasibly sloppy behaviour. Although, oddly enough, he never scored again for Spain in a World Cup, he stands third in the all-time list of top scorers for the national team with 26 goals, behind Hierro and Raúl.

The smooth-talking Jorge Valdano, restored to Madrid in 2000 as director of football, played alongside Butragueño in the 1980s. He told me that Butragueño had been the most important player at Madrid since Di Stéfano, but for reasons of style, not trophies:

> For many years Spanish football was associated with La Furia (the fury), meaning aggression and directness. Those were the qualities most respected and sought after, but it was difficult to convert into any particular style. There was no beauty to it, but it dominated for decades. Then Emilio came along and was an instant hero despite representing the total opposite of the furia stuff. The fans have a certain weakness for players who give 110 per cent,

but now they also like the stylists – because of Emilio. He seduced the Bernabéu. He won them over completely, because he was unique. Nobody has ever played quite like him. He changed the way the Bernabéu viewed the game, and the legacy has grown.

With the *quinta* and Hugo Sánchez, Madrid went on to win five consecutive league titles from 1986 to 1990, a run that was finally stopped by Barcelona's Dream Team. In the last season of the run, Real scored a record 107 goals under Toshack and Sánchez equalled Zarra's record of 38 in a single season. The success seems all the more remarkable considering the almost permanent rumours of hostility between Sánchez and Michel, the latter accusing the former of greediness and over-provocative behaviour – which was a bit rich coming from Michel, whose smooth Armani exterior hid an almost rabid *madridista*.

The gossip still has it that the *quinta* did away with Toshack in the end, as well as Sánchez and anybody else they weren't too keen on. Sánchez's famous statement that he belonged to '*La Quinta de los Machos*' (the real men's squadron) went down like a lead balloon with Michel and company, implying, as it did, that the *Buitre* was effeminate and that he and his mates lacked what it took to be true winners. Sánchez, never one to hide from the headlines, has repeated this since, and it remains a cold fact that the major failure of the *quinta* to win a European Cup has always placed a question mark or two against an otherwise legendary side. They lost three semi-finals, to PSV Eindhoven, Milan and Bayern Munich, a rare trinity of failures.

Butragueño's gentle behaviour on the field and his boyish face hid, according to some, a vengeful nature and a back-stabbing mentality. Along with Michel's acidic wit and Sanchís's deliberate nastiness to newcomers, the three allegedly ran the club from the dressing-room, so much had they besotted their chain-smoking president, Ramón Mendoza. He took up the post in 1985, the same year as the *quinta's* arrival on the scene. He had a lot to thank them for. Mendoza finally left in 1994 under a cloud of debt and his own cigarette smoke, leaving Michel and Sanchís as the last surviving members of the *quinta*. Despite the triumphs of winning back the European Cup in 1998, 2000 and 2002, Real are yet to foster a new generation of local players which can give the fans in the Bernabéu that specifically *madridista* feeling. Perhaps it is for this reason that the supporters have so taken Raúl Gonzáles to their heart, the successor to Butragueño and a remarkably similar player.

Like Butragueño, Raúl almost ended up across the city at Atlético, but Jesús Gil's dismantling of the junior side in 1992 meant that the 15-year-old, having already progressed through the various junior sides from 1988, was snapped up by Real's chief scout, Paco de Gracia. He had been following him for a couple of years, and when the chance came, he swooped. It ensured a smooth succession to the throne within the royal grounds of the Bernabéu. Butragueño's light was fading, but Raúl was there to replace him. After a period of political instability at the club, the problems associated with president Mendoza and the troublesome period of Cruyff's exultant Dream Team, up popped Raúl. Valdano was the manager at the time and, as with Butragueño, the young Raúl fitted his idea of 'footballing intelligence'.

Raúl, first blooded by Valdano as a 17-year-old at Zaragoza, has since gone on to be rated by the Bernabéu as second only to Di Stéfano, according to a poll published by *Marca* for the centenary. This is praise indeed, given the sheer number of great players who have pulled on the white shirt. But the poll was not so much a historical scale of Real's greatest footballers as a measure of their contribution to the *madridista* cause. This is a crucial factor in understanding the special nature of this club. At No 3 in the poll was Fernando Hierro, by no means the third best player to pull on the shirt, but certainly one of the most enthusiastic and aggressive. Ditto Camacho, who came in sixth.

Raúl, like Butragueño, has been a quiet, family type, given neither to the sound-bite nor to the clubbing scene. But he is Madrid through and through, a modest, working-class boy made good who plays for club, King and country. He is a patriot, a quiet but determined model of the *madridista*, avoiding insults and back-biting and simply focusing on scoring as many goals as possible. The closest Raúl ever came to provocation was in the Camp Nou when he looked up to the Barcelona crowd and put his finger to his lips after scoring – a photo that has since been incorporated into all manner of club merchandise.

Raúl will be around for some time yet, but the 21st century has seen a new development on the Castellana, centred around the figure of David Beckham. Since taking over as president, Florentino Pérez has signed Luis Figo, Zinedine Zidane, Ronaldo and Beckham, one at the start of each season he has been in charge. The first three were bought for reasons not solely connected to football, but despite the media space allocated to them, these deals predated the sort of cold-blooded marketing move represented by Beckham's transfer.

Of course, the Englishman is no slouch on the field, but until the summer of 2003 Real Madrid had not really been renowned for playing the commercial game for its own sake. Big-name signings and political ones yes – but the circus that surrounded Beckham and his wife on the day of the player's official presentation in Madrid, an event only surpassed in global viewing-figure history by the funeral of Princess Diana, demonstrated either that people have nothing better to do with their time, or that this was a new phenomenon. It represented a shift of a footballer into the marketing hyperspace previously occupied only by US basketball.

Valdano suggested to Beckham's advisers in July 2003 that wearing the No 23 shirt would invoke the spirit of the 'greatest sportsman of all time', Michael Jordan – a pointed statement in the direction of market-driven imagery. The next day, Beckham was all over the US front pages, an unprecedented event and probably a sign of things to come.

Real, of course, are not alone in the capital. Rayo Vallecano, from the hard working-class suburb of Vallecas, have been one of the perennial yo-yo teams of the league. After enjoying a euphoric spell which included leading the First Division for four weeks at the beginning of the 1999-2000 season, they succumbed to their historical tendencies and were relegated in 2003. Two other teams from the ever-expanding suburbs, Getafe and Leganes, habitually tread the murky corridors of Segunda A, with reasonably frequent visits down to the B category – mainly because if they show any signs of playing decently, the scouts from the other side of town pay a visit and take their talent away.

That situation is now as good as institutionalised. Satellite teams from the suburbs are often referred to as part of the main teams' *cantera*, often receiving an annual fee for the privilege of staying in the shadows. Real Madrid's official B team used to have their own name – Castilla – until the federation decided that the ambiguity might become a problematic precedent. If the B team wins Segunda A it cannot be promoted if big brother is up there in the First Division, which he logically must be. However, if you are not called 'Madrid B' or 'Valencia B', it might be possible to blur the defining lines between what is a reserve team and what is a separate entity – something the federation decided to remedy after the curious case of the King's Cup final in 1980.

Castilla made it to the final, only to come up against Real Madrid, on home territory of course. The seniors, Laurie Cunningham et al, won 6-1 but, because they had also won the league, the lambs were released into Europe the next season for an exploratory gambol in the Cup-

Winners Cup. West Ham fans will remember that the juniors won 3-1 in Madrid, though they may recall the second leg (won 5-1 by the Londoners) less well – it was played behind closed doors at Upton Park following the charmless behaviour of the travelling Hammers fans at the Bernabéu.

Far above in the pecking order, though always a step or two behind Real, come Atlético Madrid. In the spring of 2000, the *colchoneros* (mattress-makers) were plunged into the most damaging scandal in their history, namely the arrest of their president Jesús Gil for various financial crimes, chief among them being embezzling from his own club – something of an achievement even for Gil.

Amid the desperate attempts to scramble clear of this mess, several of the players were also investigated for undeclared income, while the case of the fatal stabbing of a Real Sociedad fan outside Atlético's Vicente Calderón stadium in 1998 by a member of the neo-Nazi group *Bastión* ended with the perpetrator sentenced to 20 years' jail in 2001.

Atlético bounced back from relegation in 2000 (their first visit to the second division since the 1930s), but the issue of Gil's almost permanent presence in the law courts never went away. Gil, whose tactic was always to present himself as more sinned against then sinning, finally gave up the ghost in the spring of 2003 when the Calderón, previously loyal, had finally had enough. The chant '*Gil cabrón, fuera del Calderón*' (Gil you bastard, get out of the Calderón) seemed to get to him, and instead of staging one of his usual foul-mouthed fightbacks, he resigned as president, leaving his son in sole charge of the club. Of course, Gil still owned 95 per cent of the shares, but given the various charges of financial malpractice levelled against him, the resignation looked like a way of preparing himself for the collapse of his 16-year-old empire.

His resignation took place a month after the official celebration of Atlético's centenary, an interesting affair, at least from a sociological point of view. Where Real Madrid chose Plácido Domingo to sing during theirs, Atlético invited the Rolling Stones. Where Real invited VIPs, the country's president and members of the royal family to a banquet, Atlético cooked a giant paella and fed it to the hordes gathered outside the stadium for the game against Osasuna – 5,000 of whom had walked from the Neptune Fountain (which Atlético claim as their own) carrying the world's largest scarf (red and white of course), knitted by hundreds of volunteers. Typically, they lost the game that day, but the more earthy nature of their celebrations befitted a club that has never harboured the kind of social pretensions favoured by their neighbours.

Formed as Athletic Club de Madrid by three Basques studying in the city, Gortazár, Aztorcha and Abdón, the team began as a sort of social club for homesick Athletic Bilbao fans resident in the city. It is Atlético's roots in the Basque Country which have ensured that they would always play second fiddle to Real, at least in terms of patronage and image. A group of young things met in the café *La Maison Doreé* in Alcalá street, where they decided to extend the influence of their home team by writing up the club's founding statutes in 1903 in exactly the same terms as those of Athletic Bilbao.

Bilbao had been in official existence for five years and the three men initially saw the creation of the club as a branch of the original one – perhaps thinking that they could literally start up another 'Athletic'. It was only when they were joined the following year by dissident members of Madrid FC that the club truly got off the ground. They wore blue and white stripes, as did Bilbao, but in 1911 changed to the famous red and white. This time it was Bilbao who followed them, in 1914, indicating that by then the Madrid branch was assuming a separate identity. It is sadly ironic that by the turn of the same century several of the club's followers would be in the dock for the murder of a Basque supporter. The roots were clear, right down to the name.

Atlético Madrid are one of the most complex and paradoxical of Spain's clubs. They stand in third place in the all-time Spanish league, with nine league titles and nine cups to their name, not to mention a European Cup final appearance (1974) and a Cup-Winners Cup win (1962). Nevertheless, they always seem somehow marginalised, kept at arm's length from the mainstream, out on the polluted banks of the Manzanares river, by the gas works. Their supporters, along with those of Sporting Gijón, are the most feared in Spain, and the Vicente Calderón was never a friendly place for visitors, even before the notorious stabbing incident. The two so-called *Ultra* groups, *Frente Atlético* and *Bastión*, fought among themselves for supremacy until the latter, a particularly xenophobic group, were disbanded after the court case. Both groups, however, regarded Madrid's *Ultras Sur* as a gang of sissies, beneath contempt – an attitude well documented by the journalist Antonio Salas whose excellent book *Diario de un Skin* (Diary of a Skinhead) narrates the tale of his infiltration into the murky and often surreal underworld of Madrid's neo-Nazi fraternity.

There's something slightly scruffy and unprepossessing about Atlético. Like 1970s Millwall, they prefer you to hate them. In fact they thrive on it. Gil, the former mayor of Marbella and president of his own eponymous political party GIL (laughably standing for 'Independent Liberals'), exploited this 'bad boys on the outskirts of town' image for all it was worth. He claimed constantly that the world was against the club, that every game lost represented a political conspiracy against his party, planned by the referees' association in cahoots with the football federation, all of whose pinko members belonged to the Socialist PSOE, his natural enemies and rivals in Marbella.

Before Gil was stripped of the title of mayor, his team ran out with 'Marbella' emblazoned across their shirts, a curious sight, but not the first time that the club had suffered from an identity crisis. They were not even called Atlético until 1947, having previously been known as Athletic Club de Madrid and Atlético Aviación. Having reached two King's Cup finals (both lost) in the Twenties, they were in on the first league competition in 1929, but finished bottom the next season. They returned briefly in 1934, only to be relegated the next season, under the management of the ubiquitous Samitier. The Civil War saved their bacon, for when the league resumed in 1939 they were chosen to replace Oviedo, whose ground had been totally destroyed in the conflict.

But 'they' were now called Atlético Aviación. Since eight of Athletic's best players had died in the war, the board of directors persuaded one Colonel Francisco Salamanca to merge his crack airforce team with what was left of Athletic Club and rename them Athletic Aviación – changed several months later by Franco's decree to Atlético Aviación, no team being allowed to sport a foreign name. Many of the players were from the Canary Islands, though this fails to explain why they were so good. The club was now Spanish in name and the incorporation of the Aviación players had finally put paid to any connection with the old Basque roots.

They certainly got off to a flyer. For a team that were supposed to have been playing in the Second Division, the upper tier held few fears for them and they won it in that first season after the war, 1939-40. Not content with that achievement, they did it again the next season, finishing five places and nine points above their more famous rivals over at Chamartín. For both titles they were managed by no less a figure than Ricardo Zamora, his first years in management proving as fruitful as his early years as a goalkeeper. He went on to manage Spain, if only for seven days, in 1952.

After the Second World War the club decided to drop the military association in its name and finally settled for the current name of Atlético Madrid in 1947. This was the year in which they thrashed Real

Madrid 5-0 in the Metropolitano, to date their biggest win over their rivals – in the only season when the latter have come close to relegation. Atlético took the title again in 1950 and 1951 under Helenio Herrera, having taken on one of the first black players to appear in the Spanish league, the skilful Moroccan Ben Barek.

As soon as Herrera had gone, Di Stéfano's Real Madrid took over and Atlético went into something of a decline, although they were always there or thereabouts, struggling up through the pomp and noise surrounding Real and Barcelona to make a valid claim for themselves as Spain's 'third team'. Bilbao might dispute this, but between 1951 and 1966, as white a period as you can get, Atlético were four times runners-up, three times losing cup finalists and three times cup winners.

There were even three years in which the *morbo* focus shifted from Barcelona and moved over exclusively to the capital. In 1959, both Madrid sides reached the semi-finals of the European Cup and were drawn together. Atlético came close to breaking up that famous run of trophy wins, winning 1-0 in the Metropolitano after Real had taken the first leg 2-1 at the Bernabéu. In the replay in Zaragoza, Real won 2-1. In 1960, the cup final in Chamartín was another fiesta of *madridismo*, the first time the two clubs from the capital had met in the final – both having won 8-0 in their semi-finals. Puskas opened the scoring for Real, but when Gento was taken out by Isacio Calleja and forced to spend the rest of the game hobbling, Atlético took over and healed some of the scars of the previous year, to the tune of 3-1. Next season they were back, Atlético this time winning 3-2, despite the inevitable goals from Puskas and Di Stéfano.

Just to keep the run going, Atlético finally won themselves a European trophy in 1962, knocking out Leicester City on the way to the Cup-Winners Cup final, where they beat Fiorentina 3-0 in a replay in Stuttgart, four months after the original game at Hampden Park. Unfortunately, three of Atlético's best years had coincided with their neighbours' glorious prime, which goes some way to explaining why they began to develop a chip on their shoulder. Rivalry certainly existed between the two clubs, but it was never as explicit as that which simmered between Madrid and Catalonia. It was as if Real Madrid preferred not to get too deeply involved in any extra *morbo* with their poorer neighbours, partly out of wanting to save it all for Barça and partly out of indifference. By ignoring Atlético, Real implied there was no competition. Atlético fell for it, and began to take on a rougher edge to compensate for the snub.

By 1974, when they reached their only European Cup final, they were managed by the Argentine Juan Carlos Lorenzo, whose Estudiantes side of the late Sixties had not exactly been assiduous followers of the Corinthian way. Against Celtic in the semi-final in Glasgow, the Turkish referee sent off three Atlético players, but they still managed a 0-0 draw. In the final in Brussels against the Bayern Munich of Sepp Maier, Paul Breitner, Franz Beckenbauer and Gerd Müller, Luis Aragonés opened the scoring in extra time, only for the defender Georg Schwarzenbeck to equalise with an astonishing 25-yarder, 30 seconds from the end. In the replay, Bayern walked it 4-0, and the dream dissolved before Atlético's eyes.

They made the quarter-finals again as recently as 1997, after their double year, but Ajax put them out in a close-run thing. Even then, the side were far from popular in Spain, their double having been won, according to most observers, by kicking opponents into submission. With Diego Simeone snarling in midfield and centre-back Juan Manuel López earning himself 44 yellow cards in his first 65 games for the club, the evidence seems to back up the accusations. Gil was having none of it of course, making an emotional speech then falling drunk into the Neptune fountain in Madrid.

What the new century holds for Atlético and Real Madrid will undoubtedly depend on financial (and legal) factors that were not in the frame back at the beginning of the previous one. As in the case of Barcelona, Spanish history was made here – through death, dictatorship, financial scandals and football. In the next 100 years they will more likely be looking for a little less turbulence and a lot more triumph. We shall see.

6. five taxis

Seville's healthy rivalry

Cándido is a Betis fan, which might explain his ever-so-slight frown when I ask him to take me to the Sánchez Pizjuán, the ground of their local rivals, Sevilla. 'It's a taxi-driver's duty,' he smiles. 'And anyway, my kids are all *sevillistas*, so there's no problem. I won't overcharge you, and I haven't thrown them out of the house – not yet anyway.'

Cándido is the second man I have engaged in conversation on the complex subject of Real Betis-Sevilla FC *morbo*, and since I have only been in the city for two hours, the signs are promising. Moreover, he fits my preconception of what the typical Betis fan ought to be – working class, solid, good-humoured, open, happy to talk. The rather more lugubrious old gentleman on the desk of the *pensión* I had checked into supported Sevilla, but his admission seemed a reluctant one, as if he had preferred not to be pigeon-holed so quickly by an English stranger. 'But my daughter follows Betis,' he added, shrugging his shoulders slightly. 'They all seem to nowadays.'

I put the question to Cándido, who seems to be enjoying the conversation, that Seville is like Liverpool, in that families can be divided by footballing loyalties without causing too much wailing and domestic gnashing of teeth? 'Totally,' he nods, sailing through a red light. 'It's very common.' I tell him that the perspective from outside Seville is a different one, namely that the two sets of supporters come from different sides of the tracks. I try to put this delicately, since Betis have always been considered the poorer, working-class side, drawing their almost rabid support from the tougher districts of Seville like Triana and Macarena. I don't want him to think I'm casting social aspersions.

'Maybe that used to be the case, but not so now. And anyway, Betis are as rich as Sevilla now, if not richer. The president, Lopera...' and he lifts his right hand from the steering-wheel and rubs thumb and forefinger together to signify 'loadsamoney'. I remain unconvinced, but decide to steer clear of the theme of *nouveaux riches* presidents trying to make their mark on Spanish society, out of fear of implicating the supporters as well. Cándido doesn't seem to have any hang-ups on that score, but I decide to press him just a little further, before we get to the stadium.

'But it's a political thing as well, isn't it? I thought Betis were always associated with the left.' Without answering, as if I've pressed the button at last, he pulls over and stops opposite a large but shapeless concrete shopping mall. 'Yeah, maybe so,' he begins, glancing at the red numbers. I owe him 700 pesetas. 'But don't fall for all that Felipe [González] stuff. He jumped on the bandwagon anyway. He was never a real Beti fan.' I suggest that Socialists had to be seen to support a so-called lefty club. 'Exactly,' he nods. 'It was true back then anyway, years before González. Sevilla were run by rich men, big men in the community. They attracted their own sort, if you see what I mean. And maybe that's why the workers went to Betis. Look – I can't change 5,000. Do you mind going over to that café and getting five one thousand *pela* notes?'

So the first taxi ride came to a rather more mundane end than I would have liked, but it represented a good start. It has always been my contention that to find out about a community you need to talk to the taxi drivers, and that was my intention in Seville, to try to get to the bottom of the extraordinary rivalry that exists between the city's two clubs. Cándido, faithful to his name, had been candid, and after only an hour in the city I was facing an unexpected problem. Perhaps there was no real antipathy between the two sets of supporters after all? What if the tales of *morbo* incarnate were just another set of myths about to be consigned to the rubbish bin?

As you cross the Avenida Eduardo Dato, the Sánchez Pizjuán is partly hidden by the new Nervión shopping precinct, so that the famous mosaic above the entrance, two-thirds the height of the stadium, rears up slowly into view as you pass through the concrete walkway that splits the two sides of the mall. The mosaic, impressively put together by local artist Santiago del Campo in 1982, depicts the crests of 60 major Spanish and international clubs who have visited Sevilla over the century. The dates of the visits are on most of the tiled pennants, but not Arsenal's, the only English team I could make out, gawping from the bottom. Despite the painstaking care that has been taken to represent the teams' pennants faithfully, Athletic Bilbao is written as 'Atlético', the non-English spelling forced on the Basque club by Franco during the war years. Interesting that Del Campo should have chosen to use the Spanish spelling, almost in a nod of approval to the fascists for their policy of linguistic 'purification'. I wonder what the Athletic fans think when they travel to games here. I suspect they are not amused.

Poor Sevilla. When the stadium that preceded the Sánchez Pizjuán, the Nervión, was officially opened during the Spanish league's inaugural season, Betis won 2-1. Both sides were in the Segunda A and Betis hadn't even come by invitation – it was just a fluke of the fixture list. Thirty years later, using the tracts of real estate in the Nervión district that the president – Ramón Sánchez Pizjuán – had acquired back in 1932 for a song, the club moved into the spanking new stadium that still stands today, adjacent to the old site. This time the fixtures were manipulated so that Betis could be invited to the party again, in order to ensure maximum *morbo*. At least the *béticos* weren't disappointed, running out 4-2 winners and spoiling the party for the second time.

The mosaic is about the only thing worth looking at in the district now. The land that surrounds the stadium, as you climb the slope that leads you out of the shopping precinct, lies dirty brown and unused. You can just imagine the construction firms rubbing their hands and lying in wait for the inevitable invitation to build new blocks of flats around the ground. The old president, revered by *sevillistas*, secured the club's financial future by buying up all the land back in 1932, and the taxi driver told me the shopping mall had been the brainchild of a family of rich immigrant Poles who had nevertheless been forced to fork out a substantial sum to acquire the land from the football club. Pizjuán never even lived to see his stadium inaugurated, dying suddenly of a heart attack in 1956.

He was not mourned by the *béticos*. According to taxi driver No 2, he was one of the reasons why the city split into two footballing communities: 'The son of a bitch had so much money that he financed the tramways around the city. He designed the network deliberately so that it only ran as far as Triana, which meant that the *béticos* had to walk along the river down to the Villamarín [the Betis ground]. Bastard.' This one is a bit different from Cándido. He's already told me off for flagging him down outside the Sánchez Pizjuán, claiming I should have crossed the road where there was a taxi-stand. I tell him that I didn't realise, that I'm English. So brusque is he that for a moment I contemplate telling him to stop and let me out, but I think better of it. He looks like a man who might enjoy the confrontation. He's in his mid-fifties, big and solid, with a pock-marked neck that reminds me of the New York taxi driver on the first page of Martin Amis's *Money*.

He's certainly about as friendly – but it's quite a long ride out to the

Benito Villamarín on the other side of town, and he looks like he might have something to say about football. It's just a question of finding the right moment. Fortunately, he has the local radio turned on and, being Spain, the journalist is hammering off in rapid-fire Andalusian about the fact that the next day, Javier Clemente is returning to the city on his managerial debut with Real Sociedad. The Betis fans are ready to give him a 'special' welcome, as the man puts it, due to Clemente's famous insult to the community the previous season, when he claimed to be 'from another country' when asked to comment on the incident in which he was spat on by a young supporter.

I lean forward in the back-seat and ask, as timidly as posssible: 'So what are you then, Betis or Sevilla?' I use the polite *usted* form of address, just to ensure that he at least responds with something. He takes his time, staring ahead into the darkening evening: 'I'm an enemy of the fucking Basques,' he growls, and for a moment I seriously think this is his preamble for a physical attack on me. How does he know I'm from San Sebastián? Do I have 'Real Sociedad supporter' written on my forehead? He senses my fear, like a man used to cowing others. 'I mean that I'm a *bético*, in case it's difficult,' he sneers, as if the average Englishman who gets into his taxi should be perfectly able to pick up the implication of his words. Nevertheless, I relax, because I understand his reply now. He means he will hate the Basques tomorrow, during the game, because of Clemente. Maybe he doesn't dislike them per se.

As he drives on into the gathering gloom, I decide to make it a personal challenge to mollify Mr Grumpy. He's so wonderfully bitter and rude that there must be something interesting behind it all. My folly is immediately rewarded when he begins to speak unprompted: 'I used to play for Betis,' he sniffs. 'That's why I'm a *bético*. But I gave in my membership card when they sold Gordillo to Real Madrid. I wouldn't piss on them now if they were on fire. The president's a shit, the young kids, the *Ultras*, stupid little *maricones*. Nothing better to do.'

I pull out my notepad. 'You played for them? When?' Again, he mugs the question: 'In the Fifties – they were crap. I only played for the first team a couple of times anyway. I played most of the time for Triana, the B team.' Triana is the working-class district over the river, the old flamenco heart of Seville before Franco's thugs forcibly cleared out the gypsies. It seems to fit the old thesis that such an area would have provided Betis with the name for their B team, at least back then. I ask him how long he played for as a pro.

'When I did the *mili* (national service), I played for the barracks and broke my leg. They took me back when I was demobbed, but I wasn't as fast. That was it. I've been doing this fucking dead-end shite ever since,' and he taps the steering-wheel in a gesture of suppressed anger. I leave him for a minute or so, then try him with the same question as I put to Cándido. 'So it's a class thing then – Betis and Sevilla? They're the posh ones and the *béticos* are the workers?' Predictably, he gives me short shrift: 'Pah – that's crap as well. The *sevillistas* just had more money. They were in with Franco as well. The only time they won the league was during the war, when everybody half-decent had done a runner.'

The *taxista*, whose name I never dared ask, was referring to a curious period in Spanish football, brought about by the country's neutrality during the Second World War. The only league title Betis ever won came in 1935, a year before the outbreak of the Civil War and only a few months before the Andalusian poet Lorca was shot by the Guardia Civil for taking the mickey out of them in his poetry. In a mythical year in the city, Sevilla also won the cup, but the spine of the Betis side was formed by Basques, the sons of families who had moved south when the early prosperity of the northern industrial revolution had begun to wane. Of the side that won the title that year, six were Basques, and all of them either fled or went underground when the Civil War broke out. The defenders Areso and Aedo took part in the successful tour of the Euskadi team that played in Europe and the Americas during the Civil War years, but the others never played again in the Spanish league.

By the time the Second World War ended Betis were in the Second Division and Sevilla were still basking in the glow of their golden era – winning the cup and finishing second in the league in 1939, the year that saw the resumption of competition, runners-up again in 1943 and champions in 1946 – like Betis, their only league title to date. To compound the contrast, the *sol y sombra* of these two sides, Betis fell into the dreaded Third Division at the end of 1946, dreaded because so many teams who dropped down never re-emerged into the light. They stayed there for seven years, probably around the time my taxi-driver friend was playing for Triana. But he tells me they were back up in the Second when he was with them, which I take to mean the late Fifties.

His dismissal of my 'class' question is similar to Cándido's, but I'm beginning to feel it's a bit of a reflex response now, something they'd rather consign to the past. It is undeniable that Betis drew their support from districts which were associated with leftist politics, union activity, gypsy culture and poverty. Seville was a city which saw its fair share of misery in the first two decades of the century and was the first city to fall to Franco's forces after the Nationalist uprising in 1936. The capture of Seville was no random act, since even before the war it had cornered the country's arms industry. Franco was subsequently to receive plenty of support from the men who mattered in the city, one of whom was the wealthy Sánchez Pizjuán.

When football officially started up again in the 1939-40 season, the King's Cup had been renamed La Copa del Generalísimo. Franco had every reason to be pleased by the fact that Sevilla won his first cup, except that they beat his home town club, the Galicians Racing de Ferrol, 6-2 in the final. The game was played in the Montjuic stadium in Barcelona and the cup was handed over by one of Franco's high-profile thugs, General Moscardó, in his new role of sports minister. Barcelona was a clever place to choose for the game, the implication being that everyone could contribute to the new political dawn, even those who had opposed it from the beginning.

Barcelona themselves had not even participated in the cup, unable to get a team together only 40 days after the end of hostilities, while Athletic Bilbao had fielded a team shorn of any of their decent players, all of whom had disappeared, had been 'disappeared' or were still on tour in the Americas. Their 8-2 elimination at the hands of their neighbours Alavés was another sign that a new era was beginning, and that the old footballing hierarchies would never again impose themselves in quite the same way. The cup was renamed La Copa del Rey after Franco's death and the restoration of King Juan Carlos, and in 1977 the first winners were... Betis. History could hardly have written the script more fittingly. In the final they beat Athletic Bilbao, back from the dead and about to pluck a crop of youngsters from their *cantera* that would return them the league title six years later.

My second driver is telling me about Sánchez Pizjuán's tramways conspiracy when I decide to ask him about the former prime minister Felipe González, the most famous celebrity fan of Betis. 'This other guy told me he jumped on the bandwagon,' I offer. 'Then he's a wanker,' comes the sure reply. 'His old man was from Santander I think,' he continues, unprompted, and I sense that he's mellowing. 'He was a miner. They're all called González up there anyway. Felipe was all right. Better than that clown [José María Aznar] they've got now. He didn't go to the games much, that's true. Some people said he was a phoney fan, but they've probably never been a prime minister. He was too busy to go to bloody football matches. Even when he was younger, as a party worker, he wouldn't have had time. No – he was all right. He went as a kid. I know he did.'

We are driving into the Heliópolis district now, and I am immediately struck by its elegance. The houses look about as working-class as Kensington – lovely mansions set back from the road, built in neo-colonial style and literally backing up to the grey concrete walls of the stadium, now renamed Estadio Ruíz de Lopera after the current moneybags president. The ground is undergoing some refurbishment and the driver swings me around the walls and into the car park, pointing out the piles of rubble and the scaffolding that will eventually support the retractable roof – a gimmick that Lopera insists will make the ground the most advanced in Europe. It's getting dark now, and the only light behind the west stand is from the club shop, still open for business. A security guard peers from around a wall, but he is little more than a shape in the gloom.

'Look,' says my driver friend, almost in a normal voice, 'if you'd come earlier, I could have introduced you to some people here. I still know a few faces. They could have told you what you wanted to know.' I thank him, whereupon his moment of friendliness defaults back to the gruff and he tells me how to get a taxi back if I need one. He points over to the west where he says I'll find the town of Heliópolis, but that it can be quite hard to get a ride back. I know he doesn't mean to tempt me back with him – he's too straight for that. He would have just told me. I hesitate momentarily, because I seem to be in the middle of nowhere, on the outskirts of a city that has a poor reputation for night safety. The contrast with the Sánchez Pizjuán couldn't be greater and I am surprised by the lack of any football surroundings – no high-rise flats with the washing flapping, no bars decked in green and white. The place seems dead.

I shake his hand and pay through the car window. He nods, a slight sadness in his eye, and he is gone, back to his world, back to his thoughts. Taxi drivers must spend a lot of time thinking, which is probably why they always have plenty to say. Cooped up for hours on end in the confines of their car, they must get plenty of time to reflect upon things, to think about what might have been – and in the case of this particular one, maybe my questions brought back the good times when he was still a hopeful youngster, turning out for Triana and getting his two games for the first team, back then when Pelé was arriving on the scene and Real Madrid were winning the first of their five consecutive European Cups. Long ago, before clubs had such silly things as official shops. I wander around it briefly, but decide against the green and white striped undies and the signed poster of Alfonso, all at decidedly middle-class prices.

Back out in the car park, the stadium looms up against the night sky. Gifted to the club by the municipality after their 1935 title victory, the stadium, then called El Heliópolis, was officially ceded to the club for a symbolic rent of one peseta a year, an amount still charged to the club's standing order today. But it had an unhappy start to its life. Two days later the Civil War began and the stadium was turned into a parking lot for a variety of military vehicles and allegedly doubled as a torture centre for Republicans unwilling to talk. Sevilla's ground, because of its more central location, was used as an administrative centre for military planning, with a permanent think-tank employed on site.

I walk through the quiet streets behind the stadium, looking for a taxi to take me to Triana. The houses are plush, maybe mid-19th century, and the streets are punctuated every few yards by small orange trees, their branches still heaving with fruit even in late October. There is no one around, most unusually for Spain. Emerging on to a main road I flag down a taxi and ask to be taken to the bar Blanco Cerrillo in Triana, the badlands across the river.

According to the European football *Rough Guide*, this is a Betis bar and the locals 'know their football'. The owner of the *pensión* told me it was in Triana, and I give the driver the address. He's a young kid, sporting a garish blue and yellow tracksuit, and no, he's never heard of this particular bar, but he'll find it for me, no problem. I ask him about the Heliópolis area, and he confirms what I have seen – it has a university, businesses, parks – he tells me that it's quite *pijo* (posh), but he uses the word apologetically, as if he doesn't want me to think he's a working-class hero. He seems calm and friendly, so I set off on my routine.

'I thought the Betis area would be much rougher than this. I'm surprised after everything I've heard.' He shakes his head. 'It's not like that here. Football teams don't always play in the districts their fans come from.' I ask him who he follows. 'Betis,' he replies quietly, as if he doesn't live and die for the cause. 'And you have friends who support Seville?' I try, since he's the youngest I've spoken to so far. I see him smile at the windscreen. 'Not many,' he offers. 'But it's no problem. I'm not an *ultra* or anything.' I ask him what the Betis *ultras* believe in. He shrugs. 'I dunno. They're Nazis or something. But the Sevilla ones are as well.' I try a joke. 'So they're all friends then?' He turns back to me for the first time, and he looks terribly young to be driving a taxi. 'No, no – there've been some murders. Drug wars and all that. They hate each other.'

We drive over the bridge into the Triana, but when he pulls over and asks a colleague the whereabouts of the bar, he gets the kind of lengthy reply which suggests that my *pensión* friend was talking off the top off his head. 'It's in Macarena,' he tells me, climbing back in, and I assure him it's OK to carry on. He heads back across the bridge and follows the road parallel to the river. 'So Macarena is *bético*?' I ask rhetorically. 'And what has it got going for it apart from that song?' The youngster seems appalled by my ignorance, but is too polite to show it. 'Er, the Basilica, lots of other churches, lots of history...' His voice falls off, embarrassed. 'And the song,' I persist. Did the Hermanos del Río (the authors of the song) come from the district?' Apparently they didn't, by which time my latest *bético* interlocutor has brought me to the end of my journey.

Down a scruffy side-street the darkness is lit by the obscurely named Blanco Cerrillo, 'the White Die'. I bid farewell to taxi driver No 3 and contemplate the object of my mystery tour round Seville. For starters, it's empty. I'd expected hordes of heaving, sweating *béticos*, all quivering to provide me with the latest gossip on the club. But I've come too far now, so I step inside, blinking slightly at the bright lights and the shiny white walls, and order a beer. Someone might come along.

The barman is in his late twenties, prematurely balding and wearing a permanent frown that probably comes with the job. A huge overweight chap waddles in with his wife and immediately begins talking about Real Sociedad with the barman, even before ordering his drinks and tapas. He says something about Querejeta, the ex-Real player turned film director, but his local dialect is so fierce that I can't catch the point he is making. Since the exchange opens no doors to me, I glance around the small bar. As it says in the book, there are caricatures of Betis players old and new on the wall and the odd signed photo, but it doesn't seem so spectacular as to warrant this mention of being a place worthy of a visit, and besides, it's well out from the centre.

Then I notice to the right, behind Mr Obese, a framed pennant of Betis dating back to 1935, the year of their league title. To its left is an identically framed pennant of Sevilla, also commemorating theirs. I catch the barman's eye. 'Excuse me,' I begin, 'but I've come here because I read that this was a bar *muy bético*, and when I look on the wall there's a Sevilla pennant. I thought that wasn't allowed.' The barman, now obviously the owner, hits straight back with the same thing I've been hearing all day. 'Pah – my mother's a *sevillista*, and my brother. It's normal here.'

Mr Obese eyes me suspiciously. I try the English humour bit with the owner. 'So you haven't murdered mum yet, eh?' I grin. The owner's reaction is not quite what I was expecting. 'Shit no – what makes you think I would do that?' he asks, frowning, as if by missing the irony of my question he concedes that there could exist certain possibilities of matricide over the football question. I change tack. I tell him that the taxi driver had told me that two twins had played in the Fifties, one for each team. I say they were the Pallaret twins, upon which the owner begins to look worried, as if he doesn't want me to know something he doesn't. He asks a shrunken little man who has just come in and is sitting on the bar-stool to my left. The little man nods sagely and goes back to his beer. I nod as well. 'So that proves it then. The two clubs are really friends.'

At this, Mr Obese cannot contain himself any longer. '*Sevillistas* are a lot of *gilipollas* (twats),' he contributes, and his tiny, birdlike wife nods in agreement, her mouth stuffed full of bread. 'I've told him to take that pennant down, but it's his bar,' he adds, also chewing on a lump of bread. 'Why don't you like them?' I ask. 'Because they're always mucking us around. They're better off in the Second Division. They should leave us in peace.'

I guess he is referring to the 1994-95 season in which Sevilla, having breathed a sigh of relief at the departure of an overweight and ineffective Diego Maradona, failed to present their year-end accounts to the federation within the time stipulated. The bigwigs met and decided to relegate the club, not to the Segunda A, but all the way down to the dreaded B league, a punishment they thought consonant with the crime. Despite Sevilla's uncontested guilt, there was uproar on the streets of the Nervión district, two directors received death threats (the committee's tribunal had comprised six First Division directors, among them Jesús Gil) and a Sevilla fan went on hunger strike. The tribunal's subsequent about-turn has never been explained, but the fact that Sevilla never cleared up their books that year yet were still allowed to stay in the top division raised a lot of eyebrows.

The Betis press had a field day, of course, and were turning the screw at every opportunity – not that their president, Lopera, has ever been the incarnation of an honest day's pay for an honest day's work. Albacete, having been relegated that season for the more conventional reason of a lack of points, were invited back to the fold to replace Sevilla. When they subsequently learned of the tribunal's about-turn, they threatened legal action. The whole messy business ended with the First Division being extended to 22 clubs and egg on a lot of faces.

By June 1997 poetic justice was done and Sevilla were relegated anyway, after a season in which they failed to replace Davor Suker, bought inevitably by Real Madrid. Bebeto, previously a hero at Deportivo, came over from Brazil to try to score some goals for the ailing side, but had to go home when the club failed to pay Flamengo the transfer fee, and then failed to pay Bebeto his wages. When they had tried to buy Robert Prosinecki from Barcelona the previous summer, their cheque had bounced. Whatever the man was referring to in the bar, it seems clear that Sevilla's reputation for being the more monied and financially cannier of the two clubs is another myth, or at least their inability to cook their books convincingly enough seems to have been at the heart of the problem. Sánchez Pizjuán was probably doing a few turns in his grave.

Back in the bar, Canal Sur, the regional station, is screening the Real Madrid v Atlético *derbi* live, and sure enough, by kick-off time at 8pm a few more football souls start to appear. Real Madrid open the scoring early on, but Jimmy Floyd Hasselbaink scores two crackers, José Marí another and Atlético go in 3-1 up at half-time, a scoreline that doesn't seem to go down too well with the barflies. They all seem to be Real Madrid supporters, presumably after Betis, and they seem genuinely put out by Atlético's cheek, leading at the Bernabéu.

Where I live, Madrid are seen as cheats, as overweening aristos, as a hegemony at the rotten heart of the Spanish state. To see these people expressing dismay at the 3-1 scoreline is something of a culture shock. However, it has to be borne in mind that Seville has for a long time been seen as the lucky city for the national side, ever since the 12-1 win over Malta which unexpectedly took them to the 1984 European Championship finals in France. Curiously, this famous game was played at Betis, where Hipóliti Rincón, the local player, scored four of the goals. But the national side was subsequently to pick the Sánchez Pizjuán as their preferred venue, probably because of the ground's larger capacity – another reason for Betis to feel that their neighbours always get the preferential treatment.

Until the 2-1 defeat in a friendly against Holland in November 2000, the *selección* had never lost in Seville, and the fans at both grounds are the happiest of flag-waving pro-Spanish patriots. The chip-on-the-shoulder feelings of Betis fans have never translated into anything anti-patriotic and, of course, the club has the prefix 'Real', which no republican fan has ever suggested they change. All of which helps to explain the bar's pro-Real Madrid attitude. Atlético, of course, are a rather hybrid beast, founded by Basques and now carried into the 21st century by Jesús Gil. For those who have no regional grudges to bear, Real Madrid are the obvious choice.

The owner opens up a little, and explains to me how his bar came to be in the *Rough Guide*. Apparently the English teacher across the road in a language academy knew someone at the publishers and was asked to write the piece on Betis before their Cup-Winners Cup game against Chelsea in 1998. Despairing of finding any pure Betis bars outside of the *peñas* – the supporters' clubs' venues – he decided to make his local watering-hole famous, and that was it. 'You're not the first one to come here because of it,' he says, in a rather tired voice which suggests my research doesn't interest him that much. Nevertheless, he gives me some fixture cards published by the bar and severely undercharges me for the steak and chips his wife has served up for me at half-time. We shake hands and I walk out into the warm, dark street. I want to go back to the centre and to the cathedral, where the city choir are to perform at nine o'clock. Enough of football for today.

It is not to be. Taxi driver No 4 has the radio on too, and lets out a huge guffaw on hearing that Real Madrid are 3-1 down. '*¡Joder,*' he shouts, '*le van a mandar a Toshack a la porra!*' (Toshack's had it now!). Not wishing to prejudge too much, I hadn't expected this one to be into football. He looks too much like Woody Allen, with the same jittery little gestures, the academic's glasses and a curious hunch over the steering wheel, as if he is seriously myopic. 'I'm not so sure,' I say, leaning forward. 'It'd be too expensive to sack him now.' Woody considers this one, pushing his glasses back up the bridge of his nose and squinting into the passing headlights. 'Maybe so,' he nods thoughtfully. 'So you're English?' he asks rhetorically, casting a rapid little glance at me in his mirror. 'What you here for – Day of the Dead?'

He is referring to Monday's *Día de los Difuntos*, a pan-Iberian event, but one that inevitably has plenty of colour in Seville, city of a thousand *fiestas*. 'You mean Clemente tomorrow?' I joke, and he breaks into an alarming cackle, almost letting go of the steering wheel. 'Ha! Good one that!' he roars. 'So you like football?' 'Yes,' I tell him. 'So much so that I'm going to Huelva tomorrow to see Recreativo play.' This time he really does almost crash. 'Huelva! What the fuck are you going there for?' he hoots. 'What are you – some kind of masochist?' I nod. 'I guess so. I'm writing a book about Spanish football, and I wanted to see where it all began,' I explain. On hearing this Woody turns more serious. 'That's good,' he says, cutting the cackle and adjusting his glasses again. 'They started it all, and now no one cares about them very much. No one remembers them now, because they're shite, but that's not their fault. Huelva's too close to this place. A lot of the kids there are *sevillistas*.' Now he has given me the chance, I ask him the inevitable question – Betis or Sevilla – but he has a surprise in store.

'Neither!' he roars again. 'Can't stand either of 'em. I support Valencia.' I suggest that he cannot be local. 'Sure am!' he proclaims. 'I'm the local weirdo here. My mates could never understand me.' I ask him why Valencia. 'I don't know really. I always liked the colours – white shirts, black shorts. A true contrast. Not many teams like that.' He goes quiet, as if what he has said is getting a bit too deep. He seems like a closet intellectual, reluctant to let it all come out.

I steer the topic away from him. 'But it's amazing,' I point out, knowing that he will add something I want to know, 'everyone here talks about football. Everyone belongs to Betis or Sevilla, and yet they tell me there's no real problem between the two clubs, that it's just a friendly kind of *morbo*.' By the time I get the question out we are passing the cathedral to our right. He pulls over and parks two wheels up on the kerb, smack in the tourist heart of town, oblivious to the heavy traffic behind. He wants to answer me properly.

'It's true. It's a *rivalidad sana*,' he declares, as if he wants me to quote him in the book. He means that it's a healthy rivalry. 'There are some kids – jerks, Nazis – nothing better to do, that have warmed it up a bit, but that's just testosterone,' he says to the central mirror, shifting his eyes every time I look back at him. 'You have to be one or the other here, or else you're nobody. If there's no *fiesta*, what do you talk about? Even the grannies are into football here. The *béticos, hombre*, they're the best fans in Spain. There's no debate. They'd follow the team down to the Third Division – they wouldn't care. In Madrid, no way. Bilbao – nah, not even them. Look at Sevilla. The crowds down by half when they went down. At Betis the crowds were just the same. That's the big difference. It's a social thing. Sevilla are more bourgeois – they say it's changed but it hasn't. If Sevilla go down, half the fans go to the gym on a Sunday,' and he affects what I take to be a middle-class Andalusian accent. 'Women in fur coats – they get them out as soon as the weatherman says summer's finished and sit there in the Pizjuán looking bored while their hubbies chew on fucking great cigars. I can't stand it. That's why I support Valencia.'

His speech at an end, he almost forgets to charge me. I pay and thank him, then for some reason decide to tell him that taxi driver No 2 was an ex-Betis player. It just seems to me, as I'm opening the door, that he might be interested. He responds immediately. 'Yes, there is a guy works the cabs – old guy I think, called Alejandro. Can't remember his surname. Played for Triana. Grumpy old shit.' I laugh an affirmative and leave Woody to get on with his job. As he drives off, I am almost tempted to take the registration number, to phone him again and talk to him more about the whole Sevilla-Betis thing. I seemed to get him on my wavelength, and besides, he had stopped the car and turned the engine off, just to gather his thoughts and tell me what he really thought. By the time I have my pen out of my pocket the car is too far down the road. I shrug and decide that might be pushing things too far. Ships that pass in the night. Best to leave it at that.

'Bourgeois' – a strange word in the circumstances. *Burguesa* had been the actual word he used, a very loaded term in Spanish with all sorts of connotations in the subtle contexts of Spanish class warfare, most of which I wasn't sure I really understood. The Betis war-cry of *Viva er Beti manque pierda* would indeed seem odd coming from fur-coated ladies, it has to be said. Couched in deliberately colloquial Andalusian, it would sound a bit like those earnest Pathe News chaps concluding a report on the Cup final with a jolly 'And up the Arsenal!' in a voice somewhere between Quentin Crisp and the Duke of Edinburgh.

The Betis phrase is well-known throughout Spain, and has contributed to the idea that the club is run and supported by good working-class stock. *Er Beti* should be *el Betis*, but Andalusian famously drops its terminal 's' sounds and strangles its 'l' consonants into something like an 'r'. *Manque pierda* should read *aunque pierda* in standard Castilian, and the whole phrase means 'Up with Betis, even when they lose!'. It's an unusual attitude to find in Spanish football culture, which is not generally given to making public declarations in favour of the more long-suffering aspects of fandom.

The historic catchphrase seems to accept that Betis are potential losers – not a sentiment shared by a pushy president at the end of the 20th century who invested (wasted, some would say) £22 million on the Brazilian Denílson and then decided that such an act alone merited renaming the stadium after himself.

As for the 'healthy rivalry'? I was coming to the surprising conclusion that it was just that. The historical evidence suggests as much. Apart from the extraordinary year of 1935 (and the equally extraordinary year of 2000, when both were relegated), the two sides have spent an oddly inverted sort of coexistence, as most of the chroniclers of the two clubs repeatedly point out. Juan José Castillo, a venerable Spanish sports writer who contributed some particularly tedious pages to the *Historia del Fútbol Español*, written in monthly collectable instalments in the magazine *Epoca* in the Seventies, insisted on this aspect of Seville in order to use up every possible metaphor known to the language which might illustrate the Spanish love of duality.

His essays on the two clubs talk of *cal y arena* (lime and sand) to describe the emergence of the powerful Sevilla side of the war years while Betis went into a seemingly irreversible decline. He then throws in *cara y cruz* (face and cross – two sides of the coin) to describe Betis' curious 1977-78 season in which they made a decent stab of their first venture into Europe – 'Eurobeti' as they called themselves for that year's Cup-Winners Cup – knocking out AC Milan and Lokomotiv Leipzig before bowing out to Dynamo Moscow in the quarter-finals. After celebrating their heroes' welcome on their return from the Soviet Union (*cara*) they spent the rest of the season staggering around with a hangover, and were finally relegated (*cruz*). The Moscow game was switched to Tblisi because of heavy snow in the capital, but Betis remain convinced the whole thing was a scam, prompting the then manager to write (literally) a letter to Brezhnev complaining that a side with such deep-running socialist traditions should not have been treated in such a shabby way.

Although Radio Moscow had defended their 'proletarian' brothers in 1949 (see chapter one) they seemed to have forgotten the socialist brotherhood line by 1978. The journalist Castillo was with the team on their odyssey, and claimed that they were given no food, cold showers after the game and a hotel without any heating.

As if all this were not enough, the relegation at the end of the season was shrouded in controversy. Betis went down despite finishing above Elche and Cádiz and level on points with Hércules and Español with a far superior goal difference. Unfortunately for them, the system then in operation was a fearsomely complex one based on comparing home defeats with away wins and down they went. But what aroused passions at Betis was not that injustice but the so-called *complot de Alicante* in which Sevilla, safely tucked up in the middle of the table, allegedly threw their game against Hércules of Alicante in order to get their neighbours relegated. It was neither the first nor the last time such allegations were to surface.

There is plenty of *sol y sombra* to report with regard to Sevilla, too. In 1934 they won promotion from the Second Division by winning at Atlético Madrid on the final day of the season. On the way home, the train carrying the Sevilla supporters hit a stationary goods train on the same line, killing nine fans and seriously injuring more than 100, an event which still counts as Spain's worst football-related tragedy. The acts of celebration were suspended and a week of official mourning declared over the city.

But Sevilla in cahoots with the fascists? On the trip back to Seville airport, the day after Huelva, I ask taxi driver No 5. He seems an easy-going sort, and we've already been over the subject of Recreativo Huelva after only 30 seconds in the car. But I haven't much time left, and there are still a couple of things I need to ask. He's a *bético* as well, making it four out of five. 'Fascists? Well, I've never heard that before. Why?' He is a middle-aged, friendly-looking family man, and he seems taken aback by this suggestion.

'Well – the side in the Forties were called *Los Stukas* weren't they? A bit dodgy, no?'

He laughs. 'That's just because they scored so many goals. I remember my old man telling me about them. He was a *sevillista*. Played for the juniors. The Stukas beat Barcelona 11-1, I think it was, in the Nervión.' I try to appeal to his sense of history. 'But it was a bit like calling them the Luftwaffe, wasn't it?' Again he laughs. 'I don't think that's fair. If Betis had had a high scoring side, they'd have been called Stukas as well.' And then, the best put-down of the four days of football and taxi rides: 'What should they have been called – the Spitfires?' Then he adds: 'But there were some funny goings-on.' The warm wind is rushing through his window and I'm finding it difficult to hear him properly. 'Funny goings-on?'

'Yeah – like there was that president during the war, what's his name, Pérez de Vargas, who was the Count of Contadero – loads of money. He was the mayor of the city later on. They said he only did a stint at the club so as to ensure his election. But he bought [Juan] Arza. He was a great player. They'd never have bought him without the guy's money. The *béticos* have never had anything like that, not until now anyway. They reckon Vargas was in with the Nazis, but who wasn't?' My note book is out again. It's astonishing. Five minutes with any taxi driver and the most detailed and interesting stuff pours liberally forth from their willing mouths. Can any city in the world match this?

The last thing I need to know is about Lopera, the Betis president.

Since driver No 2 was in full misanthropy mode when asked his opinion, I need a little more from someone less bitter. I ask how Lopera made his fortune. 'He used to rent out second-hand radios and televisions I think – back in the days when folks couldn't afford to buy them outright. They say he used to conjure up these renting contracts that said that after a certain period of rent you had to buy the appliance. They say that the contracts were written so that people never saw the clause.' I shrug. So what happened? 'He sent round "colleagues" to demand the money. If people didn't pay up...' I suggest that even if this were true, it didn't seem the quickest of ways to get rich. 'Nobody really knows. All of a sudden this second-hand dealer is a rich man overnight.'

He laughs. '*Hombre* – they're all crooked. I'd be more surprised if one of these presidents turned out to be honest. Look at Gil. No one can touch him now. He's paid them all off! If they sent him to prison, he'd buy the property. But anyway, Lopera's put us on the map. Before he came, we had to sell everybody, like Gordillo and Del Sol, but now we can buy good 'uns, like Alfonso and Finidi.'

We pull into the airport and he climbs out to get my bags from the boot. 'Well – have a nice time back in England,' he says, shaking my hand and hauling out the luggage with the other. 'You've taken my mind off what has so far been a bad day,' and he points ruefully down to the kerbside rear door of his white Peugeot, which I see is badly dented. 'Bloody motorbike – just five minutes before I picked you up,' he spills out, needing to tell someone. 'He hits me in the side – bam – at a crossroads. I get out to see if he's OK. He's on the floor. Young kid. And he picks up the bike, never looks me in the face, and buggers off. Not a word. Bastard. This'll cost me a packet.' I ask if he's insured. 'Sort of, you know, third party. Comprehensive's too much. Anyway, look, it was nice talking. *¡Viva er Beti!*' he manages a little lamely, and waves me off.

Inside the swish airport, completely refurbished for the 1992 Expo, it occurs to me that despite the welter of information communicated to me over two days, I am, in many ways, none the wiser. Seville seems to be a city very aware of itself, of its traditions, of its history, of its significance in the wider scheme of things, and of the particular nature of its football-related *morbo* – and yet no one has really wanted to analyse or be drawn into any sort of discussion which might disturb the underlying consensus that the rivalry is a 'healthy' one, to quote driver No 4.

Have I been trying desperately to unearth a rich vein of *morbo* where maybe only a smallish one exists? If the folks insist it's all good clean fun, then that is the way it will ultimately have to be interpreted. Yet events such as the very birth of Betis might still lead you to the opposite conclusion, namely that it's a nasty business and it always has been. Betis came into being for reasons unlikely to have surrounded the foundation of any other club.

Four years after the founding of Sevilla FC in 1905, and 19 years after the first organised game on Spanish soil had been won by the British employees of Seville Water Works, three of Sevilla's newly elected directors refused to sanction the signing of a player whose family, housed in Triana, were of working-class stock. The two directors who stood up to them pulled out of the club and formed Betis, in 1909. (The name refers to the Roman word for Andalucía, Baetica.) Little wonder, then, that the club immediately attracted a leftish reputation. The record books usually quote 1907 as the year of foundation, but this refers to the first year of Sevilla Balompié (*balón* = ball, *pie* = foot), the club whose eventual merger with Betis in 1913 created the Real Betis Balompié of today.

Five years after the merger, on the eve of a regional cup play-off between Sevilla and Betis, the guards of the Seville barracks where five of the Betis players were doing their military service period were ordered to lock the gates and allow no one to leave. In protest, Betis sent out their junior team who were traumatised to the tune of 22-0, a scoreline which Sevilla fans still chant on *derbi* days. When squad numbers were introduced to shirts in the early Nineties, Lopera refused to allow the No 22 shirt to be included, though he has since relented. The 'conspiracy' has never been proved, but dirty goings-on always seem to have been par for this particular course. Healthy rivalry?

On December 17, 1999, four Sevilla players were arrested in the early hours for a brawl in a bar off the Nervión, close to the Sánchez Pizjuán. They were all left out for the game the following Sunday, a 4-2 defeat at Oviedo which left them bottom of the table in what would prove to be a relegation season whose nightmarish qualities were diminished only by the fact that Betis went down as well. The players' testimony makes interesting reading. They claimed that they were with their wives – although it is unclear whether their wives were aware of this – and that some 'supporters' had been barracking them in the bar. The Sevilla players, after ignoring the insults for several minutes, marched across the bar and began to lay into their interlocutors, one of whom ended up with a fractured jaw.

'They were *béticos*,' added one of the players, as if this were somehow surprising information. In *Marca*, the *béticos* gave their version of events. 'We were sitting having a quiet drink, and they came over to us and told us we couldn't stay in the bar with Betis shirts on. We told them to take a running jump, and they laid into us.'

Healthy rivalry? Pull the other one.

7. raining champions

The unexpected challenge from Galicia

August 2002 was a cruel month. Instead of the usual weeks of sunshine, most of Spain was covered by a wet blanket of stubborn grey cloud. It is a tradition that absolutely nothing gets done during this month. Everyone goes on holiday, and everything is shelved until September when Spanish society reconvenes and the football cranks up again. The general angst and bad mood caused by the poor weather that summer prompted Spain's national television channel, TVE1, to put together a documentary looking at how people were coping.

Curiously, the region that normally suffers from an average of 320 days of rain a year – Galicia, up in the north-west – was enjoying its best summer for 50 years, baking under cloudless skies while the rest of the country shivered in the rain. Approaching a young couple on the beach at La Coruña, the TVE1 reporter held out a microphone to the bikini-clad girl and asked her how she felt for the rest of Spain. With an indignant flick of her sun-bleached blonde hair, she tersely replied *'Que se jodan'* (Fuck 'em).

It seemed impossible to avoid the phrase that summer. The rest of Spain was outraged at the girl's tetchy indifference, yet at the same time amused by the confirmation of what they had always been led to believe about the Galicians, and particularly Galician women – that they spoke from the hip, that they looked after No 1 and, most important of all, that they thought of Spain as a land-mass 'down there', hardly worth considering. *Que se jodan.* It was as if the girl had summed up, in three words, the way the Spanish regions really feel about each other.

I visited the city whose name means 'The Crown' – *A Coruña* in Gallego, the local language – in October of the same year. That was a month before the tanker Prestige went down off the Finisterre coast, unleashing a catastrophic oil spill on to the Galician shores and blackening the same beach from where the woman had spat her indifference at the rest of the country. Things were to change in the wake of the disaster, but back then the city from where the Armada sailed for England seemed peaceful and self-contained, basking in the glow of Deportivo's King's Cup win the previous season and a Supercopa victory the month before against champions Valencia, Spain's two-legged equivalent of the Community Shield.

Galicia is a weird, bleak place, battered by the Atlantic winds and soaked by the prevailing westerlies. Apart from its terrible weather, the region has traditionally been known for the pilgrimage route to Santiago de Compostela (a city that has a football team too, of course). The pilgrims still descend from the French Pyrenees to worship at the shrine of James (Iago), the mythical saint whose bones became a rallying cry for the Christian *reconquista* of Spain that finally sent the Moors packing. Galicia's claims of Celtic ties fit easily with the green, hilly landscape and the little *gaita* bagpipes whose strangled wail seems to emanate from every corner of Santiago.

Like the northern Celtic shores to which its rugged fishermen must have set sail back in the mists of time, Galicia has a history of poverty, famine and forced emigration that has determined, to an unfortunate extent, much of its cultural mindset. But there is now a growing sense of the need to fit into the new social dynamics of European integration, and, as with Ireland, football has played an interesting role. The exploits of both Celta Vigo and Deportivo in Europe of late have contributed to a change in their public profile, mirroring the desire of the region to be taken more seriously

As you drive across the roof of Spain, through the friendly arable pastures of Cantabria and Asturias, you can see the Gallego frontier from miles away. Blackish hills begin to poke up out of the landscape, the sky seems heavier and the mists come rolling in. Galicia has always been big on witchcraft, and the Inquisition had a ball up there in the isolated rural villages, confiscating the broomsticks and burning them along with their owners in a frenzy of annual purges. Luis Buñuel shot some of his bleakest films there, and the blasted heaths would make a perfect setting for the opening scene of *Macbeth*. The essence of the region lies in its wave-battered coast, the Costa do Morte (Coast of Death), so named for its fearsome reputation among sailors. Finisterre itself, of course, simply means 'the end of the world', which the area was considered to be until Columbus sailed from nearby Vigo. A greater contrast to the popular sun-baked image of Spain is hard to imagine.

The sea determines everything in Galicia – the economy, the weather, the food and the spirit of the people. Walking along the promenade in Coruña, you notice two things immediately. The first is Deportivo's football stadium, the Riazor, which looks like a giant clam from the outside. There are not too many grounds in Europe which literally sit next to the beach, but in Coruña it seems appropriate. These days the walls of the ground curl up against the vicious winds coming in off the Atlantic. But Riazor, built in 1944 and remodelled for the 1982 World Cup, was for many years a three-sided stadium, the open side giving on to the sea. In 1949 Deportivo's Rafael Franco succeeded in beating the Real Madrid goalkeeper with a ferocious shot, only to see the ball whipped back down the pitch by a sudden gale. In 1997, a stand was finally built where a wall had been improvised for the World Cup, and the ground is now quite snug inside, the four walls rising steeply from a lush green pitch.

The second thing you notice is the attitude of the people. In San Sebastián, they do their *paseo* (evening stroll) in order to have a look at each others' fur coats. In Coruña, people sit around on the sea walls or the rocks and stare out to sea, as if they expected Francis Drake to turn up again and sack the city. A contemplative lot, the Galicians. Whereas the Basque and the Catalan languages have lent to standard Spanish the vocabulary of games and food, the Gallegos have provided the wonderful word *morriña*, meaning homesickness or longing. The word derives from the tradition of the men going to sea and the women and children staying behind to work the land. They also went west by the boatload (via Vigo) in search of work and a better life, particularly to Argentina.

Before the Prestige accident, when things at last seemed to be looking up economically, it was said that a substantial proportion of Argentina's unemployed were experiencing their own attack of *morriña* and were making plans to come 'home'. Perhaps this is why Depor have been looking at plans by the architect Peter Eisenman to build a new stadium to cater for this potential new influx of converts from River Plate and Boca Juniors. Although the main reason is that after almost a century of obscurity, Deportivo have suddenly become a club that competes with the very best in Europe, never mind Spain.

The idea that remote and windswept Galicia could produce a championship-winning side would have seemed laughable even 20 years ago. But now it's a reality, with Deportivo finally winning the title in 2000, after a decade of threatening to. That event made La Coruña only the second city of fewer than 250,000 people to produce a title-winning side (the first being San Sebastián). Deportivo's president, Augusto

Lendoiro, seems to have been the spur for their change in fortune, although he breaks the mould of the usual rags-to-riches model. Formerly a local politician with the right-wing Partido Popular, he has used his contacts and persuasive personality to open others' purse-strings rather than his own.

At first his strategy was entirely based on bringing in foreigners (among them Rivaldo and Bebeto) to create the 'Tower of Babel' side of the mid-Nineties. Depor were the first Spanish club to put out a side wholly containing foreigners, against Atlético Madrid in 1996. But after that experiment backfired they brought in a sensible manager, the unassuming Basque Javier Irureta, who leavened the foreign purchases with Spanish youngsters and concentrated on playing solid percentage football. When he cut down the sometimes unwieldy squad to more workable proportions, success finally came. Even more remarkable than their silverware has been the consistency of Depor's challenge to Real Madrid and Barcelona, with eight top-three finishes in the 11 seasons since they first reached those heights, in 1992-93. Indeed, Real and Barça have each managed only seven times over the same period.

A similarly unexpected upward swing has taken place in Vigo, the city around the bend and down from the western tip of Spain, just north of the Portuguese border. Although they have yet to win a domestic trophy, Celta de Vigo have become regular contenders for European football and reached the quarter-finals of the UEFA Cup in 1999 and 2001 (when they lost on away goals to Barcelona). In 2003 they crept closer again to the honours, with fourth place taking them into the Champions League for the first time.

Celta consider themselves the more authentic Galician team, and resent Depor's recent successes. Vigo has the reputation of presenting a harder, more working-class personality, and tends to dismiss Coruña, with its more service-oriented workforce, as pretentious and idle. In San Sebastián, a week before my trip, I had asked some Galician workers who shared the same lunch spot as me if this was true. Sitting in their dusty work clothes in the smoke-filled dining room they considered my question carefully. Their unofficial spokesman, an enormous bear of a man almost too large for his seat, shrugged and avoided eye contact.

'Maybe,' he said. 'But we don't really care. It doesn't bother us. We don't have time to worry about things like that.' The answer failed to convince me. The men, from Pontevedra, were typical examples of the emigration that has always bedevilled their region. Whereas the Basque disapora was often for political reasons, the Galician one was usually economic. Between 1900 and 1981, the net outflow of people from Galicia was 825,000. Apart from a period in the 1960s, when the shipyards of Ferrol provided substantial job opportunities, Galician men have traditionally gone to sea or 'gone to Spain' in search of work. The building boom, for example, which began in prosperous San Sebastián in the mid-1990s, and which shows no sign of slowing, has been almost entirely reliant on Portuguese and Galician labour, the latter particularly being seen as dependable workers who cause no trouble.

I sensed that my question made the men feel exposed as outsiders, whose independence was compromised by circumstances beyond their control. They didn't really want to answer. Galician women may speak their minds, but the men are seen as silent types, without the 'strong'. The rest of Spain has a saying to sum up their famously non-committal attitude: 'If you meet a Gallego in a lift, you never know if he's going up or down.'

That October, my afternoon's entertainment was Deportivo against Racing Santander. The friendly press officer has reserved me a desk in the gods, right at the top of the West Stand. The view is wonderful, with the pitch down below a chilly autumn green and the hazy blue curve of the bay visible beyond the white roof of the stand opposite. Despite the rather boxed-in, symmetrical nature of the ground (in contrast to the clam outside) the place smells of football. Like Bilbao, there's something special here, something in the air. When you visit a ground for the first time you can always sense it – in the way the locals sit waiting, or in the way they unwrap their sandwiches.

If Depor win today, it will represent their 400th victory in the top flight. To put that figure into perspective, Real Madrid have won more than 1,200. As the comparison suggests, Deportivo were hardly a force to be reckoned with until the 1990s. They were founded in 1907, five years after a chap called José María Abalo did the usual trick of rushing back from England after a period of study to spread the word to his mates via the city gym – in this case the Sala Calvet. The club's first real competitive game was against an English ship, the Diligent, a year before Club Deportivo de La Coruña was officially registered. A year later they became 'Real' as well, at a time when Alfonso XIII's secretary was being kept busy by petitions from several of the newly founded clubs. Alfonso would happily grant this title to anyone who asked him, but of course not all clubs requested it.

Although neither Catalan nor Basque nationalism was in anything like full swing at this time, there was still too much of it around for sides like Barcelona or Athletic Bilbao to take the step of aligning themselves too closely with the Castilian establishment. The king got an invite to the opening of San Mamés, and that was it. Real Sociedad played in a city with 19th century royal connections, but many of their current radical nationalist supporters have come to regret the tag. Deportivo wasted no time at all in nailing their colours to the mast, and are still known today as RCD – Real Club Deportivo. But, as we shall see, Galician nationalism has always been a rather complicated beast.

For the next 80 years, Deportivo spent most of their time flitting between the First and Second Divisions, even dropping to the dreaded regional Third as recently as 1974. When the professional league began in 1929 they missed out on the tenth place (up for grabs via a series of regional play-offs) by losing the final game to Racing Santander. They finally got to the top flight in the 1940-41 season, despite having several players killed during the Civil War.

Bebel García, the team's left-winger in both footballing and political terms, was captured by the Nationalist forces in 1937 and shot. Shoved up against a wall quite close to the present stadium, legend has it that he was asked by the firing squad's leader whether he had any last requests. García replied that he did, and gestured for the man to come over. When he was within range, García undid his trousers and let fly with a stream of piss on to the pressed uniform and polished shoes of the Nationalist commander. He was shot seconds later, but for the Galicians Garcia's determination to die laughing made him a Gallego to the last – defiant in the face of adversity.

By 1950 Deportivo had a half-decent team and were top for the first half of the season, eventually ceding the title to Atlético Madrid. It was to be their best finish until 1994, when poor Djukic blew the famous penalty. Depor's alleged 'golden decade' of the 1950s is only referred to as such because of the three famous players it produced – Mañuel Pahiño, Luis Suárez and Amaro Amancio.

Pahiño came up through the ranks of rivals Celta, but was knocking them in for Depor by the time Real Madrid came snooping for a cheap goalscorer. Pahiño did well in Madrid, but by 1953 Alfredo di Stéfano was in the sights of Santiago Bernabéu, and on his arrival Pahiño was shown the door. Suárez, probably the most gifted Spanish player of all time, was taken away by Barcelona, and Amancio, a Coruña man through and through, was a fixture in Madrid's attack between 1962 and 1976. During Madrid's centenary celebrations, he was rated by Pelé as their best player of the 1960s. It seems appropriate that they all went to seek their fortunes elsewhere, mirroring the sad story of Galician exile.

The Santander players trot on in their tracksuits for a warm-up, and are booed half-heartedly by the as yet sparse crowd. At my side sits Eugenio, from the newspaper *Xornal Depor*. He has a beard and looks like the virtuous sailor on the old Players' cigarette packets. I ask him about the *morbo* quotient with regard to today's opponents, at which he rubs his balding head with his biro: 'They're OK, the Cantabros. I've got no problem with them.' He taps his colleague on the shoulder, another enormous man, engaged in chatting up the woman from the local Gallego TV station. He leans over conspiratorially: 'I like the Cantabros,' he smiles. *'Tienen mala hostia.'* (They're bad-tempered.) Like the Navarros. But that's good. Their teams are always full of fighters.'

What about Celta? Eugenio starts to nod his head compulsively and wiggle one of his legs up and down, as if his trousers have inexplicably caught fire. He lets out an obscenity with the curious lilting tones typical of the local accent: 'That's another matter.' His large friend once again squares up close to my face. 'When they come here, we always treat their journalists well, but when we go there...!' and the two of them roar with laughter. 'Last time we went to the bar at half-time, we asked the woman at the bar for a sarnie, and she says to us: "You can fuck off! Don't your wives know how to wrap a sandwich? We only serve real men round here." And she turns her back on us, the bitch! Can you believe it?'

I ask if this is typical of the reception the Coruñeses get in Vigo. Eugenio tries to enlighten me: 'They think we're a bit posh up here. It's because they've got more industry, more of a working-class community. There's a famous saying from Vigo – *Mientras Vigo trabaja, Coruña relaja* (While Vigo works, Coruña relaxes).' I ask him which of the two cities considers itself more Gallego. He considers the question carefully as the teams line up. 'Well, I guess they do, but then again so do we. Maybe you'll hear more Gallego there than here, if that's what you mean, but we don't use that as a measure.' He taps his heart several times. 'It's here. *Es un sentimiento.* Nothing more.'

In terms of mere football Celta appeared later on the scene than their cousins, in 1923. When the national league began in February 1929 they found themselves in the Second Division, along with Deportivo. But their start was inauspicious, finishing in the relegation zone, one place behind their local rivals. As a result the third division was briefly graced by Vigo's Balaídos stadium, then one of Spain's best-equipped grounds, which had been built in 1928 in anticipation of the professional era.

It took them until 1936 to win top-flight status, only for the Civil War to postpone their triumphant entrance for three seasons. But the fact that they finally reached the First Division a couple of seasons before Deportivo seems to have contributed to the idea (disputed in Coruña, of course) that Celta are historically the more important team. In 1939-40, just to rub things in further, Celta had finished in the relegation play-off position, but beat Deportivo to deny them promotion. They made it to the domestic cup final in 1948 too (they lost 4-1 to Sevilla) in what is considered to be their golden period under the management of Ricardo Zamora. Celta's record of 43 seasons in the First Division compared to Deportivo's 33 seems to give them a slight historical edge. However, although both have achieved unprecedented feats in the past decade, it is now Celta who are struggling to keep up with their neighbours' progress.

But Celta lie second in the division today, and the way this particular game is going, with Santander looking far the better side, Deportivo's rivals from Vigo are more likely to be the region's top side at least for tonight. When Deportivo go behind to a lame goal, Eugenio looks at me and shrugs. There are some whistles from the crowd but on the whole the reaction is stoical and dignified, less histrionic than down in Huelva, for example. But while the Gallegos may seem less demonstrative than the average Iberian, not everyone has seen it like that. John Toshack, for example. In 1995, he took over as coach from the local legend Arsenio Iglesias, who, with Lendoiro, had dragged Deportivo up from the depths of the Second Division in the late Eighties. Arsenio not only came within a whisker of the championship in 1994, but also took the Galicians to their first trophy, the 1995 King's Cup, albeit under bizarre circumstances. Alfredo scored the winner for Depor against Valencia in the famous '11-minute final' in Madrid, after the original game had been washed out by torrential rain in the 80th minute three days earlier, with the score at 1-1.

Following Arsenio was never going to be easy for Toshack. Like most cultures in Spain, the Galicians like to feel that those who come to work on their behalf are doing it because they feel some empathy with the place. The Depor fans suspected that Toshack's love affair with Real Sociedad was only on hold, and that they were nothing more than the temporary mistress. The Welshman kept his house just outside San Sebastián, and made the mistake of flying back too many times to play golf with his neighbour and chum, Javier Clemente. During a barren spell at home, Toshack stood up and faced the crowd as they celebrated a rare goal, famously mouthing '*¡Sí – aplaudid cabrones!*' (Yeah – you're applauding now, you bastards!). When he got back to his hotel that night, at the other end of the prom from the Riazor, someone had slashed his tyres. As he crouched down in the dark to survey the damage, a man emerged from the shadows brandishing a knife. Toshack somehow persuaded his would-be assailant to think twice and hop it, but he knew his days in Galicia were numbered.

The Russian Valery Karpin was another who got on the wrong side of the Depor fans. He made his name at Sociedad before moving briefly to Valencia and then for much longer to Celta. For the 2002-03 season he went back to his Spanish league roots, to play out his career with the Basques. 'He's probably said how happy he is to be back at Real Sociedad and all that,' Eugenio tells me, 'but the truth is he wanted to come here to Depor when his contract expired. The fans were split over the issue, and there was a poll on the club's website. A majority voted against him being signed, because of the anti-Depor things he'd said in the past. He had a cheek thinking he could play for us. He's good, mind you. We could have used him. But the attitude thing is more important. People know the things Karpin said. And in the end they stopped him from coming here.'

One interesting aspect of the rivalry between the two cities is expressed in the names they use for each other. The fact that Depor fans refer to people from Vigo as *Portugueses* stems from the unfortunate, if predictable, feeling of cultural superiority that the Spanish in general have towards the Portuguese. If the miserable postwar period in Spain contributed to the country's inferiority complex towards northern Europe, there was always Portugal to look down on. Even poorer than Spain, its proximity provided some measure of comfort to a nation that itself felt patronised by the richer, more industrially developed countries to the north. Vigo's position just north of the Portuguese border meant it was always the first port of call for migrant workers. Its industry and shipbuilding also attracted vast swathes of the rural population of Ourense and southern Galicia. Ninety per cent of the city's present population, according to the sociologist Joaquin Bueno, identify themselves as being from 'elsewhere'.

Celta's fans, in an ironic riposte to their own nickname, call the Depor followers *Turcos* (Turks). This slightly obscure description allegedly dates from the *reconquista*, when the Moors (assisted by large numbers of Turks) were finally sent packing from Andalucía, leaving the driving-over-lemons area of Las Alpujarras depopulated. The region was resettled by Galician settlers (who else?) on the orders of the Spanish

Crown, and most of them were craftsmen from the Coruña area. These people were seen as harmless softies (another accusation levelled at Coruña from Vigo), but the term 'Turks' has stuck. The real Turks returned to raid the Ría de Vigo in 1617 and destroyed the settlement of Bouzas, now a part of Vigo. Referring to Deportivo as Turks thus tars them with the same historical brush. They are both the enemy.

Deportivo and Celta both have their *ultras*, of course, as do practically all Spanish clubs. On the whole the Galicians have been at the more pitiful end of the spectrum, trading infantile political insults on the web, each trying desperately to appear more neo-Nazi than the other. It's often hard to take this sort of testosterone-fuelled stuff seriously. As Antonio Salas, the undercover journalist who infiltrated Madrid's neo-Nazi scene, pointed out, 90 per cent of the *ultras* who manage to find themselves a steady girlfriend retire from the active scene. As far as Galicia is concerned, despite the generally right-wing atmosphere of the region (and Spanish *ultras* are, by definition, right-wing) the fights between the local gangs had been pretty low-key affairs until a shocking incident in October 2003.

At a King's Cup match, 31-year-old Manuel Ríos tried to intervene to prevent fellow Depor fans beating up a 14-year-old Compostela supporter. The assailants turned on Ríos, kicking him in the ribs – the rib perforated his liver and he died on the spot. Paradoxically, the reaction to Ríos's death suggested that this did not signal any intensification of feeling between the Galician clubs. His assailant apologised (for what that was worth) and the *Riazor Blues* group of *ultras* announced on its website that it was voluntarily disbanding, in a surprisingly articulate article. Small comfort for the Ríos family, but not something you would have expected from Atlético Madrid's *Bastión* thugs, for example, who had been responsible for Spain's previous hooliganism-related death in 1998 (see page 142).

It will already be apparent that regional nationalism plays a less obvious role in Galicia's football than in the Basque Country or Catalonia. The pro-independence party, the BNG (Bloque Nacional Gallego) draws most of its support from Vigo, but it has never had much influence on the football scene there, certainly not in the way that the PNV marked out the political territory of Athletic Bilbao. Deportivo, as we have seen, were the first Spanish club to field a team entirely composed of foreigners. At the time they were experiencing a dip in fortunes after the 1994 near-miss, despite having won the King's Cup for the first time the following year, and the finger was pointed at the 'Tower of Babel' side. But there was no sense, as in the Basque Country, of this being a problem because it was keeping local players out.

The last Galician to play for Celta was Michel Salgado (subsequently of Real Madrid and Spain), and only the midfielder Fran has managed to keep the Coruña connection intact at Depor over the past decade. It's as though the Galicians' own tradition of moving away from the region has made them more tolerant of diversity at home – a side full of foreign mercenaries is fine, just as long as they show keen. It is difficult to see how either Depor or Celta could be regarded as sporting conduits for a nationalist sentiment, a sentiment that is a complex one to fathom anyway. Perhaps in Vigo something might have been born, but the diverse roots of the city's dwellers seem to have prevented the consolidation of a nationalist outlook. Working-class and proud, but that's as far as it goes.

Karen Warner, a student at Yale University, was featured on Spain's Channel 5 in the summer of 2000 for her PhD thesis, which studied the issue of Galician nationalism expressed though its football. On her website she admitted she 'quickly realised that the relation of soccer fandom and nationalism in Galicia does not play out in the same way researchers have portrayed the situation in Catalonia and the Basque Country'. So far, so obvious. She goes on: 'Instead of finding in soccer a decidedly consolidating force for Galician nationalism, the more salient issues to arise related to local rivalries between cities and towns, with nationalist issues mostly met with denial or ambivalence.'

Denial or ambivalence is about right. For the Basques and the Catalans, the question of football as political is like asking whether bears do what they do in the woods. The role of football in their political history is so central as to make the question absurd. But in Galicia, militant politics (both nationalist and industrial) have always been compromised by several factors – the most obvious one being the lack of a fixed and settled male workforce. Unions cannot be militant if they are losing members each year. Neighbouring Asturias, by contrast, has always had a more stable economy and an industrial base – mining in particular – that lends itself to a more radical political tradition .

The male diaspora from Galicia has resulted in its reputation as Spain's only truly matriarchal region. The rest of Spain jokes about Galician men being *calzonazos* (henpecked) – probably a reflection of the fact that Galician women have always had to get on with things by themselves. That may have made them tough, independent and resourceful, but not necessarily in a position to organise politically.

In Coruña's attractive main square, the Maria Pita, there is a rather curious monument. Coloured by a permanently flickering flame at its base, a collage around all four sides shows Maria herself, sleeves rolled up and brow multi-furrowed, beating back the invading English as they attempt to scale the city walls on May 4, 1589, when Francis Drake's men were carrying out a reprisal raid for the Armada. Like something from a Delacroix painting, Maria is getting stuck in, the word 'Freedom' carved into the monument above her head. Drake, it would seem, got fed up with trying to get past the defences to sack the city and returned home to face the wrath of Queen Elizabeth. Maria won the day, and has since come to represent the Galician female – spunky and courageous in the face of impossible odds.

The men of Depor certainly could have used some of Maria's spirit against Santander, and run out 2-0 losers. To make matters worse, Celta's last-minute goal at Valencia has put them top of the league just hours before the start of a holiday in Coruña to mark the day of the city's patron, Nuestra Señora del Rosario. The atmosphere is fairly sour down in the subterranean bowels of the stadium, where the after-match press conference is held. 'Jabo' Irureta shuffles in, wearing his habitual hang-dog expression. He has long ears and a drooping mouth, like a basset hound. He played with some distinction for the Atlético Madrid side that lost the 1974 European Cup final to Bayern Munich after a replay, but he is one of those men whose appearance as they get older makes it seem inconceivable that they were ever athletic young footballers.

Irureta is a contemplative soul, like his adopted Gallegos. A week after Depor had won the 2000 league title, he walked part of the pilgrim route of St James, from near Ponferrada all the way to Compostela. He did it alone too, with an enormous stick and an old rucksack. But he does not seem to inspire affection. A friend of mine who played for Real Sociedad's B side when Irureta was the first-team manager (he is from the Basque border town of Irún) told me he had found Irureta depressing to be around – like being managed by a funeral director.

As he responds to questions in his unfortunately whiney voice, I get the impression the local journalists don't like him either, that they think he is weak and over-cautious. The first question immediately annoys him: 'Why do you think we always play poorly against the poorer sides? Are the players not motivated?' Irureta sighs and looks at the journalist witheringly, like a teacher who knows the pupil only too well. 'Look, it's not a question of that,' he replies. 'How about Racing? They played well.

They never let us settle. How about focusing on them?' In all his years as a coach, Irureta, nice chap though he is, seems to have developed that uncanny ability to annoy people whenever he opens his mouth.

Irureta is the only person to have managed both the major Galician sides, Celta and Depor, and the two major Basque teams, Athletic Bilbao and Real Sociedad. But it is one of the great mysteries of the contemporary Spanish game that he is rated neither by the Gallegos nor by the Spanish football public at large, despite his monumental successes after taking charge of Depor in the aftermath of the Tower of Babel crisis and the bad vibes created by Toshack.

Later in the season, against Alavés, he would go on to complete his 500th game as a coach in the top flight. In 1998-99 he hauled Depor into the UEFA Cup and took them to the semis of the King's Cup. The following season Depor took their first league title, and 2001 saw them finish as dignified runners-up and quarter-finalists in the Champions League. The next year they won the King's Cup, beating Real Madrid in the Bernabéu to ruin their centenary, and pulled off a double win over Manchester United in the group stage of the Champions League. Their win at Old Trafford that season (when they also won at Highbury) had the international press drooling over them, calling them the best side in Europe – yet Irureta's approach continued to be challenged at home.

During a training session in January 2002, the talented but wayward Brazilian Djalminha (too wayward to be an ever-present in an Irureta side) head-butted his manager during a tactical altercation, an incident that was recorded on camera. Irureta, instead of disciplining the player to preserve his own authority, simply shrugged it off and let the matter drop. Djalminha was sent out on loan to Austria Vienna the next season, but it was a measure of what the quiet Basque has had to put up with. He would seem to be a man condemned by his manner and appearance, for which success has been no remedy. Maybe the Coruñeses have never forgiven him for managing Celta for a season before he was tempted over to Deportivo by the persuasive Augusto Lendoiro.

By 2002, Deportivo could boast the fourth best club side in the world (according to FIFA), from whose ranks emerged one of Europe's best midfielders, Juan Carlos Valerón, the chief architect of Spain's progress to the World Cup quarter-finals in Korea. The likelihood of both Deportivo and Celta staying at the top seems to depend largely on their ability to hang on to this type of player, and that is conditioned, as always, by the skill with which they can carry on balancing the books. All good things can come to an end, of course, but those who saw the rise of

Galicia in the 1990s as a temporary phenomenon have so far been forced to eat their words.

The almost simultaneous rise of the two clubs from the same region has no trite and easy explanation, but may have had something to do with simple good husbandry as well as sheer coincidence. Both clubs found shrewd, forward-thinking presidents at around the same time. Both also had the luck or the foresight to sign influential foreign players who turned out to be more than also-rans and who paved the way for others to follow. Players like Rivaldo and Bebeto for Deportivo have been followed by Roy Makaay, Mauro Silva and the ageless Donato, still turning out in 2003 and scoring from corners at the age of 40. For Celta, the Russians Valery Karpin and Alexander Mostovoi stayed around to good effect, ably abetted by the Israeli Haim Revivo, Brazil's Mazinho and even Lubo Penev.

Add to this the more than decent smattering of Spanish players who were then attracted to the region by the emerging feel-good factor, and you have something approaching an explanation. With the exception of Michel Salgado, neither Barcelona nor Madrid has yet managed to make any significant snatch-and-grab forays into these largely settled squads. It could happen, of course, but for the near future at least, the force seems to be staying with Galicia.

Regardless of what happens in future on the field, the success of the two clubs – and Deportivo in particular – has already thrown an intriguing light on Galicia's slowly changing relationship with the outside world. While in Coruña I picked up a copy of the club's official magazine – a well-produced, glossy monthly. Such publications remain rare in Spain, where even the match programme has yet to catch on as a concept. The Spanish prefer to talk about their football. The idea of the crowd collectively grasping its thermos at half-time and then turning its silent attention to the delights of 'Manager's Notes' would seem both surreal and impolite to the Spanish. Here, the length and breadth of the peninsula, the fans unwrap their *bocadillos* and begin to argue about the game, struggling to hear above the din of the local oompah band.

Even more surprising was the very odd cover of Depor's magazine. It featured Manuel Fraga, the elderly president of the Galician autonomous government (the Xunta), dressed in a Deportivo shirt. The shirt was on back-to-front, and sported the name 'Don Manuel', below which there was a large black No 1. The implication, one assumes, was not that Fraga was a decent goalkeeper but that he was a decent fellow, a leader of men, a No 1. And yet in fact he looked ridiculous, not simply because he is 81 and sports a healthy wine-gut, but because the back-to-front nature of the shirt and the old man's awkward smile made him look faintly senile, as if he had forgotten how to dress himself.

As a nationalist leader Fraga is out of a very different mould from those of the Basque Country, and it comes as a shock to see him so closely identified with Depor. Not that all valid nationalism has to be like the Basque version – it can simply be a form of expressing cultural independence, something the Galicians clearly feel. But Fraga! No wonder the Riazor does not embrace enthusiastic outpourings of Galician nationalist sentiment, when the president of their Xunta was Franco's right-hand man. (Franco himself was a Galician too, of course, from Ferrol.) Fraga became a prominent member of the regime of terror, promoted through the ranks until he was awarded the post of Minister of Information, cutely named the Agitation and Propaganda Department.

This was the man who brought in the repressive Law of Press and Printing, which became a pillar of Franco's centralised administration and effectively muzzled all opposition. He spent a couple of years in London as ambassador, returning to Madrid on Franco's death in 1975 and was miffed to be overlooked as his successor. He was allegedly instrumental in the notorious murder of two left-leaning Carlists in 1976, on Montejurra hill near Pamplona, which was a key turning point in the transition to a provisional government under King Juan Carlos of a type that had at least been envisaged by the dying Franco.

Nevertheless, a year later, worried by the inevitable push for democracy and regional autonomy, Fraga founded the Alianza Popular party. This was in order to fight against what he called 'the most dangerous enemies in Spain: communism and separatism'. The following year, 1978, he voted against the legislation that converted Spain into a series of autonomous regions – effectively voting against his own region's semi-independence from Madrid. Yet 25 years later, the buddy of Pinochet, Gadafy and other such icons of 20th century democracy is still the leader of the Xunta, sporting a Depor shirt on the cover of the club's magazine.

Fraga wasn't even born in Coruña, hailing from Villalba, over to the east. But Depor have become fashionable, and he wants to get in on the act. The inconvenient fact that he was also awarded the first Honorary Membership of the Fundación de Celta de Vigo at its inception in 1997 is probably overlooked by most Gallegos. The significant thing is that Deportivo are prepared effectively to endorse Fraga's desperate attempt to cling on to the modern scene, to preserve his political life for a few last gasps through the convenient conduit of football. It is acts like these that condition the rest of Spain's attitude to Galicia. It is hardly surprising that they regard the region as an interesting but eccentric throwback that is forever promoting its cultural independence, yet allows an ex-Francoist (perhaps not so ex) to run its autonomous government. Fraga, despite his claims to be Galician through and through, would not be seen dead speaking Gallego in public – a language he has always considered to be the preserve of uneducated peasants.

When the Prestige went down off the Galician coast in November 2002, Fraga's luck began to run out. He had decided to spend the weekend hunting outside Madrid, and when news of the sinking reached his country cabin, his reaction was to shrug his shoulders and dismiss the crisis. Only when the extent of the accident became clear did he react, returning hastily to take charge, by which time it was too late. The tanker was towed out to sea and sunk, but the oil slicks had begun to hit the coast and the economy. Galicia, almost totally dependent on tourism and fish, faced ruin. Both Fraga and the central government of the Partido Popular (a party that was the bastard offspring of Fraga's own creation) suffered a torrent of criticism, and the hitherto tolerant Gallegos began to turn on their ageing leader.

One of the main mistakes of the PP was to turn down outside offers of technological help in the aftermath of the Prestige accident, preferring to bluff and blunder their way through the first vital weeks. Deportivo's new status as one of European football's leading clubs made them a logical outlet for a protest that aimed to embarrass the regional and national governments over an issue that was both local and – as a widely reported environmental catastrophe – international. A fortnight after the crisis began, Deportivo took on Juventus in a Champions League qualifier at the Riazor. A group of Deportivo supporters produced an enormous banner for the game, realising the message would be relayed across Europe. The words *Zona catastrófica Xa* (Disaster Zone Now) were unlikely to be palatable to the government, since declaring a state of emergency would have represented an immediate (if more honest) admission of defeat and a simultaneous cry for help, both technical and financial.

From the Juventus game onwards, the government was dragged through the oil-stained mud anyway until the prime minister, José María Aznar, was finally compelled to admit his cabinet's mistakes. Spanish football jumped in, as ever, with both political feet, in a show of active solidarity with the stricken community. Clubs organised a host of fund-raising events, players laid out banners of the now famous *Nunca Máis* (Never Again) slogan in the centre of various pitches before the games began – and in the Riazor there was a game between the scary-sounding Coast of Death XI and Deportivo. Celta got in on the act too, their supporters coming up with a clever banner which proclaimed *Naufraga*, punning on the Xunta leader's name and *naufrago* (shipwreck).

The Prestige affair may have put Galicia briefly in the world spotlight, but as ever it is football that has done so most effectively. As Mercedes Peón, Galicia's famous Sinead O'Connor look-alike singer, has commented, when she performs in Europe now, everyone knows what she is talking about when she tells them she is from Coruña. 'Ah – Deportivo,' they all nod. Thanks to Lendoiro, Arsenio and Irureta, the rainy north is no longer obscure and unknown.

8. a fire in the east

Valencia's hard road to the top

Valencia is Spain's third city, famous for its oranges and paella, and, after consecutive Champions League final appearances in 2000 and 2001, its football team. They lost them both, the first in Paris to Real Madrid, the first final to feature two sides from the same country since the competition began in 1956. Then, by losing out the next season too, they became only the second side to lose two consecutive finals, Juventus having pipped them to the post for that honour three years before. Nevertheless, it seemed to suggest that another of Spain's nearly teams was finally ready to make a more sustained challenge to the big two.

Valencia's relative lack of success until recent years is by no means due to any lack of desire or passion for football in the city. When Valencia met Deportivo in the '11-minute' Cup final in 1995, 10,000 Valencia fans turned up for the proceedings in Madrid, even though (bizarrely) it was televised live. Admittedly entrance was free, but they still had to get there. Valencia's fans showed up, and showed that they cared. Aside from Betis, it is hard to think of a club with a more committed or fiercely loyal set of supporters. Mestalla, the ground originally built in 1924, has for some time been one of Spain's most intimidating stadiums, from whose apparently sheer vertical walls the baying hordes holler their allegiance. It seems to function as a microcosm of the city itself, also an incredibly noisy place.

What Valencia lacks in landmarks of cultural or architectural interest it makes for up in sheer rowdiness – an attitude summed up in the name of one of its bars, Vivir sin dormir (Live without sleeping). Equally well known for making an interminable racket is Spain's most famous fan, Manolo del Bombo (Manolo – the guy with the drum), a Valencia man through and through, who has a bar named after him just down a side street from the Mestalla. Manolo failed to make the 2002 World Cup finals, allegedly because smoking was banned in the stadiums, but he has nevertheless come a long way on a beer belly and a drum.

La Mestalla (formally known as Estadio Luis Casanova) has also taken on a certain significance in both British and Spanish folk memory, since it was there that Gerry Armstrong blasted the famous goal through Luis Arconada's legs that relegated the 1982 World Cup hosts to second place in the table and confirmed to the Spanish public that their team was unlikely to progress much further in that tournament. Since then, apart from the 1992 Olympics, the ground has only occasionally been used by the itinerant national side, apparently on grounds of superstition.

But there may be other reasons. Two qualifications have to be made about Valencia's supporters, one of which leads back on to the *morbo* trail. One is that, noise and passion notwithstanding, Mestalla's denizens have a reputation as *duros* (hard), but in the sense of being hard to please, not violent. Managers have come and gone, and more than a few have noted that they were not appreciated, Claudio Ranieri and Hector Cúper in particular.

Both Ranieri and Cúper made substantial contributions towards putting Valencia back on the football map in the 1990s. They had spent many years in the wilderness, going without a trophy between Graham Rix's famously missed penalty in the Cup-Winners Cup final shoot-out of 1980 and a King's Cup win against Atlético Madrid in 1999. The league championship, won under manager Rafa Benítez in 2002, was their first since 1971 – three decades which seem to have bred a certain amount of impatience among the club's support, and a certain amount of nostalgia for a supposedly golden period that has probably been exaggerated in the club's official history. In the all-time table (see page 61) Valencia hold firmly on to fifth spot, but of their five championships, three came in their truly golden era, the long-distant 1940s.

One of Valencia's most famous traditions is the *Fallas*, the festival in which the locals spend months building effigies of the city's most reviled characters to celebrate the end of winter (it dates from the Middle Ages). The effigies are burned on the last day of the festival, a fate awarded to Hector Cúper in March 2002, after his Inter side had knocked Valencia out of the UEFA Cup. The fireworks exploded and the locals applauded furiously as he went up in flames. You'd have thought they would have been more appreciative of the rather dour Argentine who took them to the two Champions League finals, but they never seemed to like him, accusing him (shades of Irureta) of being over-cautious and defensive, and of wasting the talents of Gaizka Mendieta and Claudio López.

The 2003 *Fallas* came just too early to see Cúper featured again, but even ritual burning might have been insufficient punishment for the crime of Inter knocking Valencia out of the Champions League quarter-finals, two games that were described as *morboso* a record number of times by the Spanish press and which featured a sterile display of defensive pragmatism on the part of Inter whose cynicism was almost obscene. Valencia won the second leg in Mestalla but went out on away goals, Inter's 'efficiency' over the two legs plumbing new depths – two attacks, two goals. Maybe the Valencia fans were right after all about Cúper.

This is not a community that forgives too easily. Down in Seville, they'll support their teams unconditionally, and wave the flag with almost mindless enthusiasm when the national team visits, but the Valencianos are a bit more complex. The team that is known as *Los ché* (the mates) takes its nickname from the local dialect – or language, depending on your politics. Valencia was the last city to fall to Franco in the Civil War, and has traditionally been linked to the left of the Spanish political scene. But times have changed, and since democracy there has been a slow shift to the right, particularly on the nationalist scene where a group of linguists began a determined campaign, financed by the regional government, to prove that Valencià (as it is known locally) was a language in its own right, as opposed to a variety of Catalan.

A glance at the map shows Valencia to be a good way down the east coast from Barcelona, with Madrid roughly the same distance inland. But the area in which Valencia is the most prominent city, the Levante (East), also has Valenciano-speaking communities further north, closer to Catalonia, places like Castellón and Tarragona. Here the Catalan link has remained less of a problem, but for Valencia – geographically more distant and with a growing industrial base to compete with the best that Barcelona can offer – the move towards 'independence' has been perhaps inevitable. Older Valencia supporters will tell you that until the early 1990s, it was sometimes hard to tell which was the home side when Barcelona visited Mestalla. Valencia's residual affection for Barcelona was perhaps logical given the former city's troublesome relationship with Franco's regime. The local dialect (say it carefully) had also, like standard Catalan, been banned from the streets, causing resentment in some quarters at least.

But by the time Barça's Dream Team was visiting Mestalla, the home fans were much less divided in their loyalties. The less friendly relationship between the two cities was apparent even at the time of the 'old stone' incident in the mid-Eighties. A group of local archaeologists, linked to the nationalist movement, claimed to have found an ancient stone etched with Valenciano. Since the inscription allegedly predated Catalan, there was quite a fuss around this extremely significant 'break-through' in the history of the two tongues. Unfortunately for the nationalists, when the stone was carbon-dated it was traced back to the local brickworks, circa 1963. The Catalan press were understandably amused, and wasted little time in poking fun at their southern cousins, further buoyed by the fact that most neutral academics continue to view Valenciano as a dialect, not a language.

It wasn't until 1919 that the football club named Valencia took shape, set up in a bar (of course) called El Torino. There had been a Valencia Foot-Ball Club before, founded in 1909 on the occasion of the formation of the Federación Regional de Clubs de Foot-ball in Valencia in March of that year. A tournament was organised as witness to the occasion, with Barcelona, Español, Gimnástica de Madrid and the aforementioned Valencia FC the participants. But that club had effectively dissolved by the time the Valencia FC we know today began its life.

They've made up for lost time, but the fact of their late birth seems rather curious, given that the city has always been significant in terms of population, commerce and industry. Its position on the coast, and easy access to Madrid and Barcelona, ensured its early development. As Spain's late industrial revolution began to take hold, Madrid's land-locked position made it increasingly dependent on Valencia's port as a conduit for markets to the east. Business interests in Madrid began to drift east, especially as land was cheaper on the outskirts of Valencia. Unsurprisingly, when Franco's forces rose up and began to win the day, key regional centres like Seville and Valencia were immediately targeted as priorities – but the latter was to hold out until the bitter end.

The club's foundation appears to have been a better-late-than-never attempt to form an institution more representative of the city than the teams already in existence. FC Levante (founded in 1909), although they regularly claim to have been the city's pioneering club, were actually beaten to it by Cabanyal, an outfit which had been hanging around since 1903. Alongside Levante were other sides such as Gimnástico and Hispania, none of whose names conjured up the necessary spirit normally encapsulated by the simple use of the city name.

Levante's earliest games were played on a pitch near the docks, a plot of land which was the property of a perfume entrepreneur. Their next ground, Campo del Camino Hondo, was also close to the port area and the club came to identify itself with its working-class background.

Others, particularly Valencia, were seen as come-lately snobs. This rather easy division of teams in Spain's larger cities into pigeon-holes of class should always be regarded with some scepticism, not least because the social patterns of cities can change enormously over the span of a century.

But it does seem that part of the spirit of *morbo* resides in at least the folk-memory of such divisions. The Levante websites are full of class-based insults towards Valencia (and vice-versa), particularly as the former side has now found itself a rich president and brought in a star like Predrag Mijatovic, formerly of Real Madrid, but more importantly of Valencia. To rub things in further, Levante wear the same colours as Barcelona, and although it may be a historical coincidence (they adopted the *azulgrana* strip as late as 1935) it is more likely that they were trading on Barça's reputation and managing to annoy their neighbours at the same time. Levante's name is another divider, suggestive of the region and its maritime connection, rather than just the city.

Of course, in historical terms, Levante cannot really compete with Valencia. The first game between the two took place just after the foundation of the bigger-boys-to-be in 1919 to inaugurate Valencia's first ground, Algirós. Inauspiciously for Levante, they lost 1-0, and since then have had only a few occasions to cheer. The two clubs did not meet again for three years, this time at Levante's ground, where Valencia won 5-0. The local paper reported that:

> This encounter, as in the previous game held on the occasion of the inauguration of Algirós, was full of violent incidents and colourful arguments between the two sets of players and supporters, some of which resulted in physical aggression.

'Colourful arguments' is a very Spanish phrase, typical of the formal style still predominant in the press. But whatever the arguments consisted of, it obviously hadn't taken long for the rivalry to grow. In 1934 Valencia established their credentials by reaching the King's Cup final (although they lost to Real Madrid). The following year Levante, not to be outdone, reached the semis, beating both Valencia and Barcelona on the way, only to fall to the eventual winners, Sevilla. After sinking into postwar obscurity, Levante had to wait until the early Sixties for two rose-tinted seasons when they played in the top flight. They didn't last long, but managed to do the double over Valencia in their first season up, and when they went down the following year the ship managed to sink with the band playing, otherwise known as a 5-1 win over Barcelona.

Almost the only event worthy of note for Levante between 1965 and the signing of Mijatovic in 2002 was the surreal capture of the 34-year-old Johan Cruyff in 1981. Money worries had brought him back to Spain from the Washington Diplomats and he was to turn out on ten occasions for Levante, scoring a couple of goals. Perhaps he liked their colours, but he didn't stay for long, packing his bags and returning home to help Ajax win the Dutch league in 1982.

However, depending on your reading of history, it may not be entirely accurate to maintain that Levante have never won a significant trophy. In fact, for many, they won the most significant of the lot. When the Civil War broke out in 1936, the league programme was, of course, suspended 'until further notice'. In the area that had not fallen to Franco, the Republican civil authorities formed La Liga del Mediterráneo (The Mediterranean League) and La Copa de la España Libre (The Free Spain Cup), both played in 1937. There is a whole book waiting to be written about these tournaments, but suffice to say that for those of more democratic sensibilities, their political resonance outshines many a subsequent one, with apologies to Real Madrid.

The idea was that the knock-out tournament, to be played in venues in Valencia and Barcelona, would feature the top four finishers in the league competition, which consisted of eight teams from the region. The league, after 14 games, was won inevitably by Barça, with Español in second place, followed by Girona and Valencia. But Barcelona were then invited to tour Mexico and the United States in a fund-raising venture for the Republican cause and so Levante, who had finished fifth, took their place – and went on to win the final in Barcelona, 1-0 against Valencia.

Levante are rightly proud of this win, which is generally relegated to a historical footnote due to the Spanish federation's refusal to recognise the tournament as official. Both Levante and Valencia supporters, in rare acts of solidarity, have from time to time lobbied the authorities to change their policy and inscribe the result in the official records, but they have been met with firm refusals. You can imagine the political rumpus that would be caused by recognition of the tournament, despite the fading memory of Spain's fascism.

Just in case you thought the romantics might be winning the day too easily, it should be noted that the Republican authorities in both Valencia and Barcelona turned down Real Madrid's application to join the wartime league. Madrid, despite its later associations with the fascists, was one of the last cities to fall to Franco, and in 1937 its most famous football club was being run by a communist, Antonio Ortega. As noted in chapter five, official histories of the club pretend that he never existed, and cite Rafael Sánchez Guerra as the president during this period, a particularly sordid piece of revisionism by those who would prefer to pretend, for reasons best known to themselves, that Real Madrid have always inclined to the right of the political spectrum.

Why Madrid were excluded in 1937 is open to all kinds of political and practical interpretations. Maybe the Valencianos were unsure of Madrid's ability to stave off Franco's forces as the military situation worsened. But a less sympathetic historian would cite the exclusion as a good example of the inability of the Republicans to come to terms with themselves and make up their minds who they really wanted in their ranks. The antagonism that was to develop within the unholy mixture of anarchists, communists and just-about-everythingists eventually proved to be Franco's ace card. From a purely footballing perspective, however, hard-core Levante supporters have always cited this trophy as proof of their credentials.

The last concrete chapter in the Levante-Valencia relationship was written in 1999 when the two clubs met in the fourth round of the King's Cup at Levante's Estadi Ciutat de Valencia, Valencia winning 3-0. The ground, built in 1969, is north of Mestalla on the city's outskirts, and has moved the club slightly away from its dockside roots. As if to further emphasise the gap that had opened up between the two clubs, Valencia went on to win the final.

Indeed, as early as the 1950s, the public variety of this intra-regional *morbo* had definitely shifted to the rivalry between Valencia and Barcelona, although as mentioned earlier, it was of a rather bland variety until the official arrival of democracy in 1978. Nevertheless, there have been some classic encounters between the two sides, the first of which occurred in the final of the domestic cup in 1954, in which an inspired Valencia hammered Barcelona 3-0, reviving dreams of a return to the glory days of the 1940s. The successes of that era seem to contradict the thesis that it was only the sides that were in political favour that managed to rise from the smoking ruins of the Civil War.

Barelona's argument for their own quickish recovery is that despite all of Franco's attempts to crush them, they simply would not lie down. Valencia have never gone in for this type of political chest-beating, attributing their emergence instead to the accession of Luis Casanova to the presidential seat, and to the fact that most of their prewar squad returned after the fighting. Many other clubs lost players to exile or execution, but despite the resistance of the city, Valencia's young squad remained virtually intact. Mestalla, almost ruined in the fighting, was restored and in 1942 Valencia won their first league title, ushering in an eight-year period in which only Sevilla (1946) managed to wrest the trophy from teams in cities that had been on the republican side (Barcelona and Valencia) or which belonged to communities culturally opposed to Franco's centralism (Bilbao).

Valencia's 1942 title cut short the postwar dominance of Atlético Aviación (soon to be known as Atlético Madrid), and seemed to herald a period in which football could, theoretically at least, redress the political and military balance. Valencia's forward line, the famous *delantera eléctrica* (electric attack) consisted of Epi, Amadeo, Mundo, Asensi and Gorostiza, legends in Valencian circles and the simplest reason of all for Valencia's domination of the period.

After the 1954 cup win, Valencia went through a lull until they decided to make the old Fairs Cup their personal property in the early Sixties, establishing the club's image as an achiever in Europe, if not in Spain. This image has stuck, and has been reinforced by the recent Champions League runs, but the statistics are not as convincing as the legend. The club did appear in the Fairs Cup final for three consecutive seasons, winning the first two and losing the third to compatriots Zaragoza, in Barcelona (for two seasons the final was played as a single match). The first of the two cups was won in 1962 against Barcelona themselves, with Valencia winning the first leg by the historic score of 6-2 in Mestalla.

But after 1964, this so-called European presence waited another 16 years before reasserting itself, this time at Heysel against Arsenal. Valencia would meet Arsenal again in 2001 on their way to a second consecutive Champions League final, but the period in between was mundane, brightened only briefly in the early 1980s by the decision of Mario Kempes to choose Valencia over Barcelona. Even his presence produced no trophies, but it at least gave some credence to the Valencianos' claim that their club always prized flair and attacking style. The 'European period' was perhaps more important from this point of view than for the credibility of trophies themselves. The Fairs Cup was naturally looked down on by the Spanish press, not least because of Madrid's domination of the European Cup, but Valencia's wins certainly came with a flood of goals. In 1961-62 they thrashed Nottingham Forest (7-1 on aggregate) and MTK Budapest (10-3) and the following year put out no fewer than three Scottish teams, caning Celtic and Hibs but requiring a third match in Lisbon to put out Dunfermline (1-0), after winning 4-0 in the Mestella then going down 6-2 away.

The fact that Valencia won the league in 1971 under Di Stéfano could not hide the fact that the team had lost its swashbuckling spirit, established under the auspices of players like the Brazilian Waldo Machado, Hector Núnez and Vicente Guillot. Di Stéfano, the greatest forward ever to grace the fields of Spanish football, turned out to be a manager of wholly defensive instincts. The fact that Valencia blew the double that year by losing 4-3 to Barcelona in an excellent cup final was a freak – the side only conceded 19 goals in the league that season. Di Stéfano lasted until 1973, when he left for Sporting Lisbon, and although he was to return briefly for the season 1979-1980, his period in charge is looked back upon with little affection.

The Valencia that the more recent Euro-audience has got to know is something of a combination of the flair and the defensive models. The side that emerged in the late 1990s was memorable for its sheer speed and power, overwhelming opponents with lightning-quick breaks from a midfield orchestrated by the excellent Gaizka Mendieta and Kily Gonzales, feeding the wonderful predatory skills of the Argentine Claudio López, endearingly nicknamed *Piojo* (louse) for his tendency to irritate defenders. López never shone to the same extent in the blue and white stripes of his country, but for Valencia he was simply wonderful – for many the best forward in the Spanish league between 1998 and 2000, after which he left (reluctantly) for Lazio.

When Valencia finally began to reap what they had been sowing for several seasons, it was done without López, leading to accusations in certain sections of the press that their eventual successes were based more on a defence that took no prisoners than on flair – but the supporters for once were not complaining. Goalkeeper Santiago Cañizares and his solid back-line of Ayala, Carboni and Pellegrino were indeed the key men behind the title win of 2002, with the emergence of Ruben Baraja in midfield crucial in covering the much-lamented departure of Mendieta, also to Lazio. Baraja, a more combative, less cerebral type than Mendieta, mirrored the basic change to the side, but the signing of the young pup Carlos Aimar from Argentina was enough to keep the romantics happy.

Valencia, with Deportivo, is the club that has crossed the millennium with the clearest intention of breaking the old monopoly. Spain may well have heard such claims before, but a weekly glance at the frightening line-ups of these two teams, stocked with players that Real Madrid and Barcelona would love to get their hands on, suggests there may be substance behind them this time. It seems that the political democracy that was ushered in a quarter of a century ago may finally be bringing in its wake a genuine sporting one.

9. yokels, cucumbers and mattress makers

Spanish club culture

Spain is a deeply ritualistic country. It puts an impressive amount of time and effort into preserving a kaleidoscopic array of traditions, most of them celebrated in the form of local *fiestas*. The ultimate book on Spain would be one in which the author spent each of the 365 days of the year in a different *pueblo* with a different *fiesta*. Despite the obvious problems that this would pose for the liver, the project is perfectly feasible. Apart from the ever-burgeoning number of saints' days (the day is surely not far off when a footballer will enter the distinguished list) and all the obscure local knees-ups, there are workers' days, days to celebrate the founding of the town or city, Constitution Day, sports day, love-thy-neighbour day and any manner of other occasions that provide a good excuse for a day off.

And they do it well. For a country that is so famously anti-authoritarian and seemingly so anarchic in its social behaviour, there is an awesome level of conformity when it comes to the *fiestas*. Where British youth would sneer, young Spaniards dress up and do all manner of curious things without the slightest sign of self-consciousness. Brought up on a paler diet of irony and individualism, the British settler cannot fail to be impressed by the back-slapping togetherness that he or she will encounter on a dizzying number of social occasions throughout the year. The outsiders can either choose to add their voices to the throng or retain their *forma de ser* (way of being), hiding away for years in their attics. There are plenty of examples of both choices.

Of course, all these roots and rituals were established in the soil long before football washed up on Iberian shores. Soon after its arrival, local cultures simply added football to their weekly revelries, weaving it into the fabric of their life. All the stuff about Spanish football only becoming popular under Franco – as a means of diverting the population's attention from social ills – is a myth propagated by writers whose only perspective on Spain is through a three-lens telescope: before Franco, during Franco and after Franco. As soon as you put the telescope down and begin to look closely at the development of the game in Spain, the evidence kicks you in your unprotected eye.

Football was extremely popular in the period leading up to the Civil War, and had been gathering a steady momentum even before then. Barcelona and Real Madrid disliked each other from the off, for the simple reason that they arose from such differing regional backgrounds. Football could not fail in Spain, and the team that was named after its *pueblo* quickly became an extension of its soul. Almost any team in Spain that has been within sniffing distance of the top division has come to represent its community more strongly than either their *fiestas*, their people or their histories.

That they have become more famous than the sum of their cultural parts should nevertheless not blind us to the fact that they still retain the essence of their *pueblos* much more than do almost all the big English teams (Newcastle is perhaps an exception). Manchester United and Manchester City may once have represented distinct communities in the city, but neither has ever encapsulated Manchester in the way that Barça have embodied the spirit of their community. Manchester United have created their own set of signs and are an institution in their own right, rather than an extension of their local culture.

In Spain, however, the club is its surrounding community incarnate, and the two still feed off each other in a highly-charged symbiosis. Even the massive influx of foreign mercenaries has not changed that. When Atlético Madrid were relegated at the end of the 1999-2000 season, several players had their tyres slashed in the club car park and were subjected to all manner of abuse during open-door training-sessions. Logroñés, relegated the same year down to Segunda B, needed police protection for the manager Marco Boronat after the final game, and the players were trapped in the dressing-room for several hours by gangs of marauding fans looking to punish those they held responsible for besmirching the community image. Oviedo's players were subjected to similarly frightening levels of abuse from their fans when they took the same route down at the end of the 2002-03 season.

The success of Michael Robinson's weekly TV programme *El día después* lies in the fact that it is less about football than about the culture that football springs from. Sections of the programme concentrate on odd rituals, nicknames, ground names, eccentric supporters and so on. It sounds like a familiar fanzine-type approach, but it is much more than that, because it always focuses on the community, however small. The characters who come out of the woodwork to explain the semiotics of their clubs are always *del pueblo*. The football is somehow secondary. The programme would die a quick death in England, but has deservedly prospered in Spain because it understands how the local stadium has become a four-sided enclosure of everything that lies outside, an easy expression of the particular colour and crumble of the soil. It should hardly come as a surprise, then, that the symbols of the clubs, their colours, nicknames and songs are of paramount importance.

The importance of club colours in Spain is indicated by the fact that the press have developed a writing code that insists on referring to teams as, for example, *los verdiblancos* (the green and whites). The phenomenon appears in reports as far back as the 1920s and has now even spread to Basque, so that Real Sociedad are referred to in the local Spanish-language press as *El equipo txuri-urdin*, a curious mixture of Spanish (*el equipo*) and Basque, where the final compound means 'white-and-blue' – perhaps uniquely in the football world, putting the white first. While the power of the plain colour has been diminished everywhere by shirt advertising (except Barcelona and Athletic Bilbao – and now they too seem to be only waiting for the right offer), in Spain something survives, for although the kits change from year to year, the basic designs remain unchanged. To muck about too much with the colours would be seen as an affront to the *pueblo* and its values, and as a lack of respect for history. In a land that does not forget easily, symbolism is important. Clubs' colours have also, in some cases, become powerful tokens suggestive of specific ideologies – Barcelona's distinctive colours, for example, being part and parcel now of Catalanism.

The colours of many of the clubs are simply those of their town or city, as portrayed on the city *escudo* (shield). This probably explains why few Spanish clubs go in for flamboyant kits. There are some exceptions, of course. Real Valladolid, although they stuck faithfully to the city colours and the colours of Castile, must have regretted at some point in their history their decision, taken in 1922, to play in violet and white stripes. In fact the exact shade lies somewhere between lilac and lavender and is the oddest colour I can recall seeing a football team play in. The club's nickname is *Los Pucelanos*, which the innocent observer might assume to have something to do with puce but which in fact refers to the Roman name for the city.

Real Madrid have a smidgen of the same Castilian colour on the trimmings of their shirts, although the club itself perversely insists that the colour is blue. It was the Englishman Arthur Johnson, the same man who scored Real Madrid's first ever goal against Barcelona in their original 1902 meeting, who suggested that they wear all-white with blue(ish) trimmings – the colours of Johnson's favourite team back home, Corinthians. Johnson also proposed that for friendly games, the team should wear a diagonal purple slash across the white shirts, but that for official ones they should sport white shirts and shorts with black socks, not forgetting, of course, the *de rigueur* cloth cap – which in this case had to be dark blue. Johnson's insistence on a strict code of dress seems to have been an attempt to import what he saw as the discipline and organisation of the Corinthians into the Madrid set-up, a fussiness that was not apparent in the colours and kit of the other embryonic organisations of the time.

It seems curious that Madrid did not show a little more imagination on the colour front, given that the club was founded by cloth merchants. However, there has been little variation in their colours since the turn of the century, a sure sign that they have been happy with the talismanic qualities of their choice. The colours (or lack of them) of Spain's most famous club gave rise to their nickname *Los Merengues* (the Meringues), said to have been coined way back in 1913. It seems a rather sissyish nickname for such a powerful, self-conscious club.

Colour was originally a sign of modest wealth in football circles. At the turn of the century, less than 50 years after the first artificial dyes were produced by the Englishman William Perkin, it was simply a cheaper option to play in white. Of the first four important Spanish clubs, Huelva and Real Madrid made the simpler choice of white shirts, Athletic Bilbao wore blue and white stripes and Barcelona their famous blue-reddish combination. Huelva changed to blue and white stripes in 1909, apparently after a member of the Club Colón spotted an English sailor walking down the main street in such a shirt. The sailor explained that it was a left-over from a batch his ship had delivered to San Sebastián en route from England. That was his story anyway.

It's certainly true that Real Sociedad first wore the stripes in that same year, their predecessors Club Ciclista having also gone in for all-white. The blue and white colours are those of the city, as indeed they are of Huelva. Whatever the truth about the origins of Barcelona's colours (see chapter four) it is interesting that the club which most strongly represents the idea of the 'community flagship' never bothered to adopt red and yellow, the colours of their region since the tenth century, well before they came to represent Spain.

morbo

Athletic Bilbao, as mentioned in chapter three, finally settled on red and white in 1914, apparently in homage to Sunderland, although others claim it was to cement the relationship the city enjoyed with Southampton, for nautical reasons. The problem with the Sunderland theory is that it seems to have arisen out of convenience – Bilbao's bar-room historians having realised that it offered more kudos. The Southampton one seems much more likely, given the relative closeness of the port.

There is, of course, a purely aesthetic side to all of this. As the Sky advertisement said, when you pick a football team you pick them for life, but since you are usually taken along for the first time by a parent you don't have much choice about your adopted team's colours. In many cases, you have to learn to love them, and yet the first time that you see a game live, perhaps in the mellow light of an August Saturday afternoon, you cannot fail to be captivated by the colours of the teams. The colour of the opponents' shirts becomes fixed in your head like a folk-memory which cannot be dislodged. The aesthetic is purely subjective, all yours, and is nourished with every subsequent game.

The colours teams wear often determine your disposition towards them, so that I always had a soft spot for Wolves as a kid, so fond was I of their golden shirts. Arsenal I never liked, their white sleeves clashing too garishly with their spring-tomato chests, and any teams that went in for over-colourful patterns or combinations were instinctively marked down as losers, as if they were compensating for something that was lacking in their football. Sunday League Division Eight teams always go in for rainbow kits. The taxi driver in Seville who told me he had decided to support Valencia because he liked their plain colours as a child was expressing something almost fetishistic that I immediately understood. Why on earth should someone from a strong footballing city like Seville decide to support a team from another place simply because they wore white shirts and black shorts? The fact that he didn't like the green and white stripes of Betis struck me as incidental. There is no rational explanation for such behaviour – which is surely the whole point.

When I first came to Spain it was like being a child all over again. Watching the Sunday night round-ups of teams I had never heard of and whose traditions I knew nothing of defaulted me back to a child's perspective where all the sights and sounds take on a heightened significance. My reactions to the teams' colours was immediate and unforgiving. Valladolid's shirts struck me as unsettling and a crime against all reasonable taste. Cádiz were bottom of the First Division at the time and the reasons were written all over their canary yellow shirts with blue trimmings. On the other hand, I immediately took to Oviedo, whose simple Evertonian combination of blue shirts and white shorts came over as workmanlike and honest.

There were an awful lot of stripes about, nine of the 20 teams then in the First Division sporting them. No fewer than four wore red and white stripes – Bilbao, Logroñés, Sporting Gijón and Atlético Madrid – which seemed disproportionate. I later discovered that in the early years of the century these were the cheapest stripes to manufacture because the same combination was used for bed mattresses. The cloth, already prepared and dyed for the bedding industry, could easily be converted into football kits. Although Bilbao and Atlético Madrid started out with blue and white stripes, the discovery that red and white was cheaper seems to have helped persuade them to change. Atlético did so first, earning themselves the nickname *Los Colchoneros* (the mattress-makers) which has stuck to this day.

Logroñés, from the wine region of La Rioja, allege that their stripes represent red and white grapes – a rather dubious claim since the region is only really famous for its red, and anyway the grapes that produce the white wine are green. Still, they wouldn't have got very far with red and green stripes, so maybe what they say is true. Sporting Gijón simply took the red and white stripes that figure on the city's coat of arms and their club is more famous for other reasons – for example, that they have the supporters with the most violent reputation in the land and that their ground, El Molinón, is the only major stadium in Europe to have been designed by a female architect.

Espanyol were one of three clubs wearing blue and white stripes – along with Deportivo de La Coruña and Real Sociedad – although with a thick, blue, central stripe down the middle which came over as stodgy and unimaginative. Espanyol are one of the few clubs in Spain to have changed their colours completely from the original choice. In 1900 they first turned out as Sociedad Español de Foot-Ball in bright yellow shirts, the colour of the shorts being left to the discretion of the individual players. They were one of the first teams to go in for a truly jolly colour, but only because a friend of the club founder who ran a textile business happened to have several yards of yellow material left over after providing the table-cloths for a royal banquet. The stuff must have run out fairly quickly or shrunk in the wash because by 1901 they had changed to white shirts and blue shorts. The present-day colours were adopted in 1910 after a club member proposed that the shirts should copy the pattern on a coat of arms of a famous Catalan admiral.

Deportivo went in for fatter stripes too, but the shirts and general design were a bit cleverer, with a natty white line at the thigh end of the blue shorts, and hoops on the arms to break the line of the stripes, a little whimsy suggestive of ambition and the desire to do things a tad differently. Blue and white are the colours of Galicia, although the other two big sides in the region, Compostela and Celta de Vigo, have adopted a more Man City type of blue to distinguish themselves from the rather heavy shade of Depor's kit. Celta look fine, but Compostela's choice of a half sky-blue, half white shirt makes it look as though it has run in the wash.

Villareal, from near Castellón on Spain's eastern coast, made their debut in the top flight in 1998 and brought an unusual kit story with them. Nicknamed, rather obscurely, the Submarines (allegedly after the Beatles song) their yellow shirts date back to 1947 when the son of the club's president travelled to the nearest big shopping city (Valencia) to buy some replacement white shirts and black shorts – then the team's official colours. Unfortunately, when he got to the store there were no white shirts in stock and, with the season about to start, he panicked and bought the only batch remaining, which happened to be yellow. On returning to Villareal the players thought the shirts were fine, but that they didn't go too well with the black shorts. The president's son, decisive if nothing else, travelled to Castellón this time and bought a batch of white shorts which he subsequently had dyed blue on the vote of the players. The club still sports the combination initiated by this act of democratic aesthetics.

When I arrived in 1991 Betis were just about to drop into the Second Division, but their green and white stripes stood out on the TV highlights as something vaguely radical, certainly out of the ordinary. It is not a common kit, perhaps because green is viewed, in parts of Europe at least, as an unlucky colour. A whole multitude of teams in Muslim countries wear green, of course, the colours of Islam. Seville's Arab connections, however, have nothing to do with the adoption of the green and white stripes by Betis.

In 1912, Manuel Ramos Asensio, one of the club's founding members, brought back a dozen green and black striped shirts from a business trip to Glasgow and proposed that Betis take up the colours. The team played five games in the new strip and lost them all. A replacement set with white stripes instead of black was stitched together for the next encounter, which Betis duly won. Superstition dictated that they continue with the lucky ones, and the green and black batch were consigned to the dustbin. Santander are the only other major team who wear green, although the first-choice kit has usually consisted of a white shirt with green trimmings, black shorts and green socks. Unlike Betis, the colours are taken from their region, Cantabria.

One thing that would surprise the British spectator about Spanish football is the frequency with which similarly kitted clubs turn out against each other wearing their true first-team colours. The Basque derbies between Athletic Bilbao and Real Sociedad always feature both teams in a veritable riot of stripes – an insistence on authenticity which has not always been followed in England. Although it is often difficult to distinguish the two teams, particularly on television, it makes for an edifying sight live. It feels like a throwback to a more innocent time, when players wore only numbers on their backs and were allowed to roll their socks down in injury time. And the habit is not confined to stripes. I recall seeing Burgos v Osasuna on television in 1992, with both sides wearing almost identical red shirts. Where Osasuna had black shorts and black socks, Burgos replied with white, but it was nevertheless a strange sight and one that is unthinkable now.

In contrast to the rich histories of their colours, Spanish clubs boast a relatively poor collection of nicknames. Some may have disappeared in the mists of time due to the aforementioned tendency of the press to refer to so many of the clubs by their shirt colours – red 'n' whites, blue 'n' whites, green 'n' whites. Yet this is still surprising, given the importance of ritual and myth at *pueblo* level in Spain; fertile ground, one would have thought, for a vibrant nicknaming culture. Of course, there are some notable exceptions.

When I did my geography O-level exam, we had to mark on a map the types of industry belonging to certain towns and regions. Almost all the towns had football teams, and since I possessed a sad but unerring knowledge of their nicknames, it was a simple piece of deduction to provide the answers. I knew Northampton were called the Cobblers, which led me to the obvious conclusion that the area must have been famous for shoe production, and therefore leather. I came to the same correct answer for Walsall (Saddlers), Scunthorpe (Iron) and Sheffield (Blades), though I still don't know if the examiner was impressed by my assertion that Merseyside was famous for the production of sweets and music. Anyway, I passed, because so many nicknames of English clubs echo the original industries of their towns and cities.

In Spain, this is hardly the case at all. Almost the only club whose industrial pedigree is reflected in their nickname is Second Division Eibar, a tiny town in the Basque country whose team are known as *Los Armeros* (the Gunners) because of the previously important gun-making business there. Albacete, yo-yoing between the first and second divisions in recent seasons, are called *El Queso Mecánico* (the Clockwork Cheese), a nickname that presumably dates from the appearance of Kubrick's film, combined with the abundance of Manchego cheese in the region. The Spanish press have for some years now used the phrase *La Naranja Mecánica* (Clockwork Orange) to describe the Dutch team of the Seventies.

Mérida, from Extremadura in the south west, are known as *Los Romanos*, from which you might reasonably conclude that the town was important for its Roman remains, and you would be right. It is certainly more famous for its historical relics than for its football team, demoted from Segunda A at the end of 1999-2000 for financial irregularities and still wallowing in Segunda B at the time of writing. Betis are known as *Los Pepinos* (the cucumbers), presumably in reference to their green stripes. Osasuna, from Pamplona, are called *Los Rojillos*, meaning 'the little red ones' (their shirts are red) in allusion to the fact that the people of Navarre have a well-known and endearing tendency to put a diminutive suffix on most of their adjectives – either 'illo' or 'iko'. I once heard a native of Navarre refer to a friend as '*grandiko*', meaning literally 'little big'.

Club Deportivo Alavés, from Vitoria, the administrative capital of the Basque Country, are known as *Los Babazorros*, a strange nickname that no one seems to be able to explain satisfactorily. Indeed, when I rang the club, the official who answered my call claimed he had 'no idea'. The club's mascot is a creature that resembles a fox or coyote, and *zorros* means 'foxes'. So the name could mean 'slavering foxes', since *baba* is the stuff that runs down babies' chins. There are undoubtedly plenty of foxes in the Alava region, but it is unclear as to whether they are of the slobbering variety. Leicester City never had such problems.

However, it would appear that in fact *babazorro* is from the wholly unrelated Basque tongue and means something on the negative side of the English word 'yokel', with connotations of 'country bumpkin' or 'narrow-minded peasant'. The folks who follow Alavés are not much better off, it would seem, than Barcelona's fans, who cheerfully refer to themselves as arseholes (*culés*).

Baba in Basque is a small, hard type of broad bean which, along with potatoes (for which Alava is actually more famed), must have been the staple diet of the population in the leaner years of the century. The *Babazorros* were literally 'folks too keen on broad beans', the shorthand implication being that they had nothing else to eat and were therefore undernourished, down-at-heel yokels. As if this were not enough, another interpretation of the phrase is that *baba* is a defective shortening of the Spanish word for 'potato' and that the *zorro* is some kind of tick or aphid that blighted the crop from time to time. What must it sound like when the supporters proudly sing '*Somos los babazorros*', which literally means 'We are the potato aphids'? The club mascot should logically be a potato or a broad bean, but with Alavés' promotion to the top flight in 1998 after an excellent cup run, and subsequently wonderful romp through the UEFA Cup tournament in 2001 where they lost in an epic final to Liverpool, the marketing department at the club must have decided to stick with the salivating fox for image purposes.

Perhaps due to its oddity, the Alavés nickname was always destined to leave its native shores. This indeed happened two days before the final in Dortmund after I had mentioned the 'potato aphids' in a *Guardian* article. The *Daily Mirror* picked up on the piece and fed it to Liverpool's supporters, several of whom could be seen walking down the streets of Dortmund with the curious banner reading 'Scousers eat Aphids!'. Even for the German onlookers, many of whom undoubtedly spoke decent English, the phrase must have caused a few problems.

Competing interpretations also jostle for recognition around Espanyol's famous nickname, *Los Periquitos* (parakeets). Originally, as mentioned above, they wore yellow and were known, logically enough, as *Los Canarios*. By 1910, the team had adopted their present colours of fat blue and white stripes, but parakeets are hardly the first thing that comes to mind when contemplating this colour combination. One suggestion is that the name belonged to a small cartoon cat, El Periquito, a character in a satirical magazine published in Barcelona in the first decade of the century. Español's was the first ground in Catalonia to feature terracing and a ticket-booth – the reason, according to the magazine, why so few people turned up to the games, presumably because they would have had to pay. The Catalans have a reputation in Spain for being tight-fisted, and they themselves are often the first to agree.

The magazine, published by an editor who favoured Barça, was trying to say that only 'four cats' turned up to Español's matches – a colloquial phrase meaning 'hardly anyone'. (The most famous bohemian hang-out in turn of the century Barcelona, frequented by Picasso, was also called *Els Quatre Gats*.) But from there it is a bit of leap to suggest that because of one cat in a magazine the supporters (the four cats) became associated with *periquitos* in general. Even more obscure is the idea that the nickname originated from the tendency of those same four cats to call the stadium *La Manigua* (the jungle), due to an excess of palm trees and vegetation around the site. Of course, parakeets hang around this sort of habitat, but so do tarantulas and howler monkeys.

Another version maintains that the name became associated with the club because of an old man who used to sell nuts outside the Sarrià stadium on match days, with a couple of cheerful (blue and white) budgerigars perched on each shoulder. However, it seems unlikely that this could have occurred without someone taking his photograph and as far as anyone knows there is no documentary evidence of the phantom nut-seller and his blue and white striped birds. Whatever the truth, the club had a happy centenary in 2000, winning the King's Cup against the mattress-makers of Atlético Madrid, their first trophy since 1940, a win made all the sweeter by Barcelona's failure to win anything at all.

Valencia are known as *Los Ché* (or sometimes *Los Chés*) – nothing to do with South American revolutionaries and everything to do with the idiosyncratic habit their citizens have of greeting each other with this word, which, as we have seen, means something like 'mate' in Valenciano. The Valencians are proud of their language and take most unkindly to those who suggest it is a dialect of Catalan, even though it is. It is interesting that their nickname is one of the few that uses the regional language to advertise a particular cultural trait that is remotely positive. The arseholes of Barcelona and the yokels of Alavés hardly qualify, and none of the Galician teams bothers to use the Gallego language in their nicknames.

Indeed, when it comes to boring nicknames, the Galicians of Compostela take some beating, being known as *Compos*. The western folks of Spain in general seem rather timid in their approach to nicknaming, Deportivo de La Coruña being simply known as Super Depor and Celta de Vigo not bothering with one at all.

If nicknames reveal a somewhat restrained side to the Spanish character, it is probably because they are really more concerned with their club songs, or *himnos*. These are much closer to the crux of the matter, and reveal a side to Spanish football wholly lacking in Britain. This may be due to the fact that no British sporting audience could possibly bear 90 minutes in the close presence of an oompah band, blasting out the club song in a rather tired but determined way, trumpets parping and cymbals clashing in a manner oblivious to time, the score and sweet reason. The band is often official and is allocated a certain place in the ground, so it is possible to buy your seat as far away as possible. Nevertheless, the sound drones on, win, lose or draw. When the team is winning, however, the pace can perk up and the spectators suddenly add lyrics to the tune, a spectacle that almost casually demonstrates why surrealism found the Spanish soil so accommodating.

The curious thing about the club songs, apart from the fact that all professional teams have them, is the uniformity of their style and lyrical content. Many date back to the clubs' origins, although several have an original song and a 'modern' one, often composed in the late Forties or early Fifties, when many clubs felt reborn after the privations of the Civil War and the Second World War. Nevertheless, hardly any of these songs could be used by a historical researcher as evidence of social origins or of local culture. Instead, almost all opt for hyperbole and poetic devices that would bring an appreciative smile to the face of the most dedicated of doggerel merchants.

The club songs all have a sort of call-to-arms section, usually at the end of the final verse or as part of the rabble-rousing chorus. Each adopts a slightly different neologism to bleat out, a completely meaningless word designed to extract maximum wind from the lungs. For example, Real Madrid's rallying phrase, repeated at the end in case you miss it the first time, goes: '¡*Hala Madrid! ¡Hala Madrid!*' Celta also go for *hala*, but add the line '*Celta, Celta, ra-ra-ra*' just in case anyone was thinking of accusing them of a lack of originality. Zaragoza's chorus begins '¡*Aupa Zaragoza!*', which means more or less the same as *hala*. Real Oviedo, Sporting Gijón and Compostela are also dedicated '*aupa*' merchants. Athletic Bilbao's song, written in Basque of course, has the wonderful line '¡*Athletic eup!*', which sounds like it originated in deepest Yorkshire. Tenerife's hookline, however, seems to have come from some other space-time continuum altogether. Apparently given its first airing before a game against Murcia in 1960, it was written by the (then) popular island group *Los Huaracheros* and features a rallying-call that can only have been inspired by some early version of LSD: '¡*Riqui-raca-sumba-raca, sin-bon-ba! ¡Ria Ria Ria, rian-pun-ta!*' Follow that. Racing Santander had a decent stab in 1979, coming up with '¡*A la vi, a la vá, a la bim bom bá! ¡Racing, Racing, ra-ra-ra!*' And all of this produced and sung in irony-free zones.

The club song of Logroñés, a *pasadoble* penned by one J Eizaga way back in 1910, has some uncharacteristically interesting lines. Relegated to Segunda B in 2000, after a highly successful spell in the top division in the early Nineties, the modest little outfit from the small town of Logroño in La Rioja have a reputation for harbouring some fearsome supporters, hardened, it is said, by years of working the land. It is also said that Real Madrid's notorious *Ultras Sur* would only refuse to travel to two grounds – those of Sporting Gijón and Logroñés. The song goes:

> The wine of La Rioja, I carry in my blood
> And I am noble or hard, depending on how I am treated
> I was taught in La Rioja that the dignity of sport is reflected
> in how you play
> So depending on how they treat me, depending on how
> they treat me, I'll treat them in kind

It's as if the author anticipated the club's subsequent reputation, and it certainly sums up the peculiarity of the region, mile upon mile of lines of black vines, stretching as far as the eye can see, broken occasionally by tiny villages rising up suddenly from the mildly rolling landscape, where children back away from you and stare as if you have just emerged from a spacecraft. The whole area seems slightly time-warped, and its people rough-edged and suspicious, as in the song. Play fair with them and they'll treat you OK, but mess them around and watch out, implies the song.

I travelled to their old ground, Las Gaunas, in 1994, to see Real Sociedad take them to the cleaners, 4-0. On the way back to the coach I was to regret the scoreline as the group I had travelled with were surrounded by a large group of snarling teenagers accusing us of being Basque terrorists. Two of my companions were sprayed with red paint and another temporarily blinded by what looked like CS gas. Nasty stuff, and nothing like your average away-day experience in Spain.

Another strongly uniform characteristic of the club songs is the attempt to depict in a couple of exalted phrases the peculiar hallmark of the team – resulting in a series of absurdly overblown epithets that make *Simply the Best* look like an exercise in self-effacing modesty. Real Madrid, as one might expect, set the tone succinctly with their song *¡Hala Madrid!*, written in 1952 on the cusp of their greatest period. An engineer by the name of Luís María Segovia had previously written a *pasadoble* in 1903 imaginatively titled *¡Goal!*, English spelling and all, but by 1952 the club obviously felt the need for a new injection of spirit:

Of all the sporting glories
That excel throughout the country
See Madrid with her flag flying
Clean and white that never fades
Club of noble descent and generous spirit
All nerve and heart and sinew
Young and old, young and old
Never forget her honour...

Notice the appeal to the cleanliness of the colours and the 'noble descent'. The Spanish word is *castizo,* a heavily charged expression that suggests a purified, aristocratic blood-line running through the corridors of the Bernabéu – a significant choice of word for an institution so concerned with representing a certain vision of Spain, patriarchal and certainly Castilian. The song may be referring to the club's early backing from the Conde de La Quinta de La Enrajada. Naturally, there is no place in the song for the fact that the club's founders were Catalans.

For the centenary in 2002, the club turned to a local rock musician, José María Cano, to update the song, but to preserve the traditional feel. He certainly did that, coming up with an operatic belter entitled, surprisingly, *Hala Madrid,* which was handed to Plácido Domingo to interpret. The song is highly traditional and emotional, building up to a crescendo worthy of Handel's *Messiah.* The melody is so stirring that when it dies away and you're left with a mere football match, the bathos seems absurd. But it suited the idea of the club's centenary perfectly – patriarchal, emotional, manly – all the things that Madrid once thought itself to be.

Madrid are not alone in their pretensions, perhaps not surprisingly, since club songs are unlikely to proclaim 'We are crap' or 'We have ideas above our station', however true such sentiments may be. Zaragoza make a big point of the fact that they represent the Aragón region, and the song's author writes of the club's 'thoroughbred lineage, visible in how we play'. They go on to celebrate 'Nobility and valour, the flag and pride of Aragón... the team is a giant, bestriding the region'. That wasn't saying much in 2002, when Zaragoza were relegated, although they did bounce straight back again in the true style of thoroughbred giants.

Sevilla also boast of their *casta,* or 'good breeding', while Espanyol talk up the royal part of their name as if they were the only club to have been given the King's nod of approval. Their lap-doggish repetition makes it look as if they are clutching at straws;

> Royal Club Espanyol
> Espanyol, you're royal, truly royal
> Your nobility will justify your ends

Whatever those 'ends' might be. Some also seek, through the lenient spirit of poetic licence, to make rather grander claims for their clubs than is reflected in the prosaic reality of their empty trophy cabinets. Sporting Gijón, admittedly no slouches historically, but as yet to win a major trophy in their 98-year history, must surely blush when they sing the rousing chorus:

> Royal Sporting, famous team, made from a shining mill-stone
> With a brilliant history that shone fame upon the town
> On our ground no one can beat us
> From our quarry arose a valour
> That no one can forget
> Winner throughout the fields of Spain!

The song was penned in 1944, when the club had just come up from the Second Division and finished a decent seventh in their first season in the top flight. They went down again in 1948, but that's a minor detail. Unfortunately, the only record that Sporting have ever claimed is when they were relegated from the First Division in 1998 with only 13 points, the lowest number ever accumulated.

So colours, nicknames and songs – an unholy trinity that constitutes a sometimes baffling but endearing side to Spanish football, and one without which the game over here would be all the poorer. The phrase most beloved of local football journalists here is *sudar los colores de la camiseta* (to sweat the colours of the shirt), which is the highest praise accorded to the truly committed player. If he happens to know the words to the club song, so much the better.

10. *dark horses*

The perplexing failure of the national team

It was a warm, windy afternoon on the fashionable Ondaretta beach in San Sebastián. The tide was out and the pitch was perfect, banking down gently to the point where the waves had been breaking an hour before, with the dark sand rolled flat by the retreating water. It was 1992 and a good year for beach football. Some foreign students who had been getting together on the beach every Sunday had gradually been joined by some English expatriate teachers. By the time I wandered by one Sunday and asked for a game, the matches were almost 11-a-side and had inevitably developed into Brits v The Rest. Some weekends when the tide was up, the games would be less satisfying, with people drifting off after an hour or so, exhausted by the soft sand. This particular Sunday, however, conditions were perfect, and the Brits were looking for their first win of the month.

We must have been playing for half an hour or so when the two men appeared. They were locals, in their mid to late forties, and they asked me politely if they could play. 'Of course,' I replied, adding that one of them would have to become an honorary Brit for the duration, since for a change we had even numbers. They looked at each other and grinned. They looked a bit like Laurel and Hardy. One was stocky and going to fat, the other small and waif-like, thin as a beanpole, with a bright boyish face. The stocky one held up his hand in a voluntary gesture which I took to mean that he would play on my side, whereupon his Peter Pan friend jogged quietly on to the pitch and wandered through the ranks of Eurostudents to take his place in their defence.

I think we were losing when they turned up. We usually were, the games sadly mirroring our respective football cultures. The tubby chap who had just positioned himself in a sweeper's position behind our raggedy defence didn't look as though he was about to change our fortunes – until, that is, he got the ball. Every time the Euroboys got anywhere near our goal, the ball would somehow end up at the tubby man's feet, whereupon with a simple glance he would send the ball flying 30 or 40 yards straight to the feet of one of his new team-mates. We had obviously got lucky, for anyone with the slightest knowledge of football could see that he was an ex-pro. It was his anticipation, his immediate control of the ball and the way he could just ping it 30 yards to the feet of a pale, panting English teacher that told you.

His friend at the other end was more anonymous. The waif, when the ball arrived at his feet, simply played it square or knocked it back to the goalie. We'd obviously got the better player. Then suddenly, after about a quarter of an hour, his instincts appeared to get the better of him. Two-thirds of the way down the pitch, I pumped in a hopeful ball to one of the teachers lounging around in our opponents' goalmouth. The thin little man darted across, intercepted my pass, switched direction and shot off down the sea-slope to the wing. I ran down the bank to cut him off as he approached, but from what seemed like a trot he suddenly accelerated, made some imperceptible gesture as if to turn inside me, only to dance by on the outside as if I were a statue.

I turned to watch his progress, but it was almost too quick to register. Three or four defenders had either fallen over or been so confused by his change of pace and direction that he was already past them and shaping to shoot, his stocky friend not even bothering to intervene. Then the ball bobbled on one of the sandy divots kicked up in the previous half-hour and bounced up and away from the elf-like player straight to his waiting friend, who hoofed it high into the air and collapsed laughing, taking his friend's legs with him as he fell. The two of them collapsed in a heap, picked themselves up and then began to shoot nervous little glances around the beach. Clearly afraid of being recognised, they thanked us for the game and walked up the beach in the direction of the promenade.

After the game, several of the players were purring about the two visitors. One of 'The Rest' was a local, and when he realised what everyone was talking about he gasped in amazement at our ignorance. 'You mean you didn't know who they were?' he scoffed. 'That was López Ufarte and Miguel Echarri. The little one, López Ufarte – he played in the World Cup in 1982. He was my hero. I can't believe you didn't know who he was!'

Roberto López Ufarte, nicknamed 'the little devil', was capped 15 times for Spain, though it should have been more. He spent most of his career on the wing with Real Sociedad, scoring a more than respectable 112 goals. By the time John Toshack arrived in 1986 his powers were on the wane, slowed by a knee injury that was eventually to end his playing days. Toshack transferred him to Atlético Madrid but he returned to Real Sociedad to play deputy to a whole host of managers – which accounted for his presence that Sunday back in 1992.

Miguel Echarri, general secretary of the club and chief scout for foreign talent (none of us made the grade that Sunday) turned out for Real in the early Seventies, but had never played for Spain. But López Ufarte! One of the most outstanding wingers ever to grace the Spanish league, and a gentle, modest soul to boot. He had been happy to stand quietly at the back until some worm of professional instinct got the better of him, and then he'd exploded into life, leaving us standing. And yet he hadn't scored, although he'd clearly wanted to. He'd shaped to shoot, but the ball had bobbled away from him.

He was a brilliant player but he never quite made it on the international stage, particularly in the World Cup on home soil in 1982 where he failed, like most of his team-mates in *la selección*, to live up to expectations. Despite all the power and prestige of the Spanish league, despite all the triumphs of Spanish clubs in Europe, the national team has never really achieved anything. They have always looked as though they might do so, but when the crunch has come, they have been found wanting. The ball has bobbled up on the divot and bounced away. Fourth place in the World Cup of 1950, winners of the 1964 European Championship, defeated European finalists in 1984 in France – and that's about it. Even the runners-up medal they took home from the 1920 Olympics seems to have been won by dint of an administrative error.

Given the quality that has marched through the ranks of Spanish football during the past 80 years, it seems odd that such under-achievement should still be the hallmark of the nation's football, now institutionalised to such an extent that Spain are always the 'dark horses' of any tournament they qualify for, as if history has taught them the hard way that they must never expect too much.

Cervantes would have enjoyed the antics of the national team, for they have been nothing if not Quixotic. Their story is a faithful reflection of the adventures of Quijote and Sancho Panza – noble self-delusion, well-meaning failure and hubris by the cartload – although the pride of the Spanish has always been a complicated, neurotic sort of pride, tinged as it is with that fatal dose of inferiority.

When the Spanish football squad set out by train for Antwerp in the autumn of 1920 to compete in the Olympics (Spanish football did not turn professional until 1926), they travelled third class. Few of the players had set foot in a foreign country and the press angle at the time was all about how the involvement of the team in the tournament would simultaneously raise European awareness of Spain and enable the country, isolated down there in the Iberian peninsula, to measure itself against other nations.

It was as if they had no real conception of how good or bad they were likely to be. Before the global village, it was difficult to know what you were going to come up against, a factor that added a sort of picaresque spice to the matches, like Quijote traipsing through the countryside, never quite sure what or whom he was about to encounter. And when all the games were over and Spain went home with the silver medal, the self-delusion began to take shape.

The 1920 Games bear much of the responsibility for the subsequent 80 years of relative failure, and several of the incidents back then were to set the template for the years to come. Like England's failure to acknowledge the luck that accompanied them in 1966, the Spanish reaction of 'Well, we're not as bad as we thought' contributed to their failure four years later in Paris, where they were knocked out in the first game, 1-0 at the hands of the Italians.

The results in 1920 were quite impressive. In the opening game in Brussels they defeated Denmark 1-0, before losing to the hosts 3-1 in the quarter-final (complaining bitterly about the Dutch referee). The tournament was chaotic. Belgium won it by default, Czechoslovakia having walked off in protest in the final, dissatisfied with the (English) referee. With the Czechoslovaks banned, a tournament was quickly organised to award the silver and bronze medals, but most of the French players, accompanied by their manager Freddie Pentland, had already gone home after their semi-final defeat. So the four beaten quarter-finalists played a knockout for the right to meet the other losing semi-finalist, Holland, for the medals. Spain had already booked their train tickets home but, reprieved by this tortuous improvisation, they overcame Sweden 2-1 and Italy 2-0 and finally won 3-1 against the much-feared Holland in the second-place play-off.

Looking back at the Spanish side for the tournament, there was certainly enough quality in the ranks to explain the success. Zamora, Samitier, Pichichi, Txomín Acedo and the fearsome Basque captain José Belauste – whose full name was the no less fearsome José María Belausteguigoitia Pagazaurtundua – were players more than capable of competing with the cream of Europe's amateurs, although they were not to know it at the time.

It is obvious from the chronicle of the trip that all the strengths and weaknesses of the country were reflected in the performances, both on and off the pitch. The manager Paco Bru, having finally got the players he wanted for the tournament, received an untimely kick from the nation's achilles heel in the form of a players' mutiny the night before the game with Denmark. Patricio Arabolaza, the forward from Irún, was delegated by the majority Basque contingent to tell Bru that they thought the team for the opening game should comprise only Basques – a curious petition considering that this would have excluded Zamora and Samitier, by far the two most accomplished players.

It is unclear whether the request was motivated by political, personal or tactical reasons, but Bru, to his credit, ignored it and played the 'Spanish' contingent. They won, and Patricio got the only goal – the first player to score for Spain. The attempt to force the manager's hand was even more unreasonable when one recalls that it was Bru himself who had personally intervened in order to bring along the Basques, the federation having originally selected a 'Spanish only' squad for him.

The game against the hosts was played the next day, and the players got together more amicably with Bru to decide democratically on the line-up. Guillermo Eizaguirre, the reserve goalkeeper, having learnt during the meeting that the young Zamora was to continue between the posts, retired to his hotel room, packed his bags and caught the train home the next day. So much for team spirit. Then Belgium won 3-1 – so much for democracy.

Three days later the game against Sweden, a total bloodbath by all accounts, gave rise to the famous journalistic epithet *La furia española* (Spanish fury). The game also featured a seminal moment in Spanish football history, when, with the Swedes leading 1-0, the terrifying centre-back Belauste allegedly strode across the half-way line and hollered to the man on the ball, Sabino Bilbao, '¡A mi Sabino, que los arrollo!' (Give it to me, and I'll put it up 'em!). Sabino did as he was told, and Belauste scored a famous equaliser, to be followed by Acedo's winner in the 80th minute, by which time there were only seven Swedes and eight Spaniards left on the field. The other players were to be found in the local hospital or prostrate by the side of the pitch. The Swedes clearly contributed to the carnage, but the game became legendary in Spanish football, by serving up 'proof' that the *selección* represented a race of manly warriors.

The tricky problem for the *furia* legend – a word still used liberally by the Spanish press today – is that although Bru toughed out the Basque contingent's earlier petition, nine of the team who turned out against

Sweden were Basque. The phrase *furia española* therefore seems somewhat inappropriate, particularly if you are Basque and subscribe to the idea that Spain is a separate entity. It may be of some comfort to the more patriotic of the national team's followers that the scorer of the winner, Athletic Bilbao's *maketo* forward Txomín Acedo, was the brother of the great-grandfather of Spain's indisputably rightwing prime minister, José María Aznar. The *selección* website that eagerly offers this information also makes a point of spelling the Basque 'Txomin' in the Spanish way – 'Chomín' – an interesting little outbreak of revisionism. None of which changes the fact that the *furia* had nothing to do with the heartland of *España* – even the two 'Spanish' players in the side that day, Zamora and Samitier, were Catalans. But what the hell? Never let the facts get in the way of a good national legend.

The reporter from the *ABC* newspaper, unable to hide either his distaste for what he had seen, or his partiality, certainly did not do so:

> This afternoon witnessed the most barbaric and brutal game ever seen on a football field... the Swedes scored first and decided to protect their lead by turning to violence. Our boys responded by shouting 'Go for the man', which is exactly what they proceeded to do. We went on to win by sheer guts and resistance. The Swedes left the field beaten up and battered to a pulp, which was no less than they deserved.

The next day the limping army had to face the Italians without Samitier, Juan Arrate, Patricio, Acedo and Belauste himself – all victims of the battle. The squad was nothing if not resilient. They played the final 20 minutes with ten men, Zamora having taken an early bath after landing a right hook under the jaw of an Italian. Spain had three days to recover before meeting the Dutch, and were consequently able to put out a full-strength side which ran out 3-1 winners – the third a header from Pichichi, his first and only goal for Spain.

'Rubrik', the *ABC* journalist, underlined the symbolic significance of the success for his country's image:

> What was the impression of the other nations towards us? Enormously positive. No one had previously believed that in Spain this sport was so advanced. They all thought we were just bullfighters.

Rubrik goes on to record that the Spanish consul in Antwerp, Señor Yebra, 'praised them for having defended so sportingly and honourably the national name'. Sportingly and honourably? The infighting and outfighting hardly bear witness to such a conclusion. But the consul's words found an echo in the journalist's own summing-up:

> And on that agreeable note, our breasts filled with the lively memories of such unforgettable struggles, we boarded the train on the morrow to return to our great country, more than satisfied with our patriotic achievements.

Of course, when the train reached the Belgian border, Zamora was arrested by the authorities for smuggling out a case of cigars and the whole squad were detained for several hours at Feignies police station while they were searched. One wonders if Rubrik ever commented on what this contributed to the national image. When the squad finally got home, the federation snubbed Paco Bru and decided not to give him a medal. And so on and so forth. Although the team had proved they could compete and the European football press were eulogising Zamora, the Olympic excursion had also highlighted fissures which would plague the national team for decades to come.

Between 1920 and the 1924 Olympics in Paris, the *selección* played eight games and won six of them, leading just about everyone to the conclusion that they would win the tournament. It was the beginning of a long history of disappointments, and maybe even of the general way of thinking of an entire people. Spain lost 1-0 to Italy courtesy of an own goal by Vallana, and the press were quick this time to suggest that they'd seen it coming all along. They blamed the system of two managers – Bru had resigned and given the job to Parages and Cernuda, neither of whom had seen much point in preparing the squad, above and beyond playing some practice matches. Only three of the players who had gone to Belgium in 1920 played in the Italy game, and there were the inevitable reports of tensions between the two managers and the players. In the end, the ball must have bobbled on the divot.

Four years later, Spain tried to play it straight by sending only amateur players to the Amsterdam Olympics – the Spanish federation having embraced professionalism two years earlier – only to find on their arrival that most of the other teams had included paid players in their ranks. Mexico, their first opponents, had also stuck to the true spirit of the Games and were soundly stuffed for their good behaviour, 7-1 by a young Spanish side. Although they were amateurs, the team included several players who would go on to have distinguished careers, Jacinto Quincoces and Patxi Gamborena to mention but two.

They were then drawn to play Italy – fast becoming their bogeymen – and, to compound the luck of the draw, their opponents had brought along all their top players, six of whom had played in the 1924 encounter. The Spanish press may have been guilty of exaggeration when stating that 'almost all' the other participating countries had included professionals in their squads, but the accusation against the Italian team was true. And so appeared another Quixotic factor in the national team's character – rise to the occasion when the odds are stacked against, and fail miserably when they appear to be in their favour. Spain scored after 15 minutes, a long-range cracker by the full-back Francisco Zaldúa, and proceeded to outplay their surprised and much more experienced rivals. But the Italians equalised ten minutes from the end, brought in their rested star Levratto for the replay, and won 7-1.

These were early years, but if it is true that a child's personality is irrevocably formed by the age of six, they were the decisive ones. By the late 1920s, international football had got its act sufficiently together to see the potential in staging a World Cup competition, in order that the professionals too might measure themselves against each other. FIFA's meeting in 1929 in Barcelona decided to accept Uruguay's bid to stage the first competition (though there were other candidates, including Spain), but only four European countries travelled to South America. Spain were not among them. Too many clubs were disinclined to release their best players for the best part of two months, and besides, the federation was broke.

Had the team gone, they would no doubt have begun as dark horses, among the favourites but not at the top of the podium. A year earlier, they had beaten England in Madrid's Metropolitano, the first time the founders of the game had lost an international against a team from outside the British Isles. As further proof that they may have achieved something in Uruguay, Spain beat Italy 3-2 in Bologna in a friendly in 1930. Early in 1931 they travelled to England for the first time and were destroyed by their avenging hosts, 7-1 at Highbury, but by 1933 they were recording their biggest ever win, a scandalous 13-0 over Bulgaria in the Chamartín. Encouraged by these results, and the relatively short travelling distance to Italy, Spain were ready to compete in a World Cup for the first time by 1934.

The second World Cup came at a time when sport began to be

harnessed to more elemental struggles for supremacy in Europe. The year before, Hitler had taken power in Germany and the 1936 Olympics, with exquisitely poor timing, were scheduled for Berlin. The Italians, like their German friends, were not keen on failing either on the symbolic sporting fields or in real combat. In 1935 Mussolini was to give the order to invade Abyssinia. For now, though, the important thing was to put on a good show.

In searching for reasons for Spain's under-achievements we have so far uncovered regional rivalry among the players, indiscipline, a failure to analyse either success or failure, and a debilitating inferiority complex. Now came the turn of the referees. The national squad easily beat Portugal to qualify for the finals (they were always paired against them until 1954) and the manager, Amadeo Salazar, decided to contract Sunderland for a three-game sparring competition over in Spain. Spain drew two and lost one, perhaps a better preparation than for the previous tournaments where they had either gone in complete ignorance, with too much confidence, or with no expectations at all.

In the finals they beat a still emerging Brazil 3-1 in their first game, only to be drawn against the hosts in the next round (the tournament then being a straight knockout). Poor Spain. Italy again. The first game was in Florence and ended 1-1. Spain scored first, but Italy's equaliser, if the press accounts are to be believed, made Lofthouse's famous shove on Harry Gregg at Wembley look tame indeed. Angelo Schiavio – a survivor from the 1928 game – thumped Zamora as a corner was taken, and Giovanni Ferrari did the same to the ball, sending it into the net. The Belgian referee, Louis Baert, initially disallowed the goal but was then subjected to such pushing, shoving and Italian vernacular that he changed his mind and gave a goal instead, whereupon he was then the target for an equal amount of Spanish protest. But the goal stood. In the second half, he disallowed a Spanish goal by Ramón de Lafuente for offside – a curious decision given that the player in question had beaten four opponents before putting the ball into the net.

The replay was the next day, despite the Spanish complaints about their walking wounded. As Sweden had done 14 years earlier, the Italians had selected their targets carefully and neither Zamora, Guillermo Gorostiza nor Quincoces could play. Those that did, according to *ABC*, were 'playing practically on crutches'. Italy won 1-0, again kicking the remaining Spaniards into oblivion, and the Swiss referee René Marcet disallowed a goal by Campanal, just for good measure. Both Baert and Marcet were suspended by their respective federations on returning home from the World Cup, and it would seem that Spain were truly the victims of the fact that the Italians had to stay in the film at least until after the ice-cream interval.

History was to repeat itself 60 years later in the 1994 World Cup in the United States. The Spanish should have beaten Italy in the quarter-finals of a tournament in which they were, for once, living up to their bidding as the dark horses, coming up on the blind side, improving as the competition progressed. When José Luis Caminero equalised Roberto Baggio's first-half goal in Boston, Spain took the game to the Italians' throats. With ten minutes to go, the much-travelled Julio Salinas, on for the defender Sergi, broke clear but famously fluffed his chance. The country has never forgiven him, especially since Baggio scored the winner three minutes from the end, against the run of play.

The counterpoint with 1934 resides in the final minute when Luis Enrique, up for a corner, was elbowed in the nose by Mauro Tassotti as he made to head the ball goalwards. The blood on his shirt seemed evidence enough, but the Hungarian referee was having none of it. Cheated out of it again by those unscrupulous Italians. Football in Spain, as in most countries, has not only failed to dispel negative stereotypes of other nations, it has actively encouraged them. For those in Spain who believe in such stereotypes, the Italians are *perros* (dogs), meaning they are untrustworthy and opportunist. The history of the football matches between the two countries has unfortunately blinded the Spanish to the fact that the Corinthian spirit has hardly pervaded the fields of their own sporting culture, even if, in the two games in question, they truly deserved to win.

But as quickly as sympathy comes, she is just as soon whisked away. In the concluding paragraph of the magazine *Epoca* on the US World Cup, the writer dredges up all the old ghosts, almost despite himself:

> Regrettably, Spain were knocked out just as they were demonstrating that they could play football of the highest quality. But we know what happened then; bad luck, Salinas's miss, Zubizarreta's indecision with Baggio's first goal, a blind and cowardly referee... more circumstances pitted against us than Italy's superiority.

A less emotional resumé of the game might have highlighted the fact that whereas Salinas missed his chance, Baggio did not, and where Zubizarreta misjudged, Gianluca Pagliuca cut down Salinas's angle of approach more cleverly than most Spanish commentators were prepared to point out. It was easier to look for scapegoats, and Salinas offered himself up most helpfully. The foul on Luis Enrique should indeed have resulted in a penalty, but his team-mate Miguel Angel Nadal's clumsy tackle on Roberto Donadoni in the first half, also ignored by the referee, has never formed part of the legend.

Worse was to come. In the 2002 World Cup, Spain went out to the hosts South Korea in the quarter-finals, in a game that made the phrase 'controversial circumstances' seem hardly adequate. After cruising through the opening stages with three straight wins, then squeezing past Ireland on a penalty shoot-out, the prospect of the hard-working but tactically more limited Koreans was not exactly a daunting one. With Brazil hardly setting the pulses racing and Germany looking decidedly fallible, the growing sense of optimism was justified – if one can ever really say that in the context of the Spanish team.

Instead, the scenes at the end of the game, which the hosts won on penalties, sparked off diplomatic rows between the two countries amid accusations of match-fixing that sank to the level of semi-racist slander. Ángel Villar, president of the Spanish Football Federation, resigned from his position on the international referees' committee in protest at what he described as a 'farce'. And one has to say that he had a point.

The game featured two disallowed goals that the Egyptian referee, Gamal Ghandour, may have some trouble explaining to his grand-children in years to come. Ivan Helguera's header ten minutes into the second half looked legitimate enough, but was apparently disallowed for 'shirt-pulling'. At the end of the game, Helguera had to be restrained by security guards as he berated the officials in his finest Esperanto, but he was probably telling them, with some justification, that he had not been anywhere near an opponent's shirt.

But the second goal, where Fernando Morientes thumped a header past Lee Woon-Jae only to be informed that the ball had gone over the goalline before Joaquin's delicately chipped centre, was stretching matters even further. In one of the most replayed disallowed goals since Michel's famous effort against Brazil in 1986, the slow-motion view from behind Morientes seemed to confirm that the linesman, Michael Ragoonath from Trinidad and Tobago, was looking at the centre and not at Joaquín. The ball was not even half-way across the line when Joaquin's boot made contact, but as soon as it was clear that Morientes was unmarked, the flag was raised.

Even in the bars of San Sebastián, where the locals are normally fairly indifferent to the Spanish team's cause, they were frothing with righteous indignation. History had repeated itself and Spain were once again on a premature flight home. But it also repeated itself in a post-match orgy of teeth-gnashing which once again provided the national press with an excuse to avoid any sort of calmer analysis. The game did indeed throw up some serious doubts as to the competence of the officials, but the Spanish press preferred the conspiratorial line (shared by the Italians who had gone out in similar circumstances), muttering darkly about under-the-table deals between Nike and the Korean government and worse, dismissing the officials as *tercermundistas* (Third World). Spain were indeed unlucky again, and could easily have gone on to win the tournament, but there was no excuse for such nonsense. And once again, no one mentioned that in extra time Spain had sat back, instead of trying to overwhelm their tiring opponents. Perhaps they had concluded that there wasn't much point, but the game was another sorry episode in the incident-strewn history of the *selección*.

As a surreal postscript to this game, BBC radio had asked me to provide a post-match commentary on the 'local reaction', from some bar heaving with patriotic humanity, though I had warned them they might be better off finding someone in the heartlands, such as Seville or Madrid. In the perfectly normal bar I chose in San Sebastián, plenty of people watched the Spain games, but were not exactly Spanish flag wavers. After the match I tried to explain (truthfully) that although there was no mass mourning, the people in the bar and on the surrounding streets were muttering and slouching away, appalled by the seeming injustice of it all. Then, to my horror, some fireworks began to go off 200 yards behind me. It was the local branch of Herri Batasuna, the radical leftist nationalist party, celebrating Spain's defeat. Standing clutching my mobile, with several million people listening in, I decided to lie, for the sake of political simplicity. 'Oh, they're local *fiestas*,' I fibbed.

Many reasons have been cited as contributory factors to Spain's under-achievement, but regional tension is one which is almost never mentioned by the Spanish themselves. This is interesting, since foreign observers often wonder whether the presence of players from separatist regions in the national team causes friction in the dressing-room. They seem to have the general impression that the national side takes shelter in Seville or in the Bernabéu because there they are guaranteed the sort of unthinking, flag-waving support that they require.

Spain has no national stadium so, like a medieval king, the *selección* is obliged to wander its lands seeking morale, succour and confirmation of loyalty. Occasionally they will venture up north to Santander, but almost never to Bilbao, San Sebastián or the Camp Nou. If the *selección* do play in Barcelona, it is usually at Espanyol's ground, particularly now that they are based at the Olympic Stadium of Montjuic. As hosts of the 1982 World Cup, Spain played in Valencia, a city with a strong local culture but no great pretensions to separatism. The city could hardly be held responsible for the home side's dismal showing, but after Spain drew with England in the second phase, a result which sent both teams on their summer holidays, the critics weighed in.

Real Sociedad, champions that season, had contributed almost half their team to the cause, and this was the reason, according to most observers, why Spain had failed. Luis Arconada, certainly one of Spain's most distinguished goalkeepers, had let Gerry Armstrong's shot through his legs in the final match of the opening phase, but this was not deemed half as serious as the fact that he had chosen to wear white socks throughout the tournament, instead of the regulation black ones. The white socks, of course, were the same ones as he wore for his Basque club, Real Sociedad, and several journalists decided that this was tantamount to an unpatriotic gesture – an absurd accusation, for Arconada was no nationalist.

During the Sixties and Seventies José Iribar, another of the great Basque goalkeepers, made no secret of his allegiance to Herri Batasuna, the militant leftist nationalist party, but his dedication to the red and yellow shirt of the *selección* was never questioned. It seems that Arconada fell foul of the general feeling that the Uruguayan José Santamaría, the manager for the 1982 tournament, had relied too much on the Real Sociedad squad that summer. Worse, it was said, he had tried to get them to play like Real Madrid, when they had won the championship by virtue of their sturdy defence, not their attack.

None of their defenders was in the squad, but half their midfield and almost their entire forward line were, of whom López Ufarte, our hero from the beach, was the only real player of international class. The implication that the inclusion of so many players from one club, and a Basque club to boot, created tensions and cliques in the squad, has been vigorously denied by the players. The other half of the side was from Real Madrid, newly converted into footballing rivals – as opposed to merely political rivals – with the arrivistes Sociedad and it is said, perhaps by those who wish to believe such things, that the two failed to mix.

It is probably nonsense, as is the general idea that Spain will always malfunction while it harbours politico-cultural tensions within its football squads. *El gran fracaso* (the great failure) of 1982 still rankles, a taboo year not to be mentioned in polite conversation at dinner parties. But of course, one has to ask the inevitable question – whose national memory are we talking about? Do the Basques and Catalans support the Spanish national team?

Spain is one of the most institutionally federal countries in Europe. In its 'autonomous regions', the elected politicians preside over local governments that have wide-ranging powers over health, education and fiscal policy. As far as the constitution is concerned (drawn up after Franco's death) the Basque Country and Catalonia are just two autonomous regions among many – Galicia, Asturias and Andalucía, for example, all having equal status and equal legislative powers.

As far as the Basques and the Catalans are concerned, this is the consti- tution of the *café con leche para todos* (white coffee for everyone), deliber- ately drawn up by *Españolistas* whose intention was to subsume real regional culture and separatism under a political system that pretended to be devolving equal shares of democracy to everyone. The former *Guardian* journalist John Hooper once wrote that there are 142 ways to have coffee in Spain. It's a coffee culture. To only do it one way suggests centralism as opposed to regional variety. It's a decision that has reaped a bitter harvest among the hard-line Basque and Catalan nationalists, forced to drink their *café con leche* with all and sundry. As a result, some Basques have resorted to terrorism, while the Catalans have tried to prove they are superior in economic, cultural and sporting terms.

No other autonomous region of Spain has done anything remotely like this since the transition to democracy, mainly because, as planned, *café con leche* is no particular problem for them. In football, the lines are very clearly drawn. When Real Madrid (or the *selección*) visit places like Oviedo or Santander, they are warmly welcomed. Along the coasts, from Alicante downward, many bars run by locals will adorn their walls with posters of the country's most successful side. Even in Galicia, third in the separatist league table with a distinct cultural and linguistic identity, there is no real problem with the *café con leche*, and consequently none with the national side.

Equally, the Galician-born professionals do not get together every Christmas (during the winter break) to play for their regional *selección*, as the Basques and the Catalans do. Such gatherings, obviously banned under Franco, usually take place two or three days before Christmas and feature a game against another country, often from eastern Europe or Africa. The games are well attended and the *Euskadi* and Catalan teams gather all their top players and wear the regional colours.

There have been times when either of these teams could have destroyed the Spanish national outfit given the opportunity – a political impossibility, of course. During the Dream Team years, the Basque exiles in Barcelona made the *Euskadi* team a powerful one indeed, and they regularly won their Christmas fixtures. With Zubizarreta, Bakero, Goikoetxea, Beguiristain and Salinas they were a match for anyone, not forgetting internationals like Rafael Alkorta and Mikel Lasa at Real Madrid. The Catalans were no mugs either during that period, with Guardiola, Sergi, Albert Ferrer, Guillermo Amor and Nadal for starters. Both local federations always push for more games, and the Catalans actually got up a petition in 1999, headed by Guardiola's signature, to allow the regional team proper international status for all competitions.

Guardiola, now retired, was the local hero of Barcelona's Nineties Dream Team, and was not the sort of character, you would have justifiably thought, to turn out for Spain with his hair dyed red and yellow. And yet he captained the side and played for them with distinction on 47 occasions. A neutral observer might well ask why someone like Guardiola even bothered. If he was so committed to the regional cause, why did he not make a stand and refuse to play? And, of course, Guardiola is hardly the only example of regionalist hard-liners turning out for the Spanish national team throughout its history. Guardiola would probably have answered that he had no alternative, on one occasion commenting that by playing for Spain he was further advertising Catalan prowess. No Catalan has ever (publicly) refused to play for Spain on political grounds.

Ignacio Kortabarría, the Real Sociedad captain who carried the Basque flag on to the pitch in that famous game against Bilbao in 1976, played once for Spain, and, so the football history books tell us, was picked no more. The truth seems to be that he refused to play again, claiming in the club's official history that he found the atmosphere in the national squad 'hostile'. Iribar, his counterpart at Bilbao, although he won 49 caps, also claimed that he refused to play his 50th because 'there were those who decided that I didn't belong' – though he may have been making excuses for the fact that his powers were on the wane. It seems rather curious that no one questioned his commitment on the 49 previous occasions.

Apart from these isolated cases, the regional question seems to be the least of the national side's problems. There is no realistic threat of a break-up of the squad into several 'national' sides, unless the political map changes in totally unpredictable ways in the new century. It's a complicated business, but it is nevertheless untrue, to answer the original question, that these regions have no interest in the fortunes of the Spanish side. It may be that in the depths of some heavy nationalist bars in deepest *Euskadi* the television screen remains blank during World Cup matches but, by and large, the Basques and Catalans suffer and sigh along with the rest of the country when it comes to the big competitions. Of course, there are usually plenty of players from these regions in the national squad, to echo Guardiola's point. In many cases since 1920 they have formed a majority.

When Spain come a cropper, as in 1982, people may feign indifference, but they don't really mean it. And if the players from these regions in question have bothered to travel and identify with the national team, it is unlikely that they will play half-heartedly for the sake of principle. In 1994, two-thirds of the Spanish squad in the US were Catalan and Basque. The players, amused by the predictably stereotypical reception given to them on arrival in the country – all flamenco and castanets – decided to a man to grow the *perilla*, the small goatee beard made famous by the sailors of the ill-fated Armada and one of Spain's earliest known contributions to European fashion. The little joke was proof of the lack of tension and of the good spirit in the camp, and seemed to contribute to one of the better campaigns in their history.

A related issue, made more pertinent by the implications of the Bosman case, has been the relatively abundant presence of foreign players and managers in Spain. The Spanish league, unlike those of many other European countries, has never been afraid to put out the welcome mat for overseas players, and the golden era of its football is gilded with the names of other nationalities – Di Stéfano, Ben Barek, Kubala, Puskas, Santamaría and Platko. These players were never deemed to be bringing ruin upon the national fabric because their presence was felt to be restricting home-grown talent, as the argument often goes nowadays. The Spanish have only recently woken up to the fact that this might be the case, prompted by an overseas invasion even greater than the one that has so affected the current English scene. However, like the English they have largely accepted the argument that the influence on their home-grown players is benign. You might not be able to play like Zidane, but he sure makes a good role model.

Between the retirement of Puskas and Kubala and the signing of

Cruyff by Barcelona in 1973, the Spanish federation decided to allow only players with Spanish roots to play in the league, which more or less limited the field to South Americans. The legislation, introduced in 1965, usually allowed players in on the grounds that they had a Spanish parent or grandparent – but the policy soon became known as *el timón de Paraguay* (the Paraguayan rudder) when it was discovered that a consul in that country was earning himself a tidy sum by helping to falsify documents for a substantial number of players.

It was Agustín Montal, the Barcelona president, who called the policy into question, believing that Real Madrid, in cahoots with the authorities, were ensuring that the Catalans' requests for good players were turned down, while simultaneously rubber-stamping signings for anyone else. Matters came to a head when Montal employed a Catalan lawyer to investigate the 'roots' of all players who had been allowed into the country. His discovery that 46 of the 60 contracted had been waved through on falsified documentation blew the issue out of the water and worried the federation into changing the rules. (One Argentine, Miguel Angel Adorno, had claimed that his father had been born in 'Celta', rather than Vigo.)

There is no evidence to suggest that Real Madrid themselves got much benefit from the policy since, with some exceptions such as Adorno himself (who ended up at Valencia) and Juan Garate (Atlético Madrid), many of the players who came over turned out to be of sub-standard quality. It seems as though the Spanish ministry had passed the legislation, on the advice of someone within the Bernabéu camp, just in case another Di Stéfano were to come along. Whatever the truth, the threat that the under-the-table relationship between the Spanish federation, the ministry and shady consuls in Paraguay might be exposed was enough to lift restrictions and pave the way for Barça's signing of the Peruvian Hugo Sotil and then Cruyff, the latter's move to the Catalan club having been blocked by the authorities three years earlier, in 1970.

Of course, Cruyff, who now seems more Spanish (Catalan) than Dutch, never played for Spain, for even if he had taken up Spanish nationality, FIFA had legislated in the mid-Sixties to prevent players turning out for more than one country. Before that rule was adopted, 29 foreign players did turn out for Spain – 14 Argentines, three Brazilians, three Paraguayans, two Hungarians, two Cubans, a Moroccan, a Dane, a Filipino, a Uruguayan and a Frenchman. Six of these players won more than ten caps, and Di Stéfano was until recently the second-highest scorer of all time for the national team.

By contrast, very few Spanish players have travelled abroad. This prompts the twin conclusions that the Spanish footballer is either a parochial fellow or simply one that has failed to attract much attention. Both probably have some truth in them. And therein may lie the rather more prosaic answer to the question of why the national team has usually failed to live up to expectations – namely that there have simply not been enough top-class home-grown players. Good ones, yes; but top-drawer acts?

This is a tricky topic for a foreign author to tackle, but the facts cry out for analysis – Luis Suárez is the only Spanish player to have been elected European Footballer of the Year (he beat Puskas into second place in 1960), and only four other Spaniards have figured in the top five of the voting – Amancio (1964), Michel (1987), Butragueño (1986 and 1987) and Raúl (2001). Their numbers look feeble compared to historically middle-ranking European countries such as France (nine) or Yugoslavia and its constituent parts (eight), let alone the dominant powers of Germany, Italy, Holland and even England, who can boast 14 mentions.

Despite having to fight for air in a midfield orchestrated jealously by Kubala, the Galician-born Suárez became Spain's best home-grown player, in the opinion of many. Significantly, he was one of the few Spanish players to have attract the attentions of the Italians, signing for Internazionale in the Sixties and eventually finishing up at Sampdoria.

Gento, Zarra, Samitier and Santillana might have some claims to be rated as highly, but Spain is notable primarily for having produced a series of great goalkeepers – Zamora, Iribar, Arconada, Zubizarreta – all of whom have managed to leave their mark on the world's collective football memory. Few outfield players have managed to do the same, and only Suárez has the votes to show for it. Sir Alex Ferguson claimed in 2003, after Real Madrid had taken his team apart in the Bernabéu, that Raúl was the best player in the world, but there has as yet been no official recognition of his opinion.

The issue of managers runs parallel, for Spain has been just as keen on having foreigners at the helm of its football clubs as it has been enthusiastic in its importation of talent on the pitch. Between 1986, when Luis Molowny led Real Madrid to the league title, and 2000, when Javier Irureta did the same for Deportivo de La Coruña, no Spanish manager lifted the trophy. When the modest Irureta was interviewed after the game against Espanyol that clinched the title for Deportivo, he drew attention to the fact that the win was not just good for the game because it had broken the traditional two-club monopoly, but because it had reaffirmed the place of the Spanish manager after so many years in the shadows.

That year was in fact a triple whammy of a reaffirmation of the home-grown leader, for in addition to Irureta's feat, Real Madrid took their eighth European Cup home cradled in the arms of the modest and avuncular Vicente del Bosque (who was in the side who lost to Liverpool in Paris in 1981) and Paco Flores led Espanyol to their first trophy in 60 years, fittingly in the Catalan club's centenary, when they beat Atlético Madrid in the King's Cup final.

When you think of the great managers in the Spanish game, it is the names of Johan Cruyff, Helenio Herrera, Ladislao Kubala, Fred Pentland and Leo Beenhakker that spring to mind. The foreigners Pentland, Santamaría and Daucik all managed or co-managed the national side, albeit briefly, while Kubala clocked up 11 years in all, more than any other coach. While that assessment may risk underestimating Spanish expertise in the field, the Spanish themselves happily perpetuate this sense of their game having been shaped and defined by outsiders, as if the fact reflects well on them, and on their willingness to welcome and then assimilate a whole range of cosmopolitan influences. Despite the fact that the Spanish are so often accused of being parochial (and proud of it) the story of their football does not always reflect this.

Spain has always viewed the importation of sporting ideas as positive, rather than corrupting. It has been the European country most open to the conversion of its foreign stars into Spanish nationals ready to sweat the red and yellow shirt of *la patria*. Before the war, football enabled Spain to poke its toes into the waters of surrounding cultures, without ever getting too deeply implicated. Later, it helped to redefine the country, to such an extent that the impact of foreign flesh during the Fifties brought worldwide attention and admiration.

Franco, as has been noted, was all the happier for this, but it wasn't just Real Madrid who put a smile on his face. Even the *selección* played their part in making the early Fifties a golden period for Spanish football. Spain, left out of the Marshall Plan and resented by the wartime allies, travelled to Brazil in 1950 for the first postwar World Cup keen to prove that they could contribute in some way to the party. They had a decent side, but went with few expectations. Antonio Ramallets was another in the line of solid goalkeepers, up front they had Piru Gainza on the left and Athletic's Zarra, Spain's most prolific goalscorer. But England had a powerful side, Uruguay looked good again and Brazil were about to revolutionise the game. Spain went with modest hopes, and were rewarded for their realism.

After two fairly easy wins over the US and Chile in the group phase, they came up against the England of Billy Wright, Tom Finney, Stanley Matthews, Jackie Milburn and Stan Mortensen. Even though they had beaten England 4-3 back in 1929, the 1-0 win in the Maracaná on July 2, 1950 still counts as Spain's most famous victory. It's a game hardly anyone in England remembers, coming as it did after the much more sensational defeat against the US. But in Spain everyone knows that Zarra scored in the 50th minute, that it was a gentle side-footed shot finishing off a move between Gainza and Silvestre Igoa and that Matías Prats, commentating live on radio from Brazil that afternoon, coined the immortal phrase 'Zarra – the best head in Europe after Churchill!', referring both to his heading ability and his coolness under pressure.

By 1950, Spain had become a nation of radio listeners, and this was the first major tournament in which people could follow the games live, on crackly short-wave. The immediacy of the goal, brought into people's homes by Prats' mellifluous voice, may well be the reason why this game has lasted so long in the nation's memory, although there are those who point more to political and social reasons.

The political ones are fairly obvious. Zarra's goal was a huge raspberry blown in a northerly direction at a country whose leaders had actively excluded Spain from the postwar handouts, had sent many of its workers and intellectuals to fight for the Left in the Civil War and which was seen to be lording it a bit, now that it had supposedly saved the world. The Spanish felt isolated, victimised and undernourished, and had no particular reason for feeling 'saved'. Then, lo and behold, the two leaders of the Allied powers, the US and England (seen as equivalent to Britain of course), both defeated in the opening round!

In pure footballing terms, the Spanish were as surprised as anybody, since England had been widely expected to make the final at least. In the second phase, however, reality intruded and Uruguay, the eventual winners, should really have won the game that ended in a 2-2 draw. Nevertheless, Spain was still gathered around the radio dreaming of conquering the world when they took on the hosts two days later in the Maracaná – with over 150,000 people inside. Igoa got one for Spain, but Brazil replied with six. The next day they lost 3-1 to Sweden and caught the slow boat home.

After that, it was over to Real Madrid, because the national side failed to qualify for the next two World Cups. In a sense, they shot themselves in the foot by appealing to FIFA, along with Portugal, that they should meet different opponents in the qualifying phase – the Iberian neighbours being thoroughly fed up of the sight of each other by then. But at least Portugal had always had the decency to let Spain beat them.

In order to qualify for Switzerland in 1954, Spain came up against the unknown Turks. They beat them without much difficulty, 4-1 in the opening game in Spain, a win which convinced them too easily that the return leg would be equally comfortable. It wasn't, and they lost 1-0, a result which meant that, in the absence of the aggregate goals concept, they had to play a *desempate*, literally an'un-draw', three days later in Rome. Spain only just managed to scrape a 2-2 draw, equalising ten minutes from the end. Kubala, who had made his Spanish debut a year earlier, was the vital piece missing from the jigsaw. Ten minutes before the players were due to take to the field in the Olympic Stadium, a man claiming to be a FIFA official strode into the changing-rooms waving a letter which allegedly questioned Kubala's right to play for Spain, given that he had previously been a Hungarian international. After an altercation, Kubala stood down and Spain played poorly without him.

The next day, however, FIFA denied ever having sent a delegate to the stadium, and confirmed that they had had no objection to Kubala playing for Spain. The mystery has never been solved, but it has become another of the bad luck cards that the country believes it has been dealt over the years. The 2-2 draw meant that the two countries' names had to go into the sombrero. And it was Italy again that proved to be the bogeyman, this time in the shape of a blindfolded 14-year-old boy called Franco Gemma, who was given the task of pulling from a large silver tankard the piece of paper with the name of the team that would go to Switzerland. Of course, it said Turkey.

Four years later Spain had arguably their most powerful side ever. The team of the *cuatro leyendas* (four legends) had, on paper at least, a frightening look, with Kubala, Di Stéfano, Gento and Suárez all present. In truth, it was a squad which may have had too many chiefs and not enough indians, but the world was never to find out, at least in an official competition. Qualifying for the World Cup had become a somewhat more complicated matter by now, and Spain were obliged to face two teams, Switzerland and Scotland. Neither should have caused them many sleepless nights, but the opening game in Madrid against the modest Swiss ended in a lame 2-2 draw.

Two months later, in the spring rain at Hampden Park, the Scotland of George Young and Tommy Docherty beat them 4-2, effectively ending their chances of qualification. Three weeks later in the Bernabéu, things began to come together, but, as usual, too late was the cry. Scotland were thrashed 4-1 (the game was refereed by Barcelona's favourite Englishman, Reg Leafe) and Spain repeated the score in November in Lausanne, with two goals each from Kubala and Di Stéfano. But they were already out, victims of a cold start – a trait that has haunted them ever since – and of cold weather, the oft-repeated reason for their failure to perform in Glasgow.

The following year, Spain tried to set the record straight in the qualifiers for the first European Nations tournament, a series of two-legged affairs played on a home and away basis. Seemingly under less pressure than in the awkward qualifying phases of the World Cups, and now with Helenio Herrera on the bench, Spain made short work of Poland, 4-2 away and 3-0 at home. Franco was not too happy about the political undertones of having to visit Poland, and when the subsequent draw paired Spain with the Soviet Union, he decided enough was enough. The team was withdrawn from the tournament, meaning that Di Stéfano would never get the chance he craved – to shine on the international stage for his adopted country.

In 1962 he travelled to Chile, but was allegedly injured before the tournament even began. For that World Cup Spain adopted the now discredited method of taking along both a 'trainer', Herrera, and a manager, Pablo Hernández, who of course failed to get on with each other (no one ever got on with Herrera) and who both had doubts about their ageing Argentinian star. Herrera has since denied that he kept Di Stéfano out of the team, but there are stories of a training session in Viña del Mar, two days before the opening game with Czechoslovakia, in which the famously eccentric tactician went in unnecessarily hard on his already limping compatriot.

Czechoslovakia beat them 1-0, despite the fact that Spain still had a very useful side – including Santamaría, Puskas, Suárez and Gento. However, they could only manage a 1-0 win over a poor Mexico side in the second game, collecting their tickets home three days later after a 2-1 defeat at the hands of the Brazil of Didi and Garrincha. Spain played well, and had been leading up to the 70th minute, but Brazil and Czechoslovakia went on to dispute the final and Spain went home to think again. The next time they would get it right.

In the summer of 1964, the day after Spain had won their first international trophy by beating the Soviets 2-1 in the Bernabéu, the conservative newspaper *ABC* featured a cartoon of Franco shaking the victors' hands and telling them: 'You and I have come out winners. We've both beaten the reds.' When Spain was handed the organisation of the European Nations Cup, Franco clearly decided to play a more discreet game than he had four years earlier. The Soviets, for whom the great Lev Yashin was at his peak, were one of the top sides in the world, having won the inaugural competition in 1960, and the chance to take them on could not be passed up this time. Franco realised that by re-establishing some tentative links with opposing faiths he was enhancing rather than tarnishing his country's image. It helped to challenge the general perception of Spain as the intolerant old bastion of European fascism (even if it was).

On paper, the squad did not look anywhere near as impressive as that of 1958, and for the first time since Kubala pulled on the red shirt it comprised only home-grown players. Iribar and Suárez were the only real names in an otherwise young, experimental side, and it may have been the lack of real expectation that kept them on an even keel. Romania, Northern Ireland and the Republic of Ireland were all dispatched without difficulty. In the semi-finals Spain came up against Hungary, beating them 2-1 in an epic that stretched into extra-time.

Against the Soviets in the final, the young Jesús María Pereda put them in front with a cracking shot across Yashin after five minutes, only for Galimzian Khusainov to equalise three minutes later. The second most famous goal in Spanish football history had to wait until the 83rd minute to make its appearance – a long-range header from Marcelino Martínez that Yashin, judging by the famous photograph taken from behind the net, seems to have misjudged. In the wide-lens photo, the ball has looped down under the bar and is just falling snugly into the left corner of the net. Yashin is stooped forward, his left arm flailing at the air, while in the right corner of the picture Marcelino, partially hidden by a horrified-looking Edouard Mudrik, is just hitting the floor after his prodigious leap. *ABC* was moved to comment the following day:

> In this quarter of a century there has never been displayed a greater popular enthusiasm for the state born out of victory over communism and its fellow travellers... Spain is a nation every day more orderly, mature and unified, and which is steadfastly marching down the path of economic, social and institutional development. It is a national adventure.

Maybe so, but the onward march of its football team was less than steadfast. Spain's contribution to the 1966 World Cup was brief, two straight defeats by Germany and Argentina after a 2-1 win over the Swiss condemning them to an early return home. Worse was to come two years later, although the criticism the team received after losing the 1968 European Nations Cup quarter-final to a useful England side was hardly justified. The manager, Domingo Balmanya, who had succeeded José Villalonga only two years previously, walked before he was asked, which left the unfortunate Eduardo Toba with the job of qualifying the team for Mexico. He failed, in a campaign in which the final humiliation of a 2-0 defeat against Finland in Helsinki was considered Spain's blackest hour until the 3-2 defeat in Cyprus in 1999. Poor Toba hid in his flat for weeks on end while the federation decided that it was time to entrust the job to Kubala, drink problem notwithstanding.

For the *selección* the Seventies, like its haircuts, are best forgotten. Failure to qualify for Germany and an early exit from Argentina speak for themselves. After the miserable experience of the 1982 World Cup the expectations for the 1984 European Championship in France were hardly great. The fact that it was in some ways Spain's finest hour, suffering a defeat in the final every bit as honourable as their win in 1964, supports the idea that the Spanish rely heavily on a perverse kind of psychology, one which seems to reward them when they reach rock-bottom but which punishes them the minute they start to feel too good about themselves. There is no known cure for this condition, which explains, as much as anything does, Spain's relative failure on the international scene.

The French campaign, to borrow a word from the host's lexicon, was quite bizarre. After a bright beginning to the qualifying phase, the final round of games saw Holland heading the group on goal difference – a considerable goal difference, for Spain were obliged to defeat Malta by 11 clear goals if they were to go through. The subsequent 12-1 rout of the Maltese in Seville generated a collective euphoria sufficient to send the Madrid stock market through the roof and the Dutch into mourning, though not before several of their football journalists had pointed the finger accusingly at the Maltese goalkeeper Bonello.

However, the events of the game suggest that it was a fair fight, despite the suspiciously neat scoreline. Spain missed a penalty in the second minute, scored through Santillana 13 minutes later, only for the Maltese to equalise after another two minutes through an innocuous looking shot from Demanuelle. If Malta had been paid to lose, they were certainly creating an effective smokescreen. Spain needed 11 more, and they only had 72 minutes left to score them in – a goal more or less every seven minutes.

But they got them, Juan Señor making up for his penalty miss by scoring the decisive 12th in the 86th minute. There was still time for the referee to disallow a goal by the inspirational Rafael Gordillo, the ex-Bético who played his finest game back in his old stadium. Bonello, the unfortunate goalkeeper, had told the Spanish press before the game that it was inconceivable that he might concede 11 goals, pointing quite justifiably to the reverse fixture in Malta in which the Spanish had only just managed to win 3-2 and adding, rather less wisely, that if he were to concede 11 he would not return to his country. *Marca* joked the next day that he had let in the 12th so that he could get on the plane home. The game is filed away in Spain's archive of national legends, and everyone of a certain age remembers at least the goalkeeper's name and the order of the scorers.

Having unexpectedly reached the finals, Spain should have relaxed (according to the theory) but instead contrived to demonstrate why they had struggled to qualify in the first place. They drew their opening two games, against Romania and Portugal, but came good in the third, beating Germany at the last gasp with a famous header from Antonio Maceda in the final minute, a goal as celebrated over Europe as the Bulgarian Iordan Letchkov's would be ten years later in the US. Even the Dutch must have cheered when it flew past Toni Schumacher.

In the semi-finals Spain came up against the fancied Denmark of Preben Elkjaer and Michael Laudrup and beat them on penalties after Maceda, again, had equalised Søren Lerby's early goal. The final that June in the Parc des Princes against the wonderful French side is a more famous game now than the victory in 1964. One reason is obviously that it is more recent, but it also belongs to the period of democratic modern Spain and so lacks any nagging political connotations. Perhaps even more crucially, it featured the famous mistake by goalkeeper Luis Arconada, who allowed Michel Platini's rather weak free-kick to slide under his body and over the line at a time when the Spanish were looking as though they might seriously poop the party. Bruno Bellone's second in injury-time certainly flattered the French, and the game has gone down as the modern period's finest performance, spoiled only by Arconada's mistake.

As Arconada ruefully told a friend of mine who taught him English some years ago, he is remembered more for his one mistake than for the rest of his career. Spain's hierarchy of great goalkeepers usually has him at No 3, behind Zamora and Iribar, but the bar-room critics and the press have never forgotten his error, despite the fact that the team would never have got to the final in the first place without him. As with Salinas in 1994 and Zubizarreta in 1998, the press would find easy scapegoats for what should have been more openly acknowledged as collective responsibility. Raúl's missed penalty against France in the quarter-finals of Euro 2000 will undoubtedly become the stuff of similar legend, although the player in question was, and still is, such an icon that the press found it difficult to immediately lay the blame on his shoulders.

Will Spain continue to be the dark horses? If they are not, there is no guarantee that the country will prefer to be regarded more highly, or if it would rather retain its superstitious streak – determined never to express too much confidence too early, so as not to give the gremlins of poetic justice too much of a field day in the event of defeat. Will the beach be flattened and the divots finally disappear, or will Cervantes continue to look down with a smile on his face?

11. *lost order*

...and the limits of democracy

There's a mighty speech in Shakespeare's *Troilus and Cressida* about 'order'. Ulysses thunders that it's best not to mess about too much with the grand scheme of things but just keep them the way somebody up there intended them to be. If you don't, the consequences can apparently get a bit serious:

> Take but degree away, untune that string
> And hark, what discord follows!
> The General's disdained
> By him one step below, he by the next
> The next by him beneath...

Maybe so, but since the millennium Spanish football has so far shown all the signs of the health and buoyancy that arise from untuning that string and disdaining the General above. The discord is yet to follow. What seems like 100 years of 'the old one-two' has suddenly developed a more egalitarian streak, and the folks are flocking in through the electronic turnstiles. They always did, but now they come along, if they can afford it, to watch their team participate in a competition that looks capable of yielding a winner from more than merely two or three sides.

After the twin feats of Deportivo and Valencia, the sudden and unexpected revival of Real Sociedad's fortunes, pushing Real Madrid all the way during the 2002-2003 season, seemed yet further proof. The Spanish league is probably the most balanced in Europe, with its overall quality hardly a matter for debate. Despite the Milan-Juventus *cri de coeur* at Old Trafford in the 2003 Champions League final, the balance of power has shifted, at least for now. Neither Ronaldinho nor David Beckham would seriously have contemplated moving to Serie A in the summer of 2003, and Zidane has never tired of recounting how much more he has enjoyed his football since moving to Spain. The endorsements of such players have only served to reinforce the feeling that Spain's star twinkles the brightest in Europe's footballing firmament.

But Spain, and Spanish football, remain as stubbornly paradoxical as they were when I first discovered them. Real Madrid, forever destined to be the ogre when it comes to talk of democracy, have been trying their best to portray themselves as more powerful and filthy rich than ever, as if they wish to be seen as aloof from the present configuration, above the messy business of mere mortals. The nickname '*Los Galácticos*' became an epithet they welcomed, and by the 2003-04 season it was being used regularly by the British press. Democracy creeping in? Better do something about that.

The imperious notion at the core of *madridismo* – that winning is all – has always been accompanied by the more brutal conceit that mercy is a sign of weakness. This complex idea, central to the soul of the bullfight – that brutality and nobility are one and the same thing – is the origin of the cry of '*olé*' when one Spanish side, gorged on the blood of its dying opponent, starts to knock the ball around in an arrogant and unmerciful fashion, sometime around the 89th minute. Since the beginning of the Florentio Pérez era at the Bernabéu, the club has indulged itself in an orgy of financial '*olés*', some of which were clearly designed to broadcast the impression that although Valencia and Deportivo had recently won a couple of leagues between them, they shouldn't let it go to their heads.

In recent years Spanish clubs have been free to negotiate their own individual TV rights contracts. Atlético Madrid, Valencia, Deportivo and even Espanyol have signed decent deals with pay TV operators, but of course the big two, Barça and Real Madrid, have reached the most lucrative arrangements, with Telefónica and Sogecable respectively. Spain's old firm, still afloat on the sea of their massive collateral, continue to have by far the most clout, despite the claims from various watchdog sources that Real Madrid's annual financial reports represent prime examples of Spain's supreme art form – creative accounting.

Madrid's older habits, of keeping the lending banks at arm's length with a combination of old boy networking and back-scratching could only continue to operate if the team continued to function. Pérez, one of Spain's most successful (and some say ruthless) businessmen, saw the potential problem when he took over in 2000 and decided to modernise the club's financial base – at least publicly. He wiped off the club's debt literally overnight, through the controversial sale of the Ciudad Deportiva, Real's training ground which dated back to the 1960s. The trouble was, he sold it to the municipal council, who then declared that the land would be subsequently purchased by private property concerns. The local council, of course, was run by Spain's ruling Partido Popular, whose leader, José María Aznar, just happened to be the country's prime minister and life-long supporter of Real Madrid. With some justification, the supporters of both Atlético Madrid and Rayo Vallecano saw the council's purchase of Real's property as an abuse of taxpayers' money and an outrageous example of political favouritism.

So in Spain, 25 years after Franco's death, democracy remains a relative term. In purely sporting terms, Spain's tough, high-kilowatt league has equipped clubs of previously doubtful pedigree such as Celta de Vigo, Mallorca, Málaga and Alavés to make waves in Europe. It would have been to nice to report that this apparent levelling out of the field was somehow a parallel development, walking hand in hand with the introduction of democracy in 1978 and Spain's subsequent liberalisation.

One could argue, and several have, that the four-year dominance of the two principal Basque clubs in the early 1980s was clear evidence that Franco was dead and buried in more than the merely literal sense. Lieutenant-Colonel Tejero's coup attempt in 1981 had failed and the oppressed minorities were rising up in a flowering of cultural and sporting identity. It's a nice idea, and the absence of Real Madrid's name from the league trophy until 1986 did seem to suggest that the old hierarchies were fading away. Barcelona also chipped in to make the same point with their 1983 victory over the old enemy in the King's Cup final, followed by a title win in 1985.

But this is all too simple for a country like Spain, and crucially, it overlooks the influence of our old friend *morbo*. No one really expected Real Madrid to go away, nor for the spirit of centralism and right-leaning politics that they had come to represent to just disappear overnight. It may seem perverse to say so, but some of Barcelona's happiest years as a football community (1948-1953) came during their unhappiest years as a political one. It has something to do with the siege mentality, the collective spirit that political and cultural persecution confers unwittingly on the oppressed.

While totalitarian systems can ensure victory for real 'regime teams' (such as East Germany's Dynamo Berlin), the relationship between Real Madrid and Franco was never as direct, as I hope I have shown. And conversely, there is no necessary relationship between the relaxation of central control and the flowering of a vigorous multi-polar league. Whatever the cause of Spain's current football pluralism – particularly

235

remarkable at a time when Champions League money has had the opposite effect in England and other leagues – it is bound to be more complicated than simply the post-Franco effect.

What is certain, however, is that Spain's mental barbed-wire fences have been standing firm since the Civil War, and it will take more than mere democracy to knock them down. The terrible beauty of Spanish football is that someone, somewhere, hates your guts, and will always be delighted to demonstrate this when your team comes to town. Maybe this is the factor which ensures that the bigger clubs must remain permanently on guard. Since the *morbo* levels are vigorously maintained, no one gets an easy ride. As we have seen, it was always around in the Spanish game, even before the onset of professionalism. But with the eventual dismantling of the machinery of the dictatorship, it was only natural for those who had been silenced to come out of the shadows and make their presence felt – to concentrate on a more explicit cultivation of *morbo* – often called *reivindicación* by the post-Franco political observers.

This almost desperate laying of claim to regional identity – to make up for the lost years – is at least part of the reason why the upper half of the pyramid of Spanish football has been widening over the last few years. But the loosening of the political shackles will have an effect only in so far as the framework of *morbo* allows. Franco kept equality at bay with his thugs, but eventually came to realise that a spirit of competition was more useful to his purposes than a league too obviously dominated by one team. Any team could win back then – it's just that they were more wary. Now the fear has gone.

Given such a rich and variegated scene, my personal conversion has been swift and painless. Having been suckled on the particular milk that is English football, I am still moved by the strains of *Match of the Day* and find it difficult to adjust to life without the glorious mud of the FA Cup third round in January and the final in May. These are bonds that are hard to break, and they become a part of you, snuggled down somewhere in the soul. But aesthetically and cerebrally, I am cured. The Premiership still looks a crude offering after the Spanish version, and the general gap in technique, fitness and tactical nous seems to me to be ever widening.

Not everything in the garden is hunky-dory, of course. The culture of anti-authoritarianism, translated to the football field, becomes a little tiresome after a while. The referees in Spain look to be the worst of the European crop, but in truth it is because they are obliged to operate in a counter-productive atmosphere of 'us and them' – a mentality that has gradually soured the Premiership but one that has always been pervasive here. Spanish refs seem incapable of judging what is or what is not legitimate physical contact. Sadly, players are encouraged to cheat, and talk quite openly of the logic of the professional foul and the dive. Those employed to judge them stand little chance. In Spanish football culture, you are regarded as an idiot if you don't play the game a bit craftily, and it is widely acknowledged that the more sporting teams get nowhere. When Sammy Lee turned up for his first training session at Osasuna in 1987, he was amazed to learn that the session was to consist solely of diving practice, in and outside the box. His protests fell on deaf ears.

In this respect the game needs a big clean up, a whole new mind-set, but there is no one around to suggest how to begin the process. Most of the foreign players who have arrived in the past few years soon learn how to fit in, and cotton on with depressing speed to the required patterns of behaviour, John Aldridge's aforementioned mastery of the phrase *hijo de puta* (son of a bitch) being a prime example.

But I cannot end on a sour note. Part of my reason for settling down in this country is the joy of the football. Just before the Bosman ruling came into effect, I insisted that my son be born here, in San Sebastián, so that one day he might turn out for Real Sociedad as part of their *cantera*. It's the sort of action that guarantees that your offspring will reject football entirely, but that's fine, I suppose.

Even though there is far too much of it around, I never tire of the spectacle, of the *morbo,* of the endless, animated conversations with strangers in bars about who should be in and who should be out – of the Saturday night match live on television, the endless Sunday night summary programmes and Robinson's *El día después* on Monday night.

As the new football century stumbles into some sort of shape, it is difficult to predict the directions it will take, despite the abundance of signposts left standing from the previous 100 years. But two things that seem reasonably certain are that folks in Spain will be playing and watching football, and that the word *morbo* is unlikely to die out through lack of use.

appendix

Spanish teams in European finals

Champions Cup
1956 Real Madrid 4 Stade de Reims 3   Paris
1957 Real Madrid 2 Fiorentina 0   Madrid
1958 Real Madrid 3 AC Milan 2   Brussels
1959 Real Madrid 2 Stade de Reims 0   Stuttgart
1960 Real Madrid 7 Eintracht Frankfurt 3   Glasgow
1961 Benfica 3 Barcelona 2   Berne
1962 Benfica 5 Real Madrid 3   Amsterdam
1964 Internazionale 3 Real Madrid 1   Vienna
1966 Real Madrid 2 Partizan Belgrade 1   Brussels
1974 Bayern Munich 4 Atlético Madrid 0   Brussels (after 1-1 draw)
1981 Liverpool 1 Real Madrid 0   Paris
1986 Steaua Bucharest* 0 Barcelona 0   Seville
1992 Barcelona 1 Sampdoria 0   London
1994 AC Milan 4 Barcelona 0   Athens
1998 Real Madrid 1 Juventus 0   Amsterdam
2000 Real Madrid 3 Valencia 0   Paris
2001 Bayern Munich* 1 Valencia 1   Milan
2002 Real Madrid 2 Bayer Leverkusen 1   Glasgow

Fairs Cup and UEFA Cup
(winners in *italics*)
1958 London 2 Barcelona 0   *Barcelona* 6 London 0
1960 Birmingham 0 Barcelona 0   *Barcelona* 4 Birmingham 1
1962 Valencia 6 Barcelona 2   Barcelona 1 *Valencia* 1
1963 Dinamo Zagreb 1 Valencia 2   *Valencia* 2 Dinamo Zagreb 0
1964 Real Zaragoza 2 Valencia 1   (in Barcelona)

1966	Barcelona 0 Real Zaragoza 1	Real Zaragoza 2 *Barcelona* 4
1977	Juventus 1 Athletic Bilbao 0	Athletic Bilbao 2 *Juventus* 1
1985	Videoton 0 Real Madrid 3	*Real Madrid* 0 Videoton 1
1986	Real Madrid 5 Cologne 1	Cologne 2 *Real Madrid* 0
1988	Español 3 Bayer Leverkusen 0	*Bayer Leverkusen** 3 Español 0
2001	Liverpool 5 Alavés 4	(in Dortmund)

Cup-Winners Cup

1962	Atlético Madrid 3 Fiorentina 0	Stuttgart
	(after 1-1 draw in Glasgow)	
1963	Tottenham 5 Atlético Madrid 1	Rotterdam
1969	Slovan Bratislava 3 Barcelona 2	Basle
1971	Chelsea 2 Real Madrid 1	Athens (after 1-1 draw)
1979	Barcelona 4 Fortuna Düsseldorf 3	Basle
1980	Valencia* 0 Arsenal 0	Brussels
1982	Barcelona 2 Standard Liège 1	Barcelona
1983	Aberdeen 2 Real Madrid 1	Gothenburg
1986	Dynamo Kiev 3 Atlético Madrid 0	Lyon
1989	Barcelona 2 Sampdoria 0	Berne
1991	Manchester United 2 Barcelona 1	Rotterdam
1995	Real Zaragoza 2 Arsenal 1	Paris
1997	Barcelona 1 Paris St-Germain 0	Rotterdam
1999	Lazio 2 Real Mallorca 1	Birmingham

* *won on penalties*

European Footballer of the Year with Spanish clubs
1957 Alfredo Di Stéfano (Real Madrid)
1958 Raymond Kopa (Real Madrid)
1959 Alfredo Di Stéfano (Real Madrid)
1960 Luis Suárez (Barcelona)
1973 Johan Cruyff (Barcelona)
1974 Johan Cruyff (Barcelona)
1994 Hristo Stoichkov (Barcelona)
1999 Rivaldo (Barcelona)
2000 Luis Figo (Barcelona/Real Madrid)
2002 Ronaldo (Real Madrid)

Domestic honours in the professional era

League champions		Cup final
1929	Barcelona	Español 2 Real Madrid 1
1930	Athletic Bilbao	Athletic Bilbao 3 Real Madrid 2
1931	Athletic Bilbao	Athletic Bilbao 3 Real Betis 1
1932	Real Madrid	Athletic Bilbao 1 Barcelona 0
1933	Real Madrid	Athletic Bilbao 2 Real Madrid 1
1934	Athletic Bilbao	Real Madrid 2 Valencia 1
1935	Real Betis	Sevilla 3 Sabadell 0
1936	Athletic Bilbao	Real Madrid 2 Barcelona 1
1937	Competition suspended	Competition suspended
1938	Competition suspended	Competition suspended
1939	Competition suspended	Sevilla 6 Racing Ferrol 2
1940	Atlético Aviación	Español 3 Real Madrid 2
1941	Atlético Aviación	Valencia 3 Español 1
1942	Valencia	Barcelona 4 Athletic Bilbao 3
1943	Athletic Bilbao	Athletic Bilbao 1 Real Madrid 0
1944	Valencia	Athletic Bilbao 2 Valencia 0
1945	Barcelona	Athletic Bilbao 3 Valencia 2
1946	Sevilla	Real Madrid 3 Valencia 1
1947	Valencia	Real Madrid 2 Español 0
1948	Barcelona	Sevilla 4 Celta de Vigo 1
1949	Barcelona	Valencia 1 Athetic Bilbao 0
1950	Atlético Madrid	Athletic Bilbao 4 Real Valladolid 1
1951	Atlético Madrid	Barcelona 3 Real Sociedad 0
1952	Barcelona	Barcelona 4 Valencia 2
1953	Barcelona	Barcelona 2 Athletic Bilbao 1
1954	Real Madrid	Valencia 3 Barcelona 0
1955	Real Madrid	Athletic Bilbao 1 Sevilla 0
1956	Athletic Bilbao	Athletic Bilbao 2 Atlético Madrid 1
1957	Real Madrid	Barcelona 1 Español 0
1958	Real Madrid	Athletic Bilbao 2 Real Madrid 0
1959	Barcelona	Barcelona 4 Granada 1
1960	Barcelona	Atlético Madrid 3 Real Madrid 1
1961	Real Madrid	Atlético Madrid 3 Real Madrid 2
1962	Real Madrid	Real Madrid 2 Sevilla 1
1963	Real Madrid	Barcelona 3 Real Zaragoza 1
1964	Real Madrid	Real Zaragoza 2 Atlético Madrid 1

1965	Real Madrid	Atlético Madrid 1 Real Zaragoza 0
1966	Atlético Madrid	Real Zaragoza 2 Athletic Bilbao 0
1967	Real Madrid	Valencia 2 Athletic Bilbao 1
1968	Real Madrid	Barcelona 1 Real Madrid 0
1969	Real Madrid	Athletic Bilbao 1 Elche 0
1970	Atlético Madrid	Real Madrid 3 Valencia 1
1971	Valencia	Barcelona 4 Valencia 3
1972	Real Madrid	Atlético Madrid 2 Valencia 1
1973	Atlético Madrid	Athletic Bilbao 2 Castellón 0
1974	Barcelona	Real Madrid 4 Barcelona 0
1975	Real Madrid	Real Madrid* 0 Atlético Madrid 0
1976	Real Madrid	Atlético Madrid 1 Real Zaragoza 0
1977	Atlético Madrid	Real Betis* 2 Athletic Bilbao 2
1978	Real Madrid	Barcelona 3 Las Palmas 1
1979	Real Madrid	Valencia 2 Real Madrid 0
1980	Real Madrid	Real Madrid 6 Castilla 1
1981	Real Sociedad	Barcelona 3 Sporting Gijón 1
1982	Real Sociedad	Real Madrid 2 Sporting Gijón 1
1983	Athletic Bilbao	Barcelona 2 Real Madrid 1
1984	Athletic Bilbao	Athletic Bilbao 1 Barcelona 0
1985	Barcelona	Atlético Madrid 2 Athletic Bilbao 1
1986	Real Madrid	Real Zaragoza 1 Barcelona 0
1987	Real Madrid	Real Sociedad* 2 Atlético Madrid 2
1988	Real Madrid	Barcelona 1 Real Sociedad 0
1989	Real Madrid	Real Madrid 1 Real Valladolid 0
1990	Real Madrid	Barcelona 2 Real Madrid 0
1991	Barcelona	Atlético Madrid 1 Real Mallorca 0
1992	Barcelona	Atlético Madrid 2 Real Madrid 0
1993	Barcelona	Real Madrid 2 Real Zaragoza 0
1994	Barcelona	Real Zaragoza* 0 Celta de Vigo 0
1995	Real Madrid	Deportivo de La Coruña 2 Valencia 1
1996	Atlético Madrid	Atlético Madrid 1 Barcelona 0
1997	Real Madrid	Barcelona 3 Real Betis 2
1998	Barcelona	Barcelona* 1 Real Mallorca 1
1999	Barcelona	Valencia 3 Atlético Madrid 0
2000	Deportivo de La Coruña	Espanyol 2 Atlético Madrid 1
2001	Real Madrid	Real Zaragoza 3 Celta de Vigo 1
2002	Valencia	Deportivo de La Coruña 2 Real Madrid 1
2003	Real Madrid	Real Mallorca 3 Recreativo de Huelva 0

* *won on penalties*

index

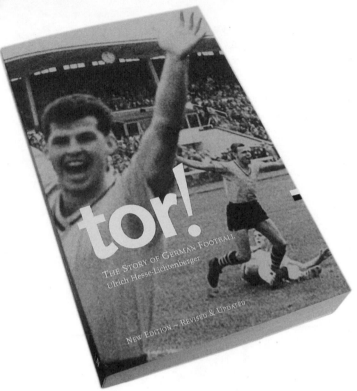

tor!
The Story of German Football
by Ulrich Hesse-Lichtenberger

Tor! follows the extraordinary story of Germany's club and international football, from the days when it was regarded as a dangerously foreign pastime, through the horrors of the Nazi years to postwar triumphs. It brings to life the fascinating characters who shaped it, not just players but unexpected heroes such as the radio commentator Herbert Zimmermann, whose ecstatic cries of 'Tor!' greeted the winning goal in the 1954 final and helped to change a whole nation's view of itself.

"Beautifully crafted... demolishes myths with the cold-blooded efficiency of a literary Gerd Müller" Times

£9.99 softback

ISBN 095401345X